# MOOD FOOD

'Where to go When, from two people
who know How'
*Paul Gambaccini, Broadcaster and journalist*

'At last someone has woken up to the fact that
eating out is as much about mood and occasion as
it is about food'
*Richard Shepherd, chef and
co-owner of Langan's Brasserie*

'The book that puts the wind up the F-plan diet
MOOD FOOD tells you where
good tastes better'
*Maureen Lipman, actress*

When You Want the Best
– The Authors' Choice of Their Favourite
Restaurant from Each Section

| | Lindsey Bareham | Stan Hey |
|---|---|---|
| *Best* | | |
| *Pre and Post Theatre* | Shu-Shan | Magno's Brasserie |
| *Treat* | Le Gavroche | Anna's Place |
| *Cheapie* | Rodos | The Lantern |
| *Romantic* | The Restaurant | The Belvedere |
| *Business Lunch* | Gay Hussar | Bertorelli's |
| *Sporting Venue* | Café des Sports | Paddock Grill, Walthamstow Stadium |
| *'Out and About'* | Bamboo Kuning | Chicago Rib Shack |
| *Sunday Lunch* | Bunga Raya | Le Caprice |
| *Entertainment* | Geno Washington's | Spaghetti Opera |
| *For a Gang* | Rasa Sayang | Porter's |
| *When Alone* | Sheekey's | Braganza |
| *With Parents* | Tate Gallery Restaurant | Fortnum & Mason's Fountain |
| *With Children* | Lucky's | British Home Stores |
| *Open Air* | Old Rangoon | The Gardens |
| *'See and Be Seen'* | Langan's Brasserie | L'Escargot |
| *'Healthy'* | Kalamaras | Mandeer |
| *Late-Night* | The Diamond | Lanes |
| *Breakfast* | Fox and Anchor | Coffee House, Inter-Continental |
| *Ethnic* | Bahn Thai | Mandalay |
| *Out of London* | Chez Max | Waterside Inn |
| *All-Purpose Venue* | Café Pelican | Café St. Pierre |

# MOOD FOOD

## THE LONDON RESTAURANT GUIDE TO SUIT EVERY MOOD, TASTE AND POCKET

Lindsey Bareham
and Stan Hey

**Illustrated by Kipper Williams**

CORONET BOOKS
Hodder and Stoughton

Copyright © 1984 by Lindsey Bareham and
Stan Hey
First published in Great Britain 1984
by Coronet Books

**British Library C.I.P.**

Bareham, Lindsey
    Mood food.
    1. London (England)—Restaurants—Directories
    I. Title        II. Hey, Stan
    647'95421        TX910.G7

ISBN 0-340-36508-0

Printed and bound in Great Britain for
Hodder and Stoughton Paperbacks, a
division of Hodder and Stoughton Ltd,
Mill Road, Dunton Green, Sevenoaks,
Kent (Editorial Office: 47 Bedford
Square, London, WC1 3DP) by
Cox and Wyman Ltd, Reading
Photoset by Rowland Phototypesetting Ltd,
Bury St Edmunds, Suffolk

**Contents**

# MOOD FOOD

## THE LONDON RESTAURANT GUIDE TO SUIT EVERY MOOD, TASTE AND POCKET

### Introduction

In our experience as restaurant critics – and that's over sixteen years and three thousand meals between us – the most common enquiry we've had from readers and colleagues is not 'do you know any good restaurants?' but 'do you know any good restaurants where I can take my mother/lover/business partner/children for an afternoon tea/romantic dinner/celebration lunch/Sunday party?'

It's that sort of question that has prompted us to write and compile this guide, because no matter how good other books may be, they seldom give you an idea of how suitable a restaurant is for your particular occasion or mood. We've identified what we think are the twenty most common eventualities which people consider when they're eating out. Then, by calling upon our extensive knowledge of the London restaurant scene and assessing such factors as formality of service, lighting, comfort, atmosphere, décor and music, we've selected twenty venues to match each of those different eventualities.

Naturally, we've used excellence of food as the basis for all our selections – there's little point in publishing completely negative reviews – but that hasn't stopped us from being critical where necessary or from campaigning against such irritations as French menus without translations, excessive mark-ups on wines or prix fixe meals whose prices are not quite as fixed as they should be.

All the reviews have been undertaken personally (and anonymously) by the two of us – no researchers have been employed nor teams of inspectors despatched. If a restaurant's in this book it's because we've been there and liked it enough to want to go back – and if you leave a restaurant wanting to return to it, surely that's the best test of all?

While we've tried to assess the chief quality of each restaurant and match it to the theme of a particular chapter, it's obvious that many places are suitable for more than one mood or occasion. So at the end of each section we've added a list of restaurants reviewed elsewhere in the book which also have the qualities relevant to that chapter. These lists, together with the other indexes, should provide you with all the information necessary to home in on the right restaurant for your needs. The price guides we've given (a three-course meal with house wine except where stated) should be reasonably accurate, and wherever possible, the times listed are for first and last orders.

On the next page you'll find our selection of the best from each section. We hope that by the time you've read and used this book, you'll be able to draw up a list of your own and have a favourite restaurant for each occasion and every mood.

Lindsey Bareham
Stan Hey
1984

## About the Authors

**Stan Hey** has written about restaurants for Time Out magazine since 1978 under the name of Ben Stanley. In 1981 he was given a free transfer to The Times and has since contributed a regular eating out column to the Preview and Saturday sections of that paper. These, like his writing for television ('Agony', 'Crown Court', 'Hazell', 'Auf Wiedersehen, Pet') and films ('Cry Wolf!' and 'G'Olé!') have been done under his own name, just in case any tax inspectors are reading this. As a journalist, he has written about sport for Time Out, The Sunday Times and The Listener. 'Mood Food' is his second book. The first, 'The Foul Book of Football No.1' which he co-edited with Andrew Nickolds, had the distinction of being the only project Tim Rice has ever lost money on.

**Lindsey Bareham** has been editor of the Sell Out and Food sections of Time Out magazine for twelve years and is currently the Food Editor, and a regular contributor to Sell Out. She has written extensively on consumer affairs, restaurants and cookery. She helped compile the Observer's London Villages Guide, wrote a booklet on English food for the British Designers' Exhibition and researched and wrote the Channel ports section of the 1984 Good Food Guide. She has also researched and written several of Time Out's guides to London's shopping and eating facilities, is restaurant editor of Time Out's Eating Out in London guide and wrote a London Shopping Guide published by Hamlyn. She is a regular contributor to Capital Radio, Radio London and BBC's Woman's Hour. She also writes regularly on consumer affairs for the Saturday section of The Times.

## About the Cartoonist

**Kipper Williams** has been a freelance cartoonist since 1976. He draws 'The Lady and The Wimp' cartoon strip for Time Out and his work appears in many other publications including New Society, Smash Hits, Radio Times and The Observer magazine.

# 1. When You're Out at the Theatre/Cinema

The major problem facing hearty eaters visiting a theatre or cinema that isn't close to home is food. Most evening entertainment starts between 7 and 8pm and that is prime eating time. There are various solutions, the most sensible being to choose a restaurant close to the venue and preferably one that serves easily digestible food. Many West End restaurants serve very reasonable set pre-theatre meals (usually under £6 a head and including a glass of wine, coffee and sometimes service) and there are now several wine bars producing tasty, wholesome and fairly priced food and brasseries (with no minimum charge) where you can eat one or two courses and top up after the production. Many theatres run snack bars (The Lyric, Hammersmith and The Almeida Wine Bar, N1 are two of the best) which are open after the show, and our list includes several late restaurants – for more see the *When You're Out Late* section. We include recommendations for places to eat close to popular venues all over town, not just in the West End.

## La Barca

80–81 Lower Marsh, SE1 (261 9221)
Waterloo tube
Open: noon–2.30pm Monday–Friday; 6–11.30pm Monday–Saturday.

The refurbishment of the nearby Old Vic has guaranteed La Barca's continued popularity with the theatre-going public of the South Bank, though, as the hundreds of signed photographs on the wall indicate, the stars of stage and screen (London Weekend TV is also close) are just as likely to eat here as the people who've been watching them. Despite the photos, the most prized souvenir on display is an Italian football shirt once worn by Paolo Rossi – effectively another Turin Shroud. Given all this showbiz bustle, it's not surprising that La Barca has a lively, brassy atmosphere and a flashy, cocky staff to go with the classic trattoria décor of tiled floors and white plaster/bare-brick walls.

Equally predictable, when so much is being staked on appearances, is the occasional lapse in the cooking, like a pollo sorpresa, cooked on the outside but still half-frozen on the inside. Safer bets then, are the simpler, 'what you see is what you get' dishes – spare ribs, lumache (snails), uovo purgatorio (baked eggs with tomatoes), steak tartar, liver and bacon and so on. Even so, if their 'what you get is what you don't see' speciality – spaghetti La Barca, served with a clam sauce in a paper bag – strikes you as good, maybe you'll be encouraged to try brains in black butter with yolk of egg and caper sauce. The flambéd bananas should be all right too.

About £35 for two.

## La Bussola

42–49 St Martin's Lane, WC2 (240 1148)
Leicester Square tube
Open: noon–3pm and 6pm–1.30am Monday–Friday; 6pm–2am Saturday.

Unusually for a theatre-land restaurant, La Bussola offers set-price three-course dinners after the show (11pm–midnight) as well as before (6–8pm), and this is the principal attraction of an otherwise tourist-orientated operation. The spacious basement room is broken up into a series of white plaster alcoves with a small area set aside for the dinner and dance set (beware – live band in operation later). Still, if you can avoid this and the ever-insistent drinks waiter, you can squeeze a reasonable deal out of what is, at £11.50, quite a high-priced set meal.

Given the cost, you'd be ill-advised to choose the likes of soup, melon or prawn cocktail from the proffered starters, or indeed a pasta as a main course. This effectively narrows the hors d'oeuvres choice down to good frogs' legs (cosciotti di rane) in a caper and butter sauce, or often over-refrigerated smoked salmon and prawns in aspic. There's a wider range among the main courses – three veal dishes, one chicken, one steak and six fish (fillets of sole mainly) – and here the piccatina of veal with rosemary and white wine is creditable, though the scampi fritti can be over-salted. Accompanying vegetables are fine though, and you eventually get your money's worth with good pastry desserts from the trolley and strong coffee in cafetières, thoughtfully served with hot milk. The house wine is good but fairly steep at over £6, so don't stray any higher or you might just as well eat at L'Interlude de Tabaillau (see page 31). The air-conditioning could come in handy on sticky summer nights.

Set dinner £23 for two (excl wine); alc about £40 for two.

## Le Café Jardin

28 Wellington Street, WC2 (836 8769)
Covent Garden tube
Open: noon–2.30pm and 6–11.30pm Monday–Saturday.

Owned by the successful Magno's Brasserie, Le Café Jardin serves a short, very reasonably priced and varied menu. The place is decorated cheerfully with red and white check table-cloths, old French advertisements and a profusion of greenery, and the atmosphere is pretty Gallic. Many people prefer the larger downstairs room.

Between 6 and 7.30pm they serve a two course meal with a glass of wine and coffee for £5.45, which is excellent value. The largely bistro-inspired menu includes fish soup with rouille, croûton and grated cheese; onion tart, various salads and eight substantial main dishes such as roast rack of lamb with wild garlic sauce, the ubiquitous steak frites (steak and chips) and omelettes. There are daily plats du jour. House wine £4.

Set meal £5.45; alc from £5 a head.

## Chez Solange Wine Bar

11 St Martin's Court, WC2 (240 0245)
Leicester Square tube
Open: 11am–3pm and 5.30–11pm Monday–Saturday.

Elegant and sombre with a strikingly stylish and very French façade, this bar in the heart of theatre-land is perfect for pre- and après-, light or substantial meals. It's run by the family who for years have run the successful Chez Solange restaurant. They serve popular French bistro dishes such as coq au vin, moules marinières and boeuf bourguignon, plus quiche, salads and pâtés. In fine weather tables are put up outside the bar in the pedestrian alleyway which cuts through from Leicester Square to Covent Garden. 120 can be squeezed into the two-floor bar where there's a choice of over-the-bar or waitress service. Their extensive wine list features several eminently drinkable house wines under £6.

Food from £3 a head.

## Corney & Barrow

118 Moorgate, EC2 (628 2898)
Moorgate tube
Open: 11.30am–3pm and 5–7.45pm Monday–Friday.

Anyone heading for the contemporary delights of the Barbican Arts Centre will find a fitting rendezvous in Corney & Barrow's strikingly stylish basement restaurant. Just a few minutes from the complex, the restaurant offers early evening drinking from 5pm and a good-value pre-theatre meals from 6–7.45pm.

Basic dishes predominate – soups, terrines, grills, pasta – and they *can* be less successful than the more ambitious, flash creations of the main card. Here you may find the likes of squid and shellfish salad, chicken in port and basil sauce or seafood sausages. As an alternative, try the snack dishes at the spectacular 'sunken' wine-bar – if you can negotiate your way round this, you'll have no trouble dealing with the Barbican's maze.

About £25 for two.

## The Covent Garden Pasta Bar

30 Henrietta Street, WC2 (836 8396)
Covent Garden tube
Open noon–3pm and 5–midnight Monday to
Friday and noon to midnight Saturday and Sunday.

After a couple of successful years mixing a comfortable sofa clad champagne wine bar (upstairs) with a stylish spotlit restaurant (downstairs), the owners of this Italian venture until lately called Nova Park, has given in to the pasta boom. Following the success of the owners Chelsea Pasta Bar (313 Fulham Road, SW10, 352 6912) Nova Park has become the Covent Garden Pasta Bar. The place has been totally re-arranged, the kitchen moved to the larger down-stairs room and the menu confined to what Nova Park was always best at, fresh pasta.

A pasta making machine has been installed and both the pasta and sauces are cooked to order. Dishes such as fettucine with smoked salmon, spaghetti vongole and trenette al pesto (with pine nuts, basil and olive oil) all make a perfect light early meal. For those wishing to split the meal; the restaurant serves a short but well chosen selection of classic Italian starters such as the fashionable carpaccio and spinach and bacon salad with avocado. Finish with zabaglione or their chocolate cream filled crepes. Their white housewine is a modest £4 and a perfect accompaniment.

From £5 for food.

## Kolossi Grill

56–58 Rosebery Avenue, EC1 (278 5758)
Angel tube
Open: noon–3pm Monday–Friday; 5–11pm Monday–Thursday; 5pm–midnight
Friday and Saturday.

A few pas de deux down from Sadler's Wells, home of contemporary dance, will bring you to the Kolossi Grill, an unpretentious but above-average Greek restaurant. The large-but-cosy open room is ideal for group dining after (or indeed before) a performance.

Imaginative alternatives to the usual array of tarahumoussaka include keftedakia (spicy meatballs) among the starters, and Armenian speciality lachmado (minced lamb in hot brandy sauce) or smoked fillet of pork with Greek sausage and egg among the main courses. Specially-bottled house wine is worth trying as a change from Othello or Demestica.

About £18 for two.

## Magno's Brasserie

65a Long Acre, WC2 (836 6077)
Covent Garden tube
Open: noon–2.30pm Monday–Friday; 6–11.30pm Monday–Saturday.

If you're on your way to the opera, Drury Lane, Aldwych or Charing Cross Road, Magno's is a convenient stopping-off point en route. Furthermore, they cater specifically for theatre-goers firstly by opening early, and secondly by providing a small set dinner that's brisk on delivery between 6–7.30pm.

The menu offers a choice of three starters and three main courses, with an accompanying glass of wine and a coffee. For the price, it's good value, even if some of the dishes are plainly the 'spare bits' from the main menu. So expect to find chicken legs rather than chicken breasts, basic stews and fish terrines. In the circumstances, you may be tempted onto the à la carte by the likes of calves' liver with bacon, fillet of pork with apple or one of the attractive sea-food dishes which appear on the daily special blackboard. The pleasant bistro-style room is a little too cramped for intimate dinners but there's an authentically French atmosphere. A companion restaurant, Le Café Jardin in nearby Wellington Street (see page 11), offers a similar menu and a similar deal.

Set meal £11.90 for two; alc about £25 for two.

## Manzi's

1/2 Leicester Street, WC2 (734 0224)
Leicester Square tube
Open: noon–2.15pm and 5.30–11.30pm Monday–Saturday; 6–10.30pm Sunday.

Since it opened in the late 1920s Manzi's has been a popular pre-and-après-a-night-out-in-the-West-End restaurant. There is a choice of two dining rooms. Upstairs, the Cabin room is more sedate and pricier with none of the charm of the bustling ground floor restaurant. Here red and white check cloths cover the tables, the Italian waiters rush around the wooden floor and there is a small oyster bar and all sorts of fishy decorations line the walls.

It's an Italian fish restaurant but fish can arrive hopelessly over-cooked. Their oysters are always the best – ask for Colchester No 1s or Whitstables. Turbot and halibut are specialities, while they serve sole in a staggering number of ways. Stick to grilled or meunière dishes and you can't go wrong, with mornay you can. Their crème caramel is authentically prepared and highly recommended, as is their house wine.

From £8 a head.

## Peachey's

205 Haverstock Hill, NW3 (435 6744)
Belsize Park tube
Open: 11am–3pm Monday–Friday; 6–11.30pm Monday–Saturday.

It's a little unfair to list this excellent restaurant in what is seemingly a 'secondary' role, since it deserves full attention in its own right. However, it just happens to be right next door to the Screen on the Hill cinema, and the two are made for each other – bastions of individuality, intelligence and quality in a world of mass entertainment and mass catering. Once a wine bar, Peachey's retains the bar and stools, but packs the rest of its small, picture-clad room with candlelit tables, creating an intimate bistro atmosphere.

Those in search of a quick snack before the flick might consider starters like deep-fried mushrooms, terrine of guinea-fowl or the smashing savoury leek tart. If you're prepared to linger, move on to

14

the stupendous casserole de fruits de mer, or the oriental-style stir-fried pork with shallots, spinach and oyster sauce. Simpler tastes are catered for by a short range of char-grills (bifstek, côtelettes d'agneau) while you can bring down the curtain with such classic French puds as chocolate mousse or crème brûlée. Additional points to note are the Friday night special bouillabaisse and the set-menu at lunchtime.

About £28 for two.

## Rowleys

113 Jermyn Street, SW1 (930 2707)
Piccadilly tube
Open: 12.30–2.30pm and 6.30–11.30pm daily.

On the edge of gents' outfitters land (it's at the Haymarket end) Rowleys is very popular with the St James's gentry who like the plain steak meals that the restaurant specializes in. Once a pie shop, the long and narrow premises are still decorated with the delightful original ceramic tiles and mirrors, with a huge wall clock dividing off the marginally more intimate salmon-pink back section.

L'entrecôte au beurre épicé is the speciality, and it's part of an all-in deal. The meal starts with salad followed by the steak (with rosemary butter) which is kept warm at each table on an individual burner and comes with a choice of French fries (as many as you can eat) or baked potato. It's a good idea but unfortunately the salad can be dull and the steak thin but the French fries are always excellent. There is sorbet or cheese to follow at £1.35 each a portion, coffee is £1.25 for two. The place has a nice bustling atmosphere and is a good spot to entertain carnivore pals.

Set meal £8.25, with dessert and wine £12 a head.

## RSJ

13a Coin Street, SE1 (928 4554)
Waterloo tube
Open: noon–2pm Monday–Friday; 6–11.30pm Monday–Saturday.

For those seeking a quieter atmosphere for their South Bank meal, RSJ is a generally reliable venue. Easily-missed because it's on a rather derelict corner of Coin Street, the premises have been basically, but tastefully, converted into an informal two-tiered restaurant serving mainly French food. The gloomy lower level is best for intimate dîners à deux, while the galleried upper level can be successfully adopted by larger parties. The gentle atmosphere may yet be shattered by development on the empty site opposite, but in the meantime enjoy simple but well-prepared starters such as seafood pancakes, avocado and tuna salad, vegetable soup or even a plate of cheeses. Successful main courses have included medallions of venison forestière (with wild mushrooms), salmon trout baked in a pastry case, grilled halibut and carré d'agneau with honey and rosemary. Chocolate and orange mousse is an attractive pud. With cheapish wines and plentiful coffee, your evening shouldn't work out too expensive either.

About £25 for two.

## Rudland & Stubbs

35–37 Greenhill Rents, Cowcross Street, EC1 (253 0148)
Farringdon tube
Open: noon–3pm and 6pm–midnight Monday–Friday; 7pm–midnight Saturday;
noon–4pm Sunday.

If you prefer to eat after your Barbican experience – then Rudland & Stubbs' commendable late-opening policy offers a useful nearby venue. A bold enterprise – a fish restaurant in Smithfield – R&S offers an extensive range of plainly-cooked seafood, ideal for late-night digestion. Jellied eels or herrings in beer may not be too smart too close to bedtime but the likes of poached turbot, Arnold Bennett omelette or grilled halibut shouldn't provoke too many nightmares. The stark white-tiled, white-clothed interior can be a little chilling in the evening, so warm up with their storming gooseberry crumble or apple and cranberry pie with custard. Meat eaters are catered for by steaks, roast beef salads or steak and kidney pie. Reasonable wines, real ale and Indian tea are other features of a thoroughly sound operation.

About £25 for two.

## Savvas Kebab House

7 Ladbroke Road, W11 (727 9720)
Notting Hill Gate tube
Open: noon–11pm daily.

Similar in style to any number of Greek and Cypriot restaurants all over town, Savvas has a strong local following for its informal atmosphere and authentic Greek food and is worth the five-minute walk from the Gate's cinemas and theatres. Not everything is to be recommended (the taramasalata is awful) but their Greek salad heavily doused with olives and feta, garlicky hummus, lemon rice soup, barbecued lamb (done on a spit in the restaurant) are outstanding. All main dishes include a salad or rice, and nothing costs more than £3 a dish. The place is unpretentious with formica-topped tables, candlelit in the evening. The Savvas family are reserved, and don't intrude with the oh-so-familiar instant Greek party spirit.

From £5 a head, Greek wine under £4 a bottle.

## Shu Shan

36 Cranbourn Street, WC2 (836 7501)
Leicester Square tube
Open: noon–11pm daily.

This is a high-quality but reasonably priced Szechuan restaurant for theatre-goers who won't worry about breathing over each other afterwards – chilli and garlic are to the fore. Simply but pleasantly furnished – half-panelled walls, white and brown table-linen, Chinese silk prints – the two-floored Shu Shan is bang in the heart of the West End, and its extensive opening times make it ideal for pre- or post-theatre dinners with a spicy difference. If you're in a hurry, the mixed hors d'oeuvres at £5 a go are excellent value, though you can obviously do better by choosing your own – sesame prawn toast, deep-fried king prawn, sesame beef, seaweed and spiced chicken have all scored well. Have a taste too of the delicious fried dumplings filled with minced pork, accompanied by a combustible chilli relish. If you're lingering, the diced chicken with cashew-nuts or sliced beef with oyster sauce are more substantial, less torrid mouthfuls, though the Szechuan smoked duck (in quarters, halves and whole) is a more typical main course. Cool off with toffee bananas or apples.

About £10 a head.

## Simeoni's

43 Drury Lane, WC2 (836 8296)
Covent Garden tube
Open: noon–2.30pm and 6–11.30pm Monday–Saturday.

Since the gentrification of Covent Garden took place most of its shops and restaurants have acquired an air of studied dandyism, as though 'Brideshead Revisited' had been brought to life again in WC2. Anyone seeking refuge from this over-poweringly effete climate, especially anyone who's been to 'Cats' or the opera, should head immediately to Simeoni's for a dose of old-fashioned Italian macho. Simeoni's announces itself with an alcove shrine dedicated to footballers of the Graeme Souness/Butch Wilkins/Marco Tardelli breed, and a veritable road-crew of muscle-bound, tattooed,

T-shirted waiters strut around the place taking orders, waving pepper mills and eyeing women. The additional decorative elements – animal skins on the wall and Italian rock and roll on the stereo – confirm that this is a hairy-chested trattoria par excellence.

The menu reflects the general robustness – big pastas, hors d'oeuvres like sausages with kidney beans or stuffed crab claws, and a strapping range of escalopes and chicken dishes. These tend to be serviceable rather than spectacular and best value is likely to be found on the list of daily specials – perhaps mussels in a wine, cream, and parsley sauce, saddle of lamb, or halibut in butter and lemon sauce. Service is brisk and efficient, in between the singing and dancing.

About £28 for two.

## Stamford's Wine Bar

7–8 Milroy Walk, Rennie Street, SE1 (633 0256)
Blackfriars tube
Open: 11.30am–3pm and 5.30pm–8pm Monday–Friday.

For those South Bank matinees when you can't face or afford a restaurant lunch, this spacious wine bar hidden in a precinct off Blackfriars Bridge is a good bet. Bare bricks dominate the walls and floors of the interior, and they even have them on the bar as match-strikers. The wooden benches, tables, stools and barrels which make up the furniture are a robust backdrop to a lunchtime menu which is fairly macho, though the clientele isn't necessarily so. Charcoal grills dominate – lamb chops, Porterhouse steaks or garlic and herb sausages, with good soups and cheesecakes flanking them. There's also a modest selection of pâtés, cheeses and salads which, unlike the grills, are available in the early evening. A good-value wine list and one or two seductive ports send you sleepily to the National's stalls.

About £12 for two.

## Strand Tandoori

45 Bedford Street, WC2 (240 1333)
Charing Cross tube
Open: noon–3pm and 5.30pm–midnight Monday–Wednesday; noon–midnight Thursday–Saturday; noon–3pm and 5.30–11.30pm Sunday.

Theatre-going can be an expensive business these days and if you combine it with a meal out there may not be much change from forty or fifty quid. It's useful then to know about this high-class Indian restaurant which has excellent, reasonably-priced food, and which is located conveniently for West End, Strand or Covent Garden. If money's no object, the de luxe tandoori at £21 for two (embracing chicken, lobster and lamb) is well worth a try, but more modest pockets can explore the tandoori specialities like king prawn, chicken tikka and boti kebab (minced lamb with capsicum, onion and tomato), or the delicately-spiced chicken curries such as chicken shahi (a cream, spice and green herb sauce). Equally appetising are the meat curries – palak gosht (with spinach) or meat kashmir (with fruit and cream). The coldly-lit interior and weird gurgling from the fish tanks in the window may disturb some, but the staff are extremely pleasant and courteous, and won't complain about any gurgling from your stomach. The pudding: banana fritters, necessarily cooked to order. Ask for them in plenty of time, like when you arrive.

About £15 for two.

## Le Tire Bouchon

6 Upper James Street, W1 (437 2320)
Piccadilly Circus tube
Open: 8.30am–9.30pm Monday–Friday.

Bang opposite Granada TV and acting as an informal canteen, Le Tire Bouchon is the perfect place for an early light snack or substantial meal before a night out in the West End. Decorated in navy blue and white with check oilskin cloths, navy ceiling and French café notices, the place is run as a brasserie/wine bar with a very short menu which majors on snacks with only two or three hot dishes daily.

Fish soup with rouille, cheese and croûtons; fillets of herring served with hot potatoes and onions; a plate of saucisson with pickled onions are typical, while the main dishes are likely to be rich and imaginative (it is said the chef did a stint at Le Gavroche), such as brochette de poisson with a saffron sauce or cassoulet Toulousain. Finish with the predominantly goat plateau of cheese which is always excellent. They offer a cheap house pichet and a small list of other wines.

Light dishes average £2, main £4.50.
In the morning they serve a continental breakfast of coffee, croissant and bread for around £2 until 11.30am.

## Vasco and Piero's Pavilion

167 Oxford Street, W1 (437 8774)
Oxford Circus tube
Open: noon–3pm Monday–Friday; 6–11pm Monday–Saturday.

If you're taking in the tasteful continental movies at the Academy Cinema, it's worth knowing that the tasteful, continental Pavilion Restaurant is directly above it – always assuming of course, that you're looking for more than a choc ice or a hot dog. In fact, Vasco and Piero's place (entrance in Poland Street) offers a high quality range of Italian specials in a cramped but brightly coloured room overlooking busy Oxford Street.

Among the starters are an interesting seafood lasagne, delicious leeks gratinati and a warming spinach soup. Main courses include grilled calves' liver with sage and lamb cutlets, though it's well worth trying their fish dishes which are especially good. Fillets of bream in a light butter and lemon sauce, or a delicious lemon sole gratinati (they certainly like their cheese here) are perfect before a soulful session in the stalls. Desserts can be a bit on the dull side, so unless you're gratinati-ed to a halt, try their well-kept dolcelatte instead. Male customers might like to note that there's a short-cut to the Academy's foyer through the gents.

About £25 for two.

*Also Good for When You're Out at the Theatre/Cinema:*
Archduke, The
Bar Crêperie
Bates
Braganza
Café des Amis du Vin
Café Pacifico
Café Pelican
Caprice, Le
Chez Solange
L'Escargot
Fakhraldine
Food for Thought
Fortnum & Mason's Fountain
Grange, The
Grimes
Han Kuk Ko Kwan
Italian Connection
Joe Allen
Jules Bar

Lafayette Bar
Melange
Messrs. C
Mon Plaisir
M'sieur Frog
No. 1
One Hampstead Lane
Palookaville
Pier 31
Rules
Sheekey's
Soho Brasserie
South of the Border
Toscanini
Tourment d'Amour
Verrey's

## 2. When You're In the Money

There are times when the cost of a meal takes on secondary importance; the times when you really want to impress or to indulge your tastebuds. London is full of expensive and impressive-seeming restaurants but they aren't necessarily value for money. Our selection of restaurants in this section are amongst London's top places and, in our view, can be relied upon for excellent food, discreet and efficient service and a good wine list, and will provide a memorable experience. Many of these places – Le Gavroche, La Tante Claire, the Terrace Room at the Dorchester and Chez Nico in particular – though excellent, really do burn a hole in your pocket (minimum £30 a head for food) so we include details of their set lunches which, at less than half the price, offer a chance to dine exquisitely, sample a high-quality wine and escape on the right side of £40 all in. A word about wine in these establishments. Very few keep a house wine; as a general rule if they do it will be a good one but there are few wines under £10 a bottle. Most keep a good list of half bottles and many include mineral water in the cover charge.

# Anna's Place

90 Mildmay Park, N1 (249 9379)
Highbury & Islington tube
Open: 7.15pm–10.15pm Tuesday–Saturday.

Although Highbury is the nearest tube to Anna's Place, it still needs a 15-minute schlepp or a bus ride after that to get there – not, you would imagine, the most auspicious preliminary for a 'big night out', but the travel's worth it. Anna's Place is a dazzlingly individual restaurant, set in the front room of a private house (yes, you have to knock on the door to get in). The tiny dining-room, with its polished wooden floor, subdued colours and displays of greenery, looks out onto a bleak and busy road but the warmth of Anna Hegarty's personality – she is an ever-present but informal hostess – and the skill of her kitchen more than make up for any sense of dislocation.

A short menu is hung by the window, but Anna takes pride in giving a detailed description to each table. The gravlax (marinated salmon with dill, served with a mustard sauce) and the oxfilé (marinated beef fillet) are reflections of her Scandinavian background, and are presented in great bowls with due pomp and ceremony. These dishes are both offered as starters, and while they're both well-reported (the gravlax especially) it seems a pity on a first visit not to try the more ambitious first courses. Of these, the kipper soufflé, served with a dish of whisky cream, is inspired, and while the combination of Stilton and celery in a mousse might seem obvious, an accompanying port and pear sauce works the magic. More prosaic but equally successful starters might include a rich Jerusalem artichoke soup or moules marinières.

Among the main courses, you're likely to find at least one game dish in season (perfect roast partridge in game sauce if you're lucky) and a quartet of seafood creations – turbot poached in lemon herb butter, sea bass en papillote with rosemary and lime, a sautéd skewer of prawns and monkfish in a ginger sauce, or marinated scallops in prawn sauce. Meat eaters might have to make do with rack of lamb or delicious fillet of beef, stuffed with Gorgonzola and served en croûte. Sumptuous puddings (prune and armagnac tart, hot hazelnut soufflé), a reasonably-priced and well-chosen wine list (some good half-bottles included) and a pleasant, relaxed atmosphere should complete a great night out.

About £23 a head.

## L'Arlequin

123 Queenstown Road, SW8 (622 0555)
Sloane Square tube and bus
Open: 12.30–1.30pm and 7.30–10pm Tuesday–Saturday, closed Saturday lunch.

It didn't take long for Nico's friend Christian Delteil and his young wife Genevieve to establish themselves as *the other* place in Queenstown Road and not the overspill for a full Chez Nico. Prettily decorated in pale lemon with a stunning display of face masks and an obligatory painting of a harlequin, the set up is formal (Genevieve 'presides' from a cash desk by the door; waiters are pristine in white; the napery has a full complement of Robin and the chairs are posh, modern wicker) but still L'Arlequin manages a relaxed ambience.

Like M. Ladenis next door, M. Delteil's cuisine is inventive, light on the stomach and typical of the nouvelle vague. At lunch he offers a superb and generally high quality (we have heard of obvious leftovers from the previous night) set meal which will be as ambitious as the carte. Fish is much favoured and feuilletés of scallops and leeks with a shellfish sauce and fricassée de lotte (monkfish) aux petits légumes have both been exquisite. Other equally complicated meat and fowl dishes have also been outstanding; silky smooth chicken liver mousse with wild mushrooms, pink, garlicked carré d'agneau and beef with foie gras have all been memorable. Crisp, light pastry tuiles are filled with raspberries and strawberries and chantilly cream in summer, tarts and sorbets follow in winter. Their cheeseboard groans with 20-odd French regional cheeses in perfect nick and accompanying salads come dressed with the now-popular walnut oil dressing. Stick to the very good house Vacqueyras '81 at £6, otherwise take pot luck with a variable list.

Set lunch £9.50; alc from £20 with wine.

## Capital Hotel Restaurant

22–24 Basil Street, SW3 (589 5171)
Knightsbridge tube
Open: 12.30–2pm and 6.30–10.30pm daily.

This restaurant on the ground floor of the stylish Capital Hotel is one of three London hotel restaurants to receive a Michelin rosette. The deceptively small (seating for 40) high-ceilinged dining-room has recently been totally redesigned by Nina Campbell and the result is a sumptuous terracotta and cream room with stunning ruched curtains (rather like the royal wedding dress), wall tapestries, engraved mirrors and a couple of lavish chandeliers. The colour scheme is echoed in the Limoges china and individual table lights give out a soft glow. The tables are well spaced and the waiting staff some of the most discreet and efficient in London.

Chef Brian Turner can be watched in action at his char-grill and he's often to be glimpsed making a lap of honour round the restaurant. Each day there is a set menu at £14.50 (three courses) and this offers outstanding value; salade d'asperges a l'huile de noix followed by wild duck breasts with four peppers and cheese or dessert (choice from the carte) plus coffee is a typical menu. From the short main menu (written exclusively in French) there is a varied choice ranging from the very plain but exquisite finest quality smoked salmon to the rich terrine of veal sweetbreads and brains and consommé with quails' eggs. Mr Turner is very keen on fish and his repertoire includes the light and delicious quenelle of salmon with champagne and tomatoes and the plainer grilled sole with chive butter. Meat dishes include the superb foie gras-stuffed quails and the excellent carré d'agneau sprinkled with herbs from Provence. Like most top chefs Brian Turner is at pains to get the best ingredients and even goes to the trouble of buying his eggs, cream and some cheeses direct from the farm and growing his own rosemary, parsley and sage. The small range of desserts (their own Roquefort pitted with walnuts is very rich) includes superb marquise au chocolat blanc with a coffee sauce and a range of fresh fruit sorbets. The wine list is unfathomably long and very expensive, though there are a few suggestions on the menu. If you can run to it we'd recommend the château-bottled Côtes de Fronsac Château Lestage 1961 at £15.

Set meal £14.50; alc from £20.

## Chez Nico

129 Queenstown Road, SW8 (720 6960)
Clapham Common tube
Open: 12.30–2pm Tuesday–Friday; 7.30–11.45pm Tuesday–Saturday.

Booking at least a week in advance is essential at this rather uninviting looking sludge-brown restaurant on a busy Battersea through road. Inside you forget the location and enter what looks like a private dining-room (with an adjoining alcove room) decorated comfortably but formally in pale terracotta with a large open dresser. Chef/owner Nico Ladenis is among London's top chefs and is almost as famous for his inability to suffer fools or late customers as he is for his superb food.

While Mr Ladenis perfects his craft in the adjoining kitchen, his charming wife will explain the short and infrequently-changed menu. Nico is a dedicated chef who takes enormous trouble to use top quality ingredients and serves food that is essentially classical but uplifted by imaginative nouvelle cuisine touches and presented like a work of art. There are seven starters and six main dishes, with the starter included in the price of the main course. Starters include Nico's sublimely smooth duck liver mousse which is served with a glass of Barsac and a nut oil dressed mâche (lamb's lettuce) salad and crisp and light asparagus feuilleté with perfect beurre blanc. Main dishes include Nico's legendary perfectly pink, bloodless grilled duck breast served fanned out on the plate with a rich red wine and herb sauce; the fish of the day will be served perfectly à point, and two quails with an almond stuffing and rich and piquant honey and raspberry vinegar sauce are a perfectly balanced combination. Vegetables come on a side plate and, though never mistreated, uphold the nouvelle influence and are on the stingy side. Superb cheeses follow and Nico has set the trend all over London for his crottin of chavignol (soft round goat cheese) grilled and served with a walnut and walnut oil dressed salad. Finish with a perfect sorbet – or more rich treats if you can cope – and good strong coffee which comes with shortbread and a stick of truffle.

To eat at dinner will cost a minimum £30 a head with wine but at lunch Nico serves a set meal at £11.50. This meal offers incredible value and the place is pleasanter to be in at lunchtime. The wine list starts at £8.50 but there is a highly-recommended house wine at £13.50 and a 1981 Sancerre at £11.50.

Alc £25 a head; set lunch £11.50.

## Ciboure

21 Eccleston Street, SW1 (730 2505)
Victoria tube
Open: noon–2.30pm Monday–Friday; 7–11.30pm Monday–Saturday.

It's all too easy in London to spend a packet in a restaurant and convince yourself you've had a good time. At Ciboure however, you're likely to feel that every penny has been well spent – indeed, every penny is itemised since the menu shows prices with and without service and VAT added, for each individual dish. A small, precisely-furnished room, done out in cream and grey, with Adrian George pastels and eye-deceiving mirrors filling the walls, Ciboure has a delicate atmosphere, compounded by serious-faced young waiters in starched white aprons and collarless shirts. Some of this foppishness spills over into presentation of the modishly light French food, but since it's all beautifully cooked (by Englishman Richard Price), you can forgive them their pretensions.

The menu changes seasonally – a smoked chicken salad with relevant vegetables appears regularly as a starter – with an emphasis on meat and game in winter, fish and offal in summer. So, noisettes de chevreuil (venison) aux fruits d'hiver will turn up in December, while June may have medaillon de ris de veau (sweetbreads) aux nouilles (noodles) fraîches. Confirmed successes are the warm royale of leeks and artichokes, the calves' liver with avocado pieces, and the perfect pink slices of filet d'agneau à l'estragon, fanned artistically across the plate. Fish fans will enjoy the stew of coquilles St Jacques. A two-course set lunch at £8.50 (£9.78 including service and VAT!) is excellent value and might offer red caviar mousse and horseradish, aubergine stuffed with crab, supreme of brill, and chicken breast stuffed with lamb sweetbreads. Eating à la carte is not that expensive by London standards (about £35–£40 for two without wine) which means that you can burn off the rest of your second dividend on their modest wines, and vintage ports and armagnacs.

Set lunch £8.50 (excl wine); alc about £25 a head.

## The Grill Room

Dorchester Hotel, Park Lane, W1 (629 8888)
Marble Arch tube
Open: 12.30–2.30pm and 6.30–10.30pm daily.

All the experts (Ronay, the Good Food Guide, Michelin and Gault Millau) agree that it takes a Swiss chef, the Dorchester's Anton Mosimann, to produce the best British food in London. Behind the revolving door and to the right of the glittery reception area, is the Grill, very comfortably and lavishly redecorated in maroon with tall tapestries on the walls, and floor to (very high) ceiling drapes across mock windows. It's a large space, well filled with tables for small and large groups; twosomes share rather curious high backed sofas and the tables are oak, refectory style. Service is suitably accomplished even if the waiters' maroon uniforms are a bit naff looking. The kitchens are vast (over sixty working chefs) so one can only expect the influence of Mr Mosimann on the food, but whatever goes on down there, you won't be disappointed.

Each day there is a lunch dish; braised oxtail on Monday (£7), beefsteak and kidney pudding (£7.50) on Wednesday and Kentish chicken pie (£7.50) on Sundays. There's roast rib (lunch) and sirloin (dinner) at £9.80 from the trolley, and a three-course lunch with a half-carafe of wine at £14.20. From the alc the chicken liver terrine (£3.50) is perfection, a masterpiece of taste and presentation – an experience one should know once – and their oysters are appropriately sound. Grill dishes use the best quality meat and whenever there is game available – we visited recently during a game promotion and enjoyed a superb braised partridge – you'll find no better.

Home-made bottled fruit, the famous chocolate torte Dorchester (all £2.50) or devils on horseback (£2.20) complete a superb meal. House wine by the carafe is a modest £6.50 but you *can* go quite mad and take advantage of their excellent list.

A meal at the Dorchester doesn't have to be a killer; you can do it for £15 a head but £25 is a safer estimate of the cost of an experience to savour.

## The Four Seasons, at The Inn on the Park

Hamilton Place, Park Lane, W1 (499 0888)
Hyde Park Corner tube
Open: noon–3pm and 7–11pm Monday–Saturday; noon–3pm and 7–10pm Sunday.

Until a few years ago, it had become unfashionable to eat in hotels, even grand ones. The suspicion was that a big kitchen, often geared to large-scale banqueting, couldn't produce the individual attention or invention of the better class of restaurant. Now however, the combination of cheaper, more accessible set-price meals and a sudden clutch of talented hotel chefs make it safe to go back in the foyer again. This is particularly so at The Inn on the Park, where the young Swiss chef Eduard Hari has been creating terrific menus every few months or so to highlight the fresh food of each season. In the ornately-furnished but by no means oppressive Four Seasons restaurant, situated on the first floor with a view of Park Lane, set price lunches and dinners give you a chance to sample M. Hari's skills. A three-course lunch, including coffee and service, costs £12.50 without wine, and will offer a well-balanced choice – a recent menu included main courses of roast fillet of beef, an escalope of fresh salmon with beurre basilic and a veal slice with kidneys in paprika sauce. Before these came starters as simple as a cream of watercress soup or as inventive as a nugget of turbot, pressed and sealed with a delicate jelly. Dinners are four-course affairs (£19.50), with perhaps a duck liver salad, charlotte de brochet (pike) with leeks, fillets of veal and lamb and finally a mousseline of rhubarb and mocha for dessert. Choosing à la carte offers slightly less adventure, with a roast daily special from the hot trolley and suprême de volaille Kiev typifying the proceedings. Good wines in useful bin end offers will complement the meal. Start with a cocktail in the piano bar to get you into that expansive and expensive mood.

About £20 a head (lunch); £30 a head (dinner).

# La Frimousse

75 Fairfax Road, NW6 (624 3880)
Swiss Cottage tube
Open: noon–3pm and 7–11pm Monday–Saturday.

Set amid a rather bland parade of shops just down from the Finchley Road, La Frimousse may not appear too spectacular a venue, despite the tasteful awning and the potted pines outside. Yet inside is what one might describe as an up-market workers' co-operative. The workers in question are all ex-Savoy stalwarts – Jacques Eza (chef), Antonio Tomas (maitre d'hôtel) and Silvino Trompetto (consultant) – with over sixty years service at the luxury hotel between them. La Frimousse, their own venture, reflects both their expertise and pedigree. The narrow, L-shaped premises have been comfortably furnished with tasteful patterned wallpaper, RAF blue upholstery, oil paintings and delicate pink napery. Oil lamps on the tables create an additional stylish touch.

M. Eza works to a classical French theme but one which is cleverly re-interpreted through modern styles. Thus the à la carte menu, changed with the seasons, might offer such standards as grilled spring chicken in a mustard and mushroom sauce, fillet of veal in rosemary sauce, and scallops and scampi cooked in butter and herbs. There are soufflés fore and aft too – a sorrel one from Languedoc as a starter, and perhaps a wonderful creation with Grand Marnier and sauce Anglaise to finish. Although the à la carte prices reflect the aristocracy of the operation, the service is both friendly and well-drilled, and the atmosphere is surprisingly relaxed. The introduction of fixed price menus for both lunch and dinner also allows a less expensive entrée to the excellence of La Frimousse.

The spectacular three course 'dîner des gourmets' menu (canapés, coffee, petits fours, wines and service charge are also included) might offer vichyssoise or a delicious crab pie to begin with, followed by perfectly roasted quails stuffed with chestnuts and celery, or a tender mignon de veau with a spinach and cream sauce. A soufflé with a light, crusty head will complete the treat.

Set lunch £6.75 a head (excl wine); set dinner £17.95 (incl wine); alc about £23 a head.

# Le Gavroche

43 Upper Brook Street, W1 (730 2820/408 0881)
Marble Arch tube
Open: 12.30–2pm and 7–11pm Monday–Friday.

Le Gavroche, the only restaurant in Britain to receive three stars from Michelin, was the Roux brothers' first restaurant when it opened in Sloane Square in 1967. In 1981 the restaurant moved to these elegant Edwardian premises and top interior designer David Milinaric transformed what was a club into a sumptuous dark-green basement dining-room with an upstairs reception lounge. Despite costing around £40 a head for food alone, Le Gavroche is full every session and reservations must be made several days, sometimes weeks, in advance.

If you can handle a late meal we'd suggest booking after 9.30pm when the staff are less pressured and a meal is altogether more relaxed. Each day there is a short 'Le Chef Propose' menu and a Menu Exceptionnel (£30 a head) plus a short carte. The Roux (the kitchens here are run by Albert) are sticklers for quality ingredients and most of their meats and poultry come from their own French butcher or are specially reared for them here, and rumour has it that their vegetables are hand-picked in the markets of France.

Everything about the place reeks money and breeding, usually from the clientele, and certainly the waiting staff are the best money can buy; you can expect perfection, from the co-ordinated ping as main course covers are lifted down to the most modest ingredient. Recent 'perfect' meals have included exquisite mousseline de homard au champagne (£12.95); huge fat slices of scallops sautéd with sliced artichoke (£14.20); pale coloured, verging on the obscenely fat pigeonneau de Bresse poêle Grand'mére (£17.80) – clearly only a distant relative of the pigeons on sale at our fishmonger – and turbot with port (£14.90). Their cheeseboard constitutes about half of Philippe Olivier's famous Boulogne shop (£7.50) and from the wide-ranging selection of desserts (unnecessary really as coffee comes with a pile of petits fours), the omelette Rothschild (for two, £21.80) is a divine fluffy sweet omelette filled with apricots. The wine list is much as you'd expect with clarets and burgundies *starting* at £20, but there are several in the £10 range, and some halves.

Set lunch £20; from £30, usually £40 a head for food.

## Inigo Jones

14 Garrick Street, WC2 (836 6456)
Covent Garden/Leicester Square tube
Open: 12.30–2.30pm Monday–Friday and 5.30–11.30pm Monday–Saturday.

Named after the fashionable seventeenth-century architect, this Inigo Jones is 17 this year and shows no signs of age. Opposite the Garrick Club and popular with its members, Inigo Jones was converted with style and elegance and shows little trace of its previous life as a stained glass factory and design studio. Upstairs is dominated by a curious dead tree which prompts a lot of speculative talk but otherwise everything is very proper. Unlike a lot of French restaurants, here the menu is thoroughly translated. A three-course set lunch features nothing from the à la carte but is equally imaginative, and the standard of all food and presentation is very high. Despite their nouvelle cuisine tag, chef Paul Gayler favours rich combinations and both the cheese terrine, prettily served in a raspberry sauce and decorated with raspberries, apples and kiwi fruit and the ragout of mussels with tomato and light curry sauce were very rich and filling. Panaché of lamb roasted with garlic and rosemary sauce proved to be a superb combination dish of lean meat, kidney and sweetbread garnished with sweet garlic. Inigo Jones keep an excellent cheeseboard which is served with black bread or biscuits. Don't economise with the house wine (£5.70 and vicious). Ideal for dining in style after the opera.

Set lunch £10.75; pre-theatre set meal 5.30–7pm; alc £30 a head.

## Interlude de Tabaillau

6–8 Bow Street, WC2 (379 6473)
Covent Garden tube
Open: noon–2pm and 7–11.30pm Monday–Friday; 7–11.30pm Saturday.

This year Interlude, the elegant, modern and almost too austere restaurant run by ex-Gavroche chef de cuisine Jean Louis Taillebaud, gets its first pestle and mortar from the Good Food Guide. Not before time. For three years Taillebaud has daily prepared a different lunch and dinner menu made up of a choice of three appetisers, six main dishes, cheese (from Philippe Olivier) a dessert and coffee served with exquisite petits fours. The all-in price also includes a champagne cocktail and half a bottle of decent wine. Perhaps the ambition of the brief he sets himself keeps the standard high, but Taillebaud's food is always interesting with light and contrasting sauces. Flan of oysters with a beurre blanc; the unlikely combination of carrot and orange in a delicious soup; turbot in champagne sauce and roast wild duck with sweet garlic are typical, and fish is always well represented. Cheeses are always in superb order.

Lunch £16.50 (house wine £7); dinner £21 (house wine £8).

## Keats

Downshire Hill, NW3 (435 3544)
Hampstead tube
Open: 12.30–2.15pm and 7–11pm Monday–Friday; 7–11pm Saturday.

The exterior of this popular haunt of Hampstead's wealthier intelligentsia, literati and stars of stage and screen gives very little away. Ring the bell and discover what owner Aran Misan did 20-odd years ago to create a setting where Keats himself would feel at home. English engravings set against red panelled walls, bookshelves lined with early editions, pretty lamps and candle-light add up to a cosy mood, the spell only broken by the brash looking attire of the waiters (colour co-ordinated to the regal purple and bright red colour scheme) and loud, eminently ear-wiggable conversations. The staff are almost all French and the menu is a fine mixture of nouvelle-inspired and classic French food; descriptions all helpfully translated into English.

At luncheon, when the place is popular with artistes being dined by their agents, local big wigs and illicit couples, Keats offer a set meal, which changes weekly, for around £10 with two choices per course. Not for the light eater; Keats will offer the likes of stuffed aubergine, a hearty salad of artichoke and fennel with an escalope of fresh salmon with chives or fillet of veal en croûte with sorrel plus a dessert to follow.

A Petit Menu Gastronomique (£15) offers even richer, more elaborate dishes (consommé a l'essence de tomate; turbot au saffron et anchoix), while the carte satisfies those wanting a light meal (fish and vegetable pâté with tomato sauce and sliced breast of duck on a celery purée) and those after a serious weight increase – fillets of sole and giant prawns in a sherry and cream sauce flavoured with tarragon; a treble fillet (for two) of beef garnished with potatoes, tomatoes, celery, mushrooms and served with three classical sauces.

French cheeses, home-made parfait, water ices and a chef's creation follow. M. Mizan keeps wines from most regions of France, and his cellar is deservedly famous. But while his list is noted for its premier cru Bordeaux (Margaux up to £100) there are plenty of halves and several good wines under £10.

Set lunch £10; Petit Menu Gastronomique £15.

## Lampwicks

24 Queenstown Road, SW8 (622 7800)
Clapham Common tube
Open: 12.30–2.30pm and 7.30–10.30pm Monday–Friday.

After some months establishing the impressive menu at Martins (see page 35) Alan Bennett has taken a huge gamble and set up on his own in this busy Battersea thoroughfare, now famous as a gastronome's place of pilgrimage. The menu is as ambitious as both of its famous neighbours (L'Arlequin and Chez Nico) but is shorter, changes more often and is cheaper; £10.50 for a two-course lunch with coffee and £14.50 for a four-course dinner that is preceded by a glass of kir and concluded with unlimited coffee.

The premises were once a lampwick factory which accounts for the name, though most recently it was a flashy bistro called A Taste of Class and Mr Bennett has inherited some flashy interior decoration but otherwise they have tried to present a plain and functional dining-room (there is a small upstairs gallery) with bright lighting, heavily-starched napery and unfussy cutlery.

Dinner begins with a kir and nibbles of delicious warm choux pastry filled with ultra smooth pâté and a tiny egg and spinach tart. Soupe à la mode de Sète en croûte (a speciality from the South West of France and typical of a regional influence in the menu) proved an excellent and novel starter of rich mussel soup cooked with a slightly sweet puff pastry crust. Duck in redcurrant sauce arrives fashionably fanned and cooked pink which contrasts prettily with the red sauce, but the three rolls of Dover sole in sauces of crab and champagne were exquisite if a little on the nouvelle (ie meagre) side. Vegetables too are nouvelle – tiny mangetouts and rolls of crisped potatoes – but perfectly cooked. Cheese – a fine selection from maestro Philippe Olivier – can be interminable, but room should be left for one of the light desserts which round off a well-balanced and nicely-presented meal; portions are just the size to enable diners to make it through all four courses. The wine list is short and fairly serious but is strong on halves; the Mâcon at £5 is particularly good and mineral water is on the house.

With wine, £15 a head for lunch; £25 for dinner.

## Lichfields

13 Lichfield Terrace, Richmond (940 5236)
Richmond tube
Open: 12.30–2.30pm Tuesday–Friday; 7–10.45pm Tuesday–Saturday.

There is nothing very spectacular about the location – in a rather dull thirties shopping parade – or the decoration – wooden panelling and an orange/lemon colour scheme – at this one-room restaurant on the edge of Richmond. However the food is quite superb and it makes you feel a touch patriotic to learn that the chef and owner, Stephen Bull, is English.

Filets de lotte en ceviche au coriandre is a superb dish of thin slices of monkfish marinated in coriander, and the rather revolting lard-like looking boudins blancs with pistachios and a mustard sauce are quite excellent. Everything on the menu (written in French and definitely requiring translation) sounds wonderful and the wild duck with onion marmalade, the selection of sea bass, brill and salmon in a beurre blanc with lime and ginger and the noisettes of lamb roasted with purée of aubergine and tomato are exceptional and irrevocably memorable. Vegetables too are given star treatment; cauliflower mousse topped with hollandaise, carrots with thyme and spinach with toasted almonds were exceptional. The cheeseboard is in perfect nick; you don't really need a puddings as petits fours come automatically with the delicious strong coffee. The wine list is varied with several vintage bargains; the house wine is incongruously Spanish.

Around £25 a head.

## Ma Cuisine

113 Walton Street, SW3 (584 7585)
South Kensington tube
Open: 12.30–2pm and 7.30–11pm Monday–Saturday.

Ma Cuisine is one of the few restaurants in London to attract solely for its food. Who would *choose* to book weeks in advance (even for lunch) and then sit squeezed next to the neighbouring table amid rather stiff petit bourgeois décor (even down to the arrangements of fresh *and* plastic flowers)? After eight years, chef/owner Guy Mouilleron has taken a back seat and installed Jean Claude Audertin in the kitchen. M. Mouilleron still has a major effect on the carte (and the day's specials – almost as many dishes as on the menu and disarmingly read out without mention of price) but is no longer responsible for everything that appears from the kitchens. M. Mouilleron comes from the South West of France and his reputation lies in the lack of pretension in his dishes, a simplicity that means all the ingredients of a dish will stand out and sauces won't disguise but enhance. Above all M. Mouilleron's continual experimentation has become his hallmark and M. Audertin is continuing his tradition.

Avocado purée with artichoke hearts and galantine chicken have equalled M. Mouilleron's scallops edged round a cream sauce with a julienne of leeks, and turbot with sorrel sauce showed the standard of ingredients remains high. Many of the dishes are on display, particularly the desserts. Though not as reliably good as it was under M. Mouilleron it's definitely one of London's top French restaurants.

Choose from the many fine burgundies and clarets or opt for the reasonable Château Senilhac 79 at £6.95.

From £20 a head.

## Martins

88 Ifield Road, SW10 (352 5641)
Earls Court tube
Open: 12.30–2.30pm and 6.30–11.30pm Monday–Saturday.

These premises have had a chequered restaurant career – most famously or infamously as Nick's Diner – but are now likely to rest with the current owners for some time. The place is rather oppressively decorated in salmon pink with high-backed chairs and scalloped curtains à la SW3 but the staff are young and informal. The short menu is, annoyingly, written exclusively in French which means to get all the subtleties of the dishes a full explanation from the waiter is essential. But once you've made your selection there are few disappointments, for the standard of nouvelle cuisine served here is very high.

Martins sensibly stick to an all-in price for both lunch and dinner and there are three or four specialities of the day which have been memorable. Like so many leading London French restaurants, they do wonderful things with fish. The petite timbale de saumon is stunning – a round sausage of salmon mousse with more salmon and white fish in a delicious crab sauce, and that's just for starters. Medallions of lotte (monkfish) cooked with saffron works wonderfully and their duck (Les aiguillettes de canard au vinaigre de Xeves) came with crispy skin, pink flesh alternating with slices of apples in a piquant calvados sauce. If you rest at this stage of the meal, you will have known exceptional value but if you follow with cheese or one of the complicated puds the bill will be dramatically affected. Best to finish with coffee (included) which comes with crisp tuiles and mouth-watering chocs. The house claret is excellent at £7.50.

Set two-course meals: £9.50 lunch, £14.50 dinner.

# Suntory

72 St James Street, SW1 (409 0201)
Green Park tube
Open: noon–3pm and 7–11pm Monday–Saturday.

There are two rooms offering a totally different experience at this stylishly austere Japanese restaurant owned by the eponymous Japanese whisky people. Decorated in black and beige with the occasional bit of stunning art or antique vessel, the colour is provided by san pan girls who shuffle around offering guests a warm flannel on arrival and serve graciously if erratically. In the first room, the lighting is bright and the menu a long à la carte with a set meal and several specials of the day (these are likely to be the most innovative dishes). Most people seem to include sukiyaki in their choice and for this purpose rather incongruously bad-taste electric griddles are set in the middle of each table.

The second room is Teppan-yaki; steak and seafood are cooked in front of you – diners sit around the central kitchen and watch the preparation which is quite an art form – pure theatre. Scallops, giant prawns, fillet steak, onions and various vegetables are served with dips of soy and the hot bright green horse-radish. Then follows clear soup, pickled vegetables and beautifully cut fresh fruit. Drink warm sake or very pricey French wine.

Set meal £9; alc from £15.

# La Tante Claire

68 Royal Hospital Road, SW3 (352 6045)
Sloane Square tube
Open: 12.30–2pm and 7–11pm Monday–Friday.

Without a doubt La Tante Claire is one of London's top restaurants. It has been awarded a pestle and mortar from the Good Food Guide, three toques from Gault Millau, two stars from Michelin and Egon Ronay has declared it his restaurant of the year. Chef and owner Pierre Koffmann was trained under the Roux brothers of the famous Le Gavroche and Waterside Inn, and his food bears the same hallmarks of simplicity, excellence of ingredients, superb light and complementary sauces and innovative combinations. The menu is short, the fish dishes change daily according to market availability and at lunch there is a three-course set meal (choice of two dishes with either cheese – from Maître Fromager de France Philippe Olivier – or any of the desserts) at £11.50 (à la carte main dishes average £11) and this menu changes daily. The restaurant, which only seats 32, is a long, narrow room with tables set along each side, with seating on olive green upholstered benches, and the only decorations are the discreet striped fabric on the walls and a selection of Klimt's most popular prints. Despite its formality and immaculate service the place doesn't overawe and its very pukka clientele make for some very interesting (and unavoidable) ear-wigging. The wine list is appropriately superior with very few half-bottles and a limited choice of wines under £10 a bottle.

Set meal £11.50; alc from £30 a head. Booking essential two weeks in advance for dinner, several days for lunch.

## Thomas de Quincey

36 Tavistock Street, WC2 (240 3972)
Covent Garden tube
Open: 12.30–3pm and 6–11pm Monday–Friday; 7–11.30pm Saturday.

Named after the famous opium eater who used to live upstairs, this is a large and comfortable but rather boringly-decorated restaurant. There is, though, nothing boring about the food. The chef, Serge Fauvez, is well-trained, having worked with luminary Paul Bocuse, and brilliant. He favours the traditional classic cuisine and food is rich, creamy and very memorable. The menu is short and divided equally between fish and meat. Terrine de poisson is a work of art, as are the poached fish set in their own juices with fresh mint, while the frogs' legs and watercress soup is so creamy and rich it is almost a meal in itself. Shellfish lovers should try the superb marinated crayfish cooked in fish stock with herbs and finished in cream. *The* dessert is a soufflé (50 minutes and for two) but the trolley too groans with delights. Needless to say all this perfection costs dear. A recent three-course lunch with one of the cheaper wines came to a staggering £68 (without a tip) but two courses are more than adequate.

From £25 a head.

## Tourment d'Amour

19 New Row, WC2 (240 5348)
Leicester Square tube
Open: 12.30–2pm and 6.30–11.30pm Monday–Saturday; 11.30am–2.30pm and 7–10.30pm Sunday.

Tourment d'Amour is a good place to go if you're making an occasion of an evening out. It's a small, pretty (Topolski sketches on the wall), slightly precious place (napkins are folded into flowing shapes in the glasses) and the food, as well as being good has a strong visual appeal. They used to offer different levels of prix fixe menus, but have now opted for the one at £13.50 for three courses, which is incredibly reasonable for the standard, and allows indulgencies in their formidable list of wines and vintage armagnacs.

A seasonally-changing menu might offer a salade gourmande (three types of lettuce, croûtons, chicken livers), poached quails' eggs in pastry or deep-fried cheese (Stilton, Gruyère) among the starters. Main courses tend to be lightly but richly sauced – lime sauce goes well with the supreme of guinea-fowl, leek accompanies poached brill, and port sauce swims around tender noisettes of lamb. Puddings might offer a pastry flan with black cherries, almonds, kirsch and cream, home-made hazelnut ice-cream or the deliciously light lemon soufflé-style tarte. With such strong and contrasting flavours around, there's a thoughtful list of half-bottles on the wine list to help you choose accordingly. The assiduous young men who provide the service are now helped by the translations on the menu – previously they were obliged to perform like recorded announcements at each and every table.

Expanded opening hours, courtesy of Covent Garden's increasingly busy week, now embrace a formidable three-course Sunday brunch, also at £13.50, which offers an overpowering (unless you're starving) array of poached eggs in brioche, scrambled eggs with smoked salmon, kedgeree, fresh haddock in cucumber sauce, a comprehensive grill-platter or a choice of entrées from the main menu. Bread, brioche, preserves, coffee or tea, Sunday papers and a glass of Buck's Fizz are also included in this bumper offer.

Set meals £13.50 a head (excl. wine)

*Also Good for When You're In the Money:*
Bell, The
Capability Brown
Chez Max
English House, The
Paris House
Waterside Inn

# 3. When You're Short of Cash

Everyone you meet will always know 'this really cheap Albanian restaurant in an alley under Westway', and indeed we've all been there – it's the Salmonella Kebab House, featuring rising damp and falling masonry, a one-armed waiter with a six o'clock shadow and a nine o'clock appointment with his probation officer, the menu includes liver you can't cut let alone eat and a wine list chosen by Dr Crippen. But you mustn't complain because it's so *cheap* . . . No, if you're going to eat on a budget in London you almost have to choose more carefully than if you're spending a packet. The trick is to look for family-run places, preferably in off-centre areas (low overheads), small menus that aren't too ambitious (fresher food) and ethnic restaurants.

# Beewees

96 Stroud Green Road, N4 (263 4004)
Finsbury Park tube
Open: 12.30–4pm and 6–11pm Monday–Saturday.

When the bank account's under strain, eating out, if it's still possible, may not seem to offer much variety – fish and chips, a curry or a Chinese are the usual standbys. Beewees however, offers a chance to branch out into Caribbean cuisine, which because of its no frills, no pretensions nature, can be enjoyed without spending too much money. There are certainly no frills about the décor here – it's more like a caff really, apart from the licence and the desert island scenes painted on the window. The proprietor is a Trinidadian of Indian extraction, so his menu offers both Caribbean and Asian dishes. The main special of the house is a stew of rice, peas, vegetables and salad served with the likes of chicken, beef and goat, all 'curried' on request. Other specials include crab callaloo (crab claw with spinach), couscous and fish stew, and their very good prawn curry. The rum punches are a treat if you can stretch to a quid a glass – and if you can, they'll make you forget your poverty.

About £14 for two.

# The Buttery Grill

31 Rathbone Place, W1
Tottenham Court Road tube
Open: 7am–7pm Monday–Saturday.

This is effectively the canteen for the huge Rathbone Place sorting office, but as well as providing the postmen with a storming English breakfast – huge fry-ups with chips, beans, toast, great cappuccino – the rear section of this formica-furnished room offers brilliantly cheap lunches to local shop assistants, students and the sort of business people who don't have Charlotte Street expense accounts. While predominantly Italian – escalopes, pastas and minestrone – the Buttery Grill also has a strong English flavour, with mixed grills, sausages, mash and onions, steak and kidney pudding, liver and bacon all featuring for less than £2 a piece. Despite the prices and the rough-and-ready look of the place, the cooking is careful and the presentation clean. Skip the rather ordinary starters – soups, prawn cocktails, melon – and leave room for one of their daily stodgerama desserts, like steamed syrup pudding with custard. If you want to make an occasion of it all, the carafes of house wine aren't too bad and the lager isn't over-priced. Because of the crowds, table sharing is usually necessary, but it's safe to eat alone. The amazingly efficient waitresses (there are only two of them) must have memories like Leslie Welch.

About £3 a head.

## The Chelsea Pot

356 King's Road, SW10 (351 3605)
Sloane Square tube and bus
Open: noon–11.30pm daily.

For years the Pot has been serving large portions of international fuel food in unpretentious bistro-ish surroundings. What's on offer never varies and everyone has their favourite dishes. Ours are a small spaghetti to start (60p) sauté of kidneys with wine and mushrooms, rice and chips (£1.05) and apple crumble with ice-cream to finish (55p) – amazing value three-course meal for £2.20! Drink lager or the Italian house wine which isn't particularly cheap at £4.30 a carafe.

From £1.50 a head for food.

## Cosmoba

9 Cosmo Place, WC1 (837 0904)
Russell Square tube
Open: 11.30am–11pm daily.

Nurses, hospital workers and students generally don't have much money to throw around these days, and certainly not on meals out. So it's an indication of how cheap, and socially useful, the Cosmoba is to see how many of its customers come from Great Ormond Street, The Italian Hospital and the university halls of residence nearby. They are attracted by the combination of cheap prices, the wide range of good Italian food, and by the always lively, occasionally chaotic, atmosphere at the Cosmoba. Both the ground-floor and basement dining-rooms are packed with tables and functional chairs. No concessions are made to privacy, as all space must be filled – so if a sixteen-stone gorilla walks in and there's a space at your table, that's where they'll sit him.

You won't mind the bluff service when you get stuck into the huge list of pastas (spaghetti vongole is recommended), pizzas, veal escalopes (£2.60–£3.40), omelettes, steaks and chicken dishes. Notable are the polpettine (meatballs), the tournedos Rossini for around a fiver, and the less-than-classical combination of Dover sole, chips and beans. Cheap carafes and cream caramel/peach melba type puds complete your budget blow-out. The basement's alpine lodge interior is better for larger groups, while the plant-

41

festooned front room is better for couples or solitary diners – you won't be alone for long though.

About £12 for two.

## Costas Grill

14 Hillgate Street, W8 (229 3794)
Notting Hill tube
Open: noon to 10.30pm Monday–Saturday.

For over 25 years the Cypriot Costa family have been providing large and cheap servings of Greek food in a pleasant, unpretentious two-room restaurant with a downstairs overflow. Several generations of family, friends and hungry cat are always in evidence and they welcome their diverse regular clientele and one-off visitors with equal zeal. Hummus (80p) is heavy on garlic and is *the* starter and kleftico (£2.90) lamb on the bone cooked in the oven is *the* main dish, though all your favourite Greek dishes, including yoghurt and honey, are available. Costas also run a fish and chippie a few doors up the road and anything on that menu is available here along with a daily-changing and somewhat surprising choice of dishes – roast pheasant and jugged hare on an autumn visit. House wines start at £3.60, 26fl oz carafe, and Retsina is £4.

From £8 for two.

## Diana's Diner

39 Endell Street, WC2 (240 0272)
Covent Garden tube
Open: 7.30am–7.30pm Monday–Friday; 9am–2.30pm Saturday.

Diana Berns opened her small and homely caff nine years ago because she wanted to prove that it is possible to produce large portions of good quality café fare and old-fashioned British food such as steak and kidney pie and stew at down-to-earth prices. The popularity of the place, which she runs with her husband and a small staff, has proved her point. The short menu is augmented by a daily special and a vegetarian dish. A proper breakfast of egg, bacon, bubble, two slices and two teas will cost around £1.50 and king-size portions of their speciality, home made steak pie with lashings of chips and vegetables, will cost £2. They aren't licensed. The café can seat 40 at pine tables and on benches; during the summer they put tables outside on the pavement. The only drawback is that Diana hasn't solved the problem of lingering cooking smells so your visit is likely to hang on in with you all day.

From £2.

42

## Le Gamin

32 Old Bailey, EC4
St Paul's tube
Open: 10am–3pm Monday–Friday.

While barristers, judges and the Fraud Squad adjourn to the Roux Brothers' swish basement restaurant, poverty-stricken legal clerks may gather in this street-level snack bar which deals in tasty titbits from the same hallowed kitchen. A narrow, functional room, furnished with bar and stools, Le Gamin will nevertheless cheer you with thick soups, a couple of hot dishes (eg, roast chicken pieces with courgettes and red cabbage), good pastries and strong coffee. Crumbs from the rich man's table they may be, but they're bespoke crumbs. Further economies are induced by the absence of a licence.

About £7 for two.

## Geales

2 Farmer Street, W8 (727 7969)
Notting Hill Gate tube
Open: noon–3pm Tuesday–Saturday; 6–11.30pm Tuesday–Friday and 6–11pm Saturday.

Nothing changes at Geales, the now 50-year-old fish restaurant which looks more like an olde worlde tea shop and is West London's most popular chippie. Check cloths cover the tables, the menu is posted on a central blackboard and the no-nonsense waitresses encourage a fast turnover – they don't take bookings. Its many regulars like it for its lack of pretension and cheap, good quality fish, though the soggy chips, nursery starters and puddings have fewer fans. A fish and chip dinner will cost well under £5 a head; drinks are ordered and paid for separately and theirs is one of the cheapest house wines in town at £2.95.

Private parties of up to 20 can be accommodated during the summer on the roof garden, and on Sundays and Mondays when the restaurant is closed the entire place is available for hire.

From £8 for two.

## Jimmy's

23 Frith Street, W1 (437 9521)
Leicester Square tube
Open: 12.30–3pm and 5.30–11pm Monday–Friday; 12.30–11pm Saturday.

Despite the smart new blue awning and a lick of paint round the entrance, Jimmy's remains *the* Soho caff par excellence. The chaotic basement room with its jam-packed formica tables and anarchic waiters attract a mixed crowd, ranging from hard-up students and jazz fans en route to Ronnie Scott's to studiously shabby Sloanes getting off on 'slumming' for the night. So your enjoyment of Jimmy's could hinge on who you wind up sitting next to. Still, the Greek food and its prices are cheerful enough – hummus for 60p and squid for a quid are among the starters. The main courses go slightly 'European' with the likes of chicken casserole and escalope of pork, pan-fried in breadcrumbs, but there are still reliable Greeks around – kleftiko, stuffed vine leaves and moussaka, with baklava among the puds. Most of this stuff is considerably better than the surroundings and the brusque service suggest, and even the house wine in carafes at just over £3 is not the throat-stripper you fear it might be. Not the place for a big night out then, Jimmy's is nevertheless great for a quick fill-up, or indeed for a break from shopping on Saturdays, when it's open virtually all day.

About £13 for two.

## Kowloon

21 Gerrard Street, W1 (437 1694)
Leicester Square tube
Open noon–midnight daily.

Although Chinese food has a reputation for being very filling while you eat it but leaving a gnawing hunger a couple of hours later, I'd defy anyone to feel peckish after a few of the buns sold at this Chinese bakery. The buns may look ordinary and uninspiring piled in the window, but virtually all of them are stuffed with a variety of curried meats or extraordinary mixtures of nuts, fruits and spices and they average 40p each. They are at their best warm and fresh from the oven (best selection around noon) and as the day progresses the choice is severely reduced as they go 'like hot cakes'. Fortunately everything is annotated in English (as well as Chinese) and we'd particularly recommend the following: glutinous rice covered and stuffed with coconut and chopped peanuts (biting into that is downright obscene), steamed water chestnut cake, croquettes of glutinous rice stuffed with lotus seed paste and rolled in sesame seed, and egg tarts. Everything is for take-away (in lurid gold and red boxes) or you can eat the buns or choose from a limited menu in the adjoining Hong Kong-style rough-and-ready tea room; the soups and crab dishes are reliably good.

From £2 a head.

# The Lantern

23 Malvern Road, NW6 (624 1796)
Kilburn Park tube
Open: noon–3pm and 7pm–midnight daily.

A largish proportion of the price we pay for West End and Central London meals goes towards the restaurant's rates and other such overheads. Just how little good food and decent service can cost when stripped of these burdens is shown by the Lantern. Converted from a shop premises in a rather scruffy terrace, and standing opposite a bleak housing estate, the Lantern is obviously not in the swishest part of town, but this finds its compensation in remarkably reasonable prices. The dining room has been simply furnished with thick curtains and butcher's block tables, bearing flowers and candles in wax-encrusted bottles, to create a snug, bistro atmosphere. The regular menu is chalked up on a blackboard, showing that all the starters currently cost just £1.10 and all main courses £2.70. Considering the prices, the quality and range of what's offered are outstanding.

Begin with the deep-fried Emmenthal with tartare sauce, pork sticks with a peanut butter dip, chicken wings in garlic butter or the tangy smoked trout pâté. Main courses include a huge lamb steak with tarragon, a chicken breast rolled with breadcrumbs, duck in Grand Marnier and oranges and a fish special-of-the-day – perhaps lemon sole. Desserts offer the wonderful princess roll (profiteroles filled with banana cream in hot chocolate sauce) and a variety of home-baked cheesecakes and gâteaux. There are eight reasonably-priced house wines covering a range of sweetness and 'body'. Plentiful coffee and informal but efficient service complete what must be the best value-for-money restaurant in London.

A companion restaurant, La Cloche, has now opened at 304 Kilburn High Road, NW6 (328 0302) boasting a similar menu and prices.

About £18 for two.

# Ooblies

78 Chester Road, N19 (263 3899)
Archway tube
Open: 7–11pm Tuesday–Thursday; 7pm–midnight Friday and Saturday.

The French cottoned on years ago to the cheap but wholesome qualities of pancakes, and here you can enjoy the original Gallic versions, crêpes, turned out before your very eyes on the restaurant's giant circular griddles. Ooblies reflects the food itself –

simple, unpretentious but tasteful, making the best of an unpromising location in a modern housing and shopping complex, with plain white walls, mirrors and large tables. Fillings for the pancakes are choice and imaginative – you can make up various combinations from elements such as asparagus, creamed leeks and chicken, or take the tried and trusted recipes. Among these the poulet Basquaise filling embraces chicken, courgettes and pimentos, and there's boeuf bourguignon or Stilton with apple and prawns in herb sauce. Sweet fillings, if you can find room for them, offer delicious combinations of liqueurs, fruit and ice-cream. Ooblies isn't licensed, so whether you bring a bottle or not is entirely between you and your wallet. The spacious tables and standard pricing of the pancakes make Ooblies a potentially useful venue for eating in groups.

About £5 a head.

## Perdoni's

18–20 Kennington Road, SE1 (928 6846)
Lambeth North tube
Open: 7am–7pm Monday–Friday; 7am–noon Saturday.

Hard by Lambeth North tube station and, should you ever need to know, equally handy for the Imperial War Museum, Perdoni's is a classic up-market Italian café – sure, the tables are formica, but they're fitted with smart tip-up seats, and the place is as bright as a button. The menu too, embraces both early morning fry-ups and such distinguished lunchtime fare as spezzatino di pollo alla cacciatore (chicken with tomatoes, onions, carrots, celery and mushrooms in a white wine sauce) and beef Stroganoff. There's a decent range of Italian wines and beers too if you really want to put on the style. Simple grills, steaks, omelettes and pizzas dominate the main card with ever-changing daily specials showing flair-cum-economy in the kitchen – tender cosciotto di miale alla Normana (leg of pork with rosemary, butter, apple rings and white wine sauce) for just £2.40 is a fair example. Finish off with delicious jam puddings, cream trifles and lemon meringue pies. Italian mammas provide bright and breezy service.

About £5 a head.

# Peter's

59 Pimlico Road, SW1 (730 5991)
Sloane Square tube
Open: 7am–10pm Monday–Saturday; 8.30am–4pm Sunday.

You'll be able to tell how full Peter's is from the number of black cabs parked outside. Number One with the capital's taxi-drivers, Peter's can sometimes seem like their private club instead of what it is – a great 'people's restaurant' serving wholesome food at non-profiteering prices. While the macho atmosphere may be forbidding to women – and the packed communal tables may mean you sit next to someone who's just wolf-whistled at you or nearly run you over – don't be put off. The range of home-made soups and pastas, steaks, liver and onions, chicken escalopes and fruit crumbles is magnificent. Considering he doesn't take notes, the waiter performs a brilliant feat of memory and is thoroughly efficient. Tips: the door opens outwards; go up and get a menu rather than wait to be given one; don't ask to see the wine list as there isn't a licence.

About £9 for two.

# Le Petit Prince

5 Holmes Road, NW5 (267 6752)
Kentish Town tube
Open: 12.30–2.30pm and 7–11pm Tuesday–Friday; 7–11.30pm Saturday and Sunday.

This small and steamy French/Algerian café acts almost as a neighbourhood kitchen. Regulars turn up with their own plates for a huge portion of the house speciality – couscous. The cracked wheat base comes with a choice of boulettes (spicy meatballs), kebab, merguez (spicy sausages), braised chicken, lamb cutlets or mutton chop, and is moistened by a bowl of vegetable broth with chick peas and spiced with a small pot of hot pepper paste. Large bowls of couscous with all the works (Imperial) will be a complete meal for two for around £12. To accompany the couscous, drink their Sidi Brahim Algerian wine, made especially to go with this dish. A small, changing menu also offers generous portions of such fillers as poulet provençale (with tomatoes, onions, garlic and courgettes), onion soup, pork cutlets baked with apples and calvados, served with boulangère potatoes (baked with onions and meat-stock), and the old favourite boeuf bourguignon. Finish with chocolate mousse, créme caramel, prunes in red wine or home-made ice-cream.

Run by young people, and now about eight years old, Le Petit Prince is an unpretentious, cosy and friendly place, complete with tortoise-shell cat, and the food served here is wholesome, filling and remarkably cheap. After the meal, sip Moroccan peppermint tea, wallow in the French jazz and imagine you're on the rive gauche.

About £8 a head.

## Rodos

59 St Giles High Street, WC2 (836 3177)
Tottenham Court Road tube
Open: noon–2.30pm Monday–Friday; 6–11.30pm Monday–Saturday.

In the shadow of Centre Point, Rodos seems to be a run-of-the-mill kebab house – a small room with a cluster of tables backing onto an open kitchen. What distinguishes it however is the welcome from the couple who run the place, and the extraordinary scale of the house's mezedakia. For £7.75, you'll get a selection of all the usual Greek dips with pitta and olives, dolmades (stuffed vine leaves), boiled and fried squid and roast quail – this is just for starters! The 'main course' embraces a huge fetta salad and a plate of grilled sausages, potatoes and meats – loukanika, kleftiko, chicken, you name it, it's on there no fewer than 15 different items! In the interests of economy (and humanity) the owner will assess the precise size of your needs – meze for two will certainly be enough for three or four people for example – and price your meal accordingly. This reduces an already reasonable cost still further and probably saves a life to boot. Just when you've surrendered, the boss will bring you a bowl of fresh dates to finish you off.

About £20 for two.

## Sree Krishna Restaurant

194 Tooting High Street, SW17 (672 4250)
Tooting Broadway tube
Open: noon–3pm and 6–11pm (midnight Friday and Saturday) daily.

It's sometimes inevitable when eating out cheaply to have to accept lower standards – of cooking, service and décor. At this marvellous South Indian restaurant however, the food, the efficiency of the staff and the comfortable, well-furnished interior would probably do justice to a place costing three times as much. Although situated right on Tooting High Street, the restaurant is cocooned from traffic noise by thick curtains, a low ceiling and wooden-slatted walls. Much of the seating verges on the communal, with long, spotlessly clean tables ranging up the centre of the room, although there are one or two individual tables dotted around – even then you may have to share just to get the queue down to manageable proportions. Bookings are taken, but it's usually a question of first come, first served.

Start immediately with one of their specials, masala dosai, a crisp pancake made from ground rice and black gram, filled with potatoes and fried rice. A bowl of sambal sauce (savoury gravy, lentils, vegetables, tamarind juice) should accompany this. Another special worth trying is the vadai, a delicious lentil doughnut. Then choose from the short range of meat, chicken, seafood or vegetable curries and biryanis (for around £2 each), accompanied by a couple of vegetables, perhaps spinach bhaji, the thin hot paratha bread, and rice flavoured with lemon or coconut. There is a short French wine list, but most people stick to lager or mineral water. This keeps the cost down still further – and then you can splash out on a taxi home.

About £12 for two.

## Sukothai

22 Bateman Street, W1 (434 2320)
Leicester Square tube
Open: noon–3pm and 6.30–11pm Monday–Saturday.

Thai food has all the fun of Chinese (easy to share, difficult to get on a fork, off-the-wall ingredients) but with a lot more bite to the sauces. For example, spicy peanut sauce is popular with the traditional pork or beef satays (kebabs) which are served as starters, while you're likely to find a very hot fish sauce lurking with intent around delicious fried pork with ginger and chillies (just try to imagine edible Vick). Other notables at this cramped, simple (plastic table-cloths) but cheerful restaurant are the crisp fried fish with chilli sauce, fried won-ton (meat-filled pancakes) and the pork with chilli and dry fungus (is that off-the-wall enough for you?) Drink European wines, lagers or Chinese tea.

About £12 for two.

## Tilley's Eats

208 Camden High Street, NW1 (485 4506)
Camden Town tube
Open: 6.30–11pm Monday–Wednesday; 6.30–11.15pm Thursday–Saturday; 1–5pm Sunday.

The no-nonsense name is a clue to this place's intentions – no 'Tilley's All British Disaster' or 'Tilley and Chilli', just cheap, wholesome eating. In fact the style of Tilley's is somewhere between a French family-run restaurant and a working-men's caff. Simply furnished and lit, it offers good home cooking – soups, grilled meat or fish and a range of mum's home-made pies (fish, steak, chicken and ham). The 'mum' is not just an ad-man's invention, she's there in the kitchen with her son, the owner. Large portions, cheap but good wine (or real ale) and classy background music (Randy Newman, Grover Washington) complete the picture.

About £14 for two.

## Tsiakkos Kebab House

5 Marylands Road, W9 (286 7896)
Westbourne Park tube
Open: 5.30–11.15pm Monday–Saturday.

Analysts of the continental ability to provide cheap restaurants usually come up with the solution that having a family-run place, with everyone pulling together, is the simplest way to cut costs. The theory would seem to hold good for Tsiakkos, a tiny Cypriot kebab house just off Harrow Road. The front-room is occupied by the charcoal grill, the refrigerated counter and the family dining-table of the people who own the operation. Beyond this is a grotto-like 'visitors' room', dark, cosy and filled with all manner of bric-à-brac, from stuffed birds and clumps of garlic to wine-flasks and Chinese prints. With the candle-lit gloom, the checked oil-cloths on the tables and the buzz of bouzouki music, you could almost be eating in the Plaka district of Athens at the foot of the Acropolis – and the prices here are just as cheap.

The meze, at £5 a head for a minimum of two people, is astonishing value – three plates of dips, pitta bread, olives and green chillies, Greek sausages and a pork kebab, large bowl of salad, moussaka, dolmades, followed by either lamb casserole or kleftico with a delicious haricot bean, cucumber and potato stew. Alternatives to this well-prepared feast are grilled red mullet, the beef stew stifado, kebabs or sheftalia. Finish off with their refreshing home-made dessert galaktobourokko – flaked pastry filled with egg custard. Tsiakkos isn't licensed, but there's a cheap, high-quality Spanish wine shop, Moreno, just a few doors away.

About £6 a head.

*Also Good for When You're Short of Cash:*
Ajimura
Antiquarius
Astrix
Bahn Thai
Bamboo Kuning

Bar Crêperie
Blue Sky
Bouzy Rouge
Bunga Raya
Busabong
Caffe Mamma
Calabash
Carriages
Cathay Restaurant
Chalk and Cheese
Chez Solange Wine Bar
Chicago Pizza Pie Factory
Chicago Rib Shack
Chuen Cheng Ku
Covent Garden Pasta Bar
Crêperie, The
Crusting Pipe
Daniel's
Diamond, The
Diwana Bhel Poori House
East West Restaurant
Filling Station
Food for Thought
Golders Hill Park Refreshment Bar
Green and Pleasant
Hampstead Patisserie
Han Kuk Ko Kwan
Harry's
Huff's
ICA Restaurant
Joy King Lau
Kentucky Fried Chicken
Linda's
Little Italy
L. S. Grunt's
Mandeer
Marine Ices
Messrs. C
Metro, Le
Mustoe Bistro
Neal's Yard Tea Rooms
Nineteen
No. 1
Parsons
Pasta Connection
Patisserie Française

Peppermint Park
Picasso, The
Pucci Pizza Vino
Quality Chop House
Raw Deal
Sabras
Sea-Shell Restaurant
Serendipity
Slinky's
Smithy's Wine Bar
Soho Brasserie
Solopasta
Texas Lone Star Saloon
Tire Bouchon, Le
Tootsies
Tuttons
Widow Applebaum's

# 4. When You're in the Mood for Romance

When it comes to a romantic dinner most people would think of somewhere with candles on the tables, soft music on the stereo and French food on the menu. But there's more to the art of seductive dining than that these days. If the candle burns your wrists as you attempt to hold hands, a Barry Manilow record brings back memories of a pet that got run over, or you order andouillettes (pigs' bladders) because they sound nice, the evening could be a disaster. And what if the Italian waiters all look like Al Pacino? Or if the couple at the table six inches away are talking about the mortgage rate? The right atmosphere, the right food and the right degree of intimacy are not always easy to find.

## Bagatelle

5 Langton Street, SW10 (351 4185)
Sloane Square/South Kensington tube
Open: noon–2pm and 7–11pm Monday–Saturday.

Elegant and chic with deco overtones and stunning black and white photos by Brassai, Bagatelle is informal yet formal enough to make an occasion of a visit. The colour scheme is beige and white, frequently uplifted by stunning arrangements of white lilies. In the summer they make use of their pretty and sweet-smelling honeysuckle and jasmine garden.

The food matches the décor – stylish and nouvelle inspired – and at lunch they serve a very good value set meal for £9 a head. The waiters are all French and serve with style, formally attired in black and white. The menu changes seasonally but we have enjoyed little cocottes of mushroom purée with egg baked (à la egg florentine) in the oven, followed by deliciously tender and pink medallions of lamb cooked in cream and tarragon. Their desserts are stunning to look at and tasty; a cold Grand Marnier soufflé piled inside a tuile and topped with candy floss, and delicate pastry shells filled with light chantilly cream and fresh raspberries are the most spectacular. The cheeseboard will arrive automatically, French-style before dessert, and offers a good ripe selection.

Set lunch £9; alc from £15 a head.

## Blakes Hotel

33 Roland Gardens, SW7 (370 6701)
Gloucester Road tube
Open: 7.30–11.30pm Monday–Saturday

The menu is international in the fullest sense of the word at the chic basement restaurant of one of London's most fashionable hotels. You don't have to rent a room to dine here and any pretensions to doing so after the meal will require a very thick wad of cash (around £100 for a very luxurious suite, all credit cards accepted). The place is very elegant from its tall trees in ali baba baskets at the electric glass doors (beware the very slippery floor). You go downstairs to the black and mirrored restaurant with its adjoining bar and heavenly and comfortable sofaed salon. Simple but stunning flower arrangements are spot-lit and an amazing collection of Thai warrior costumes are displayed in glass cabinets.

The meal begins with bowls of crudités with two dips, and there is a choice of ten starters and ten mains. Their ceviche (raw marinated fish) is a wiser choice than the warm seafood salad which looks pretty enough but has far too many flavours and is drenched in dressing. Beef Teriyaki (fine slivers of beef in a soy sauce) palls after the first few tastes but the Szechuan duck has been excellent. Finish with a delicious mango sorbet; coffee (available with cardamom) is served with dark chocolates in envelopes embossed with Blakes' logo.

One-course meals from £5, three-course meal from £15.

## Bubb's

329 Central Markets, Farringdon Road, EC1 (236 2435)
Farringdon tube
Open: 12.15–2pm and 7–9.30pm Monday–Friday.

Some of the cosiest restaurants in Paris are to be found in the bleakest settings. The Farringdon Road/Smithfield area at night is about as charmless as you can get in London, so that certainly makes you appreciate the warm atmosphere at Bubb's. It has an authentic French flavour to the décor – dark-coloured walls, lace curtains, white table-cloths – and there's a chanteuse crackling on the stereo. The jumble of rooms can usually guarantee a table with a degree of privacy, and the food is sufficiently stimulating yet sufficiently light to work the magic. Fish is a particular strong point – charlotte de turbot, marinière de poissons, salmon crêpes have all been well-received, and their daily specials often include exotic stuff like quail, roast partridge and baudroie, the principal ingredient of that Mediterranean aphrodisiac, bouillabaisse. When you step back out onto those mean streets after a fine meal here, there's only one place left to go . . .

About £35 for two.

## The Cardinal Restaurant

Wolsey's Wine Bar, 52 Wells Street, W1 (636 5121)
Oxford Circus tube
Open: noon–2.30pm Monday–Friday.

A prime consideration in choosing a venue for seduction, particularly if it's an illicit one, is 'will I be spotted by office colleagues/ friends/husband/wife?' The 'out-of-the-way' places suggested elsewhere in this section are an obvious help, but there's nothing like a good basement, with no faces peering in through the window, in which to work calmly. The atmosphere at the Cardinal, situated below Wolsey's Wine Bar, is further helped by dark, plum-coloured walls, well-spaced tables and a coal fire in winter, though a little music would help even more. The food is just right for the occasion – classy, inventive and light. They're particularly strong on fish and shellfish, with salmon, mussels, crayfish, scallops, turbot and even pike featuring regularly. Among the starters there's a smashing hot mousse of brill floating in two contrasting sauces of crayfish and watercress. Moules marinières are another possibility, although there's always smoked breast of goose with orange sauce for hairy-chested meat eaters. Fresh salmon in champagne sauce or turbot in a sauce with calvados and wild mushrooms are two known winners among the main courses and this, together with rather dry calves' kidneys with liver, confirms that the Cardinal's got a better fishmonger than he has a butcher. Ginger ice-cream might be a good dessert, though the cheese basket is crammed with high quality French produce. The wines are top-notch but reasonably-priced.

About £20 a head.

## Chaopraya

22 St Christopher's Place, W1 (486 0777)
Bond Street tube
Open: noon–3pm and 6.30–11pm Monday–Saturday.

There's a sense of elegance and style to this pretty Thai restaurant. The large, low-ceilinged room (*don't* sit upstairs) is made charmingly cosy and private by a series of screens, and there are extra-private alcove seats. Baskets of dried flowers, fresh flowers on all the tables and waitresses in traditional dress add touches of colour to the white room.

The menu is long but explicit, with several specialities and set meals. Be guided by the waitresses or take up our recommendation of Thai fish soup, which is cooked in a steamer on the table and is likely to include squid, prawns, mackerel and other white fish with Chinese cabbage in a spicy stock which you can make piquant with a chilli sauce. If you can't cope with choosing opt for one of the set meals which start around £8. French house wine £4.50, jasmine tea on the house. Chaopraya does children's portions and caters for vegetarians; and occasionally there are Thai dancers.

Set meals from £8; à la carte from £10.

## Chez Moi

1 Addison Avenue, W11 (603 8267)
Holland Park tube
Open: 12.30–2.30pm Monday–Friday; 7–11.30pm Monday–Saturday.

Holland Park is Harold Pinter's manor, and Chez Moi at lunchtime certainly has its share of those illicit-but-cool liaisons which so absorb him. It's easy to see why Chez Moi is that sort of venue – a discreet setting in a quiet street; opaque windows to prevent prying eyes; spacious, well-decorated interior with large tables-for-two; and last but not least, a sophisticated French menu. The food and its presentation have few of the pretensions of nouvelle cuisine but some of its imagination. Among the hot starters are a delicious, individual smoked salmon quiche and a ramekin of leeks and bacon in cheese sauce, while the list of cold starters includes a spinach and warm chicken liver salad. There's a short range of charcoal grilled meats, a couple of pleasant fish dishes (fillets of sole with tomatoes and artichokes) and half-a-dozen inventive specialities – poached chicken breasts in pear and Pernod sauce, for example. Linger with your forbidden fruit over chocolate truffle cake, chocolate pot with orange Curaçao, or home-made coffee ice-cream. After that, it's back to chez toi for the afternoon . . .

About £40 for two.

## La Croisette

168 Ifield Road, SW10 (373 3694)
Earls Court tube
Open: 1–2.30pm and 7.30–11.30pm Tuesday–Sunday, closed Tuesday lunch.

There's many a would-be seducer who thinks that there is nothing sexier than eating with your fingers and we all know what oysters are meant to do for your sex life. At La Croisette (the first of the three French fish restaurants run by Pierre Martin) you can eat oysters in style or spend hours picking through their famous and spectacular plateau de fruits de mer. In the basement restaurant, which is decorated in rather fussy French bourgeois style, with jolly water colours of the South of France and neat provençal print fabric, the meal is a set one. It begins with a kir and appetisers of garlicky brown shrimps and slices of hot pissaladière and you can then choose from the short menu of starter, main and dessert with a mixed leaf salad and Stilton thrown in. *The* starter is the plateau – a bed of seaweed on a large piece of cork, brimful of claire, belon and Colchester oysters, shrimps, langoustines, whelks, winkles, crabs and amandine. Follow with one of their beautifully prepared and presented fish (lobster is available). We always choose the superb turbot in champagne sauce.

Set meal £17.50, house wines from £5.50; from £20 a head.

## Crusting Pipe

27 The Market, Lower Piazza, Covent Garden, WC2 (836 1415)
Covent Garden tube
Open: 11.30am–3pm and 5.30–11pm Monday–Saturday.

A series of rooms which look more like vaults or cellars, and get darker the further back you go, comprise the Crusting Pipe wine bar. The inner rooms are candle-lit at lunchtime, as is the whole place in the evening. The Pipe is part of the Davy's chain, which means the floor is strewn with sawdust, the atmosphere is informal and the food confined to plates of cold meats (£2.20) and game pie and charcoal-grilled rib of beef or sirloin steak (just under £5). Baked potatoes, salads, Stilton, farmhouse Cheddar or double Gloucester and apple pie or cheesecake with Devon cream follow. The wine list is moderately priced with a decent house wine at £4.20 but the specialities are champagne by the tankard (£3.40), sparkling blanc de blanc (£6.50 bottle) and pint jugs of port from the wood (from £5.95). Vintage ports are decanted daily. There is also seating for up to 100 outside.

Food from £3.

## Didier

5 Warwick Place, W9 (286 7484)
Warwick Avenue tube
Open: 12.30–2.30pm and 7.30–10.30pm Monday–Friday.

Quiet spots aren't too easy to find in frenetic London, so anywhere with a restful, discreet atmosphere has a head start in the seduction stakes. Arriving at Didier, you could almost be in the country – leafy canal-side walks nearby, a nursery garden at the rear, and an art gallery and book shop adjacent, in this narrow lane off Warwick Avenue. Disarmed by the setting, your date will then be charmed by the premises – dinky, pretty in a floral, Laura Ashley way, and highly conducive to conversations of the heart.

The basic menu is rather plain (good for those in a rush) with starters as simple as avocado vinaigrette, mushrooms in olive oil with coriander, or mozzarella and tomato salad. Main courses offer two lamb's kidneys creations, one served in a mustard sauce, one grilled with bacon, with omelettes, trout with almonds and sirloin steaks emphasising the uncomplicated approach. The romantic lingerers however will enjoy the more adventurous menu du jour, which responds to seasons and market availabilities. There could be a carré d'agneau en chemise or a robust pheasant casserole. Nice desserts include crème brûlée, chocolate mousse or pear and lemon tart. Muscat de Beaumes de Venise dessert wine and various classy teas finish the meal on just the right note.

About £15 a head.

## Fisherman's Wharf at The Belvedere

Holland House, Holland Park, W8 (602 1238)
Holland Park tube
Open: noon–3pm and 6.30–10.30pm Monday–Saturday.

London is full of beautiful parks, yet none of them has anything halfway approaching a decent restaurant – except, that is, for Holland Park and the Belvedere. The Abbotsbury Road entrance will lead you through the car-park to the seventeenth-century Belvedere, flanked by lawns and rambling courtyards and cloisters. The house is probably at its best on a summer day when the airiness of the reception room and the first-floor dining gallery, the lightness of the décor and the quiet can best be appreciated – but then again, when nights close in and the lights dim, the quietness suggests you're dining in a country house rather than a central London restaurant. Up to a year ago, the Belvedere dealt in rather bland international cuisine, but now it's under the Fisherman's Wharf banner with a firm identity to offer. There are still hints of the 'international business traveller', both in prices and in some of the selections (Dover sole, bouillabaisse, venison in red wine) but now there's an invention in the cooking and a lightness in the saucing which certainly suits our purposes in this section. Starters of quails' eggs on a nest of smoked salmon mousse, orange segments flamed in sake, or oysters Belvedere (with green peppercorns and a julienne of vegetables with cream) should set you on the road to fulfilment. Progress shouldn't be halted by the likes of poached turbot in champagne sauce, sea bass in Pernod and fennel sauce or baked sole with hazelnuts and grapefruit in a white rum sauce. Even if the food doesn't do the trick, the park, the moonlight and the birdsong certainly will . . .

About £40 for two.

## Flavio

1A Lanton Street, Worlds End, SW10 (352 7414)
Sloane Square/South Kensington tube
Open: noon–3pm and 7pm–midnight Monday–Saturday and Sunday lunch.

There are several discreet corner tables at this comfortable, unpretentious Italian restaurant. It's never had the fashionable following of its neighbours La Famiglia and Bagatelle and perhaps this is why standards have remained high. The menu is short and like most Italian restaurants these days they feature several fresh pasta dishes which are served perfectly al dente. They also specialize in fish. We'd heartily recommend anything on the menu but particularly the pasta, split, grilled prawns with garlic and their liver dishes. Theirs is a superb zabaglione and their wine list features a couple of very good Sicilian wines; house wine £4.45.

From £10 a head.

## Gastronome One

309 New King's Road, SW6 (731 6381)
Parsons Green tube
Open: noon–2.30pm Monday–Friday; 7–11pm Monday–Saturday, closed August.

There's a choice of eating by the mock log fire or in the larger adjoining mirrored room at this pretty basement restaurant. Predominantly apple-green with hanging plants, the two rooms are very cosy and seating is at comfortable banquettes in the mirrored room and more formally next door. Run by a young French couple, the place has an easy atmosphere and a good adventurous chef.

They offer a series of set meals which are exceptional value, or a short à la carte. Fish is a clear favourite. Specialities include ragout de lotte du Père Martin – monkfish garnished with young vegetables and served with steamed rice, and aiguillette de canard aux petites baies – a fillet of roast duck done with young berries. Chef's daily specials are particularly recommended. Follow with their usually-ripe plateau de fromage or try the house sorbets. A pleasant, unpretentious place.

Plat du jour £4.50; set menus from £6.50 to £10; alc £12 a head for food, house wine £4.45.

## Maggie Jones

6 Old Court Place, Kensington Church Street, W8 (937 6462)
High Street Kensington tube
Open: 12.30–2.30pm and 7.30–11pm daily.

Maggie Jones, named in honour of a local royal divorcée, is tucked away in a narrow lane off Kensington Church Street. Sawdusted floors and pine tables with candles are augmented by a number of evocative nooks and crannies and one or two high-backed banquette booths in which privacy is guaranteed. A pronounced gay element among the friendly, efficient staff means that gay couples shouldn't feel at all uncomfortable here, but then neither should the most aggressive heterosexuals. The menu is ruggedly English, so careful choosing is required if you're going to stay the course. Starters are light enough – potted shrimps, chicken liver pâté, artichoke hearts in vinaigrette, haddock mousse – but might be best left alone if you're also going for a heavy, rich pudding. Main courses include grilled saddle of lamb with rosemary, steak and kidney pie, rabbit and mustard casserole, and roast chicken in creamed cucumber sauce, all cooked in decent fashion. Like its companion restaurant La Poule au Pot (see this section) Maggie Jones serves its house wine in a magnum then charges you by the glass for how much you take from it. This system can work out expensive in every sense.

About £15 a head.

## La Pomme d'Amour

128 Holland Park Avenue, W11 (229 8532)
Holland Park tube
Open: 12.30–2.30pm Monday–Friday; 7–11pm Monday–Saturday.

A suggestively-named place with illicit overtones – in fact it's an ideal venue for that sort of meeting. The conservatory at the rear with its sliding roof aids and abets seductive summer lunches, while the well-upholstered dining-room with open fire is at its best on gloomy winter evenings. The tables are thoughtfully-spaced, though on one occasion I was bombarded by my neighbour's tales of Goering's love of boar-hunting. Assuming these people aren't there, the only other obstacle to fulfilment is the richness of the French food. It is stimulating to the mind and eye – roast duckling with Grand Marnier and raisin sauce, chicken leg filled with crab mousse in a lobster sauce, snails and artichokes in calvados – but needs to be approached cautiously. Three courses of this sort of intensity would stop even Casanova in his tracks.

About £40 for two.

## La Poule Au Pot

231 Ebury Street, SW1 (730 7763)
Sloane Square tube
Open: 12.30–2.15pm Monday–Friday and 7–11.15pm Monday–Saturday.

If Gallic bluff and charm and rustic decorations reminiscent of a French country farmhouse spell romance then this is the place for you. One large room whose tables radiate around the stairwell and salad table has a couple of smaller more intimate adjoining rooms and there's a downstairs dining room. It's pleasantly cluttered with lots of secluded corners, candle-light and a busy atmosphere. White starched, lace-trimmed cloths, the odd bare oak table and copper pots, various china poules, bare brick walls, plenty of greenery and an ebullient and very fat French maître d all add up to a very pleasant place. Food is reliably prepared, portions very generous and in the evening the à la carte menu will include at least one dish per course that is your favourite French bistro dish. At lunch they do an excellent value three-course set lunch. They cunningly sell their house wine from magnums and charge you for what you drink (95p a glass), which can be very expensive.

Set lunch £6.95, alc £15 a head.

## Read's

152 Old Brompton Road, SW5 (373 2445)
Gloucester Road tube
Open: 12.30–2.30pm and 7.30–11pm Monday–Saturday; 12.30–3pm Sunday.

Though it's a small restaurant there is plenty of space between the nine tables at this attractive and subtly-lit place. The decorations are stylish but simple with pale apricot walls, huge displays of flowers and unusual bold and colourful Pichwai textiles on the walls. Large mirrors give an impression of space. The food is nouvelle cuisine at its best, prepared by one of London's few female chefs and served in style from silver trays. The menu is short, innovative and extremely reasonably-priced as is the ten-strong (from Corney & Barrow) wine list. Wild mushrooms in a sweet brioche followed by quenelles of chicken with pistachio and green pepper sauce are typical dishes and the meal starts with a radiccio salad and finishes with superb home-made truffles. Potatoes, shaped like miniature apples and pears, are presented à la Brian Turner of the Capital Hotel (he along with Anton Mossiman of the Dorchester and Quentin Crewe of Brasserie St Quentin are chef Caroline Swatland's mentors). The food will leave you satisfied but not over-laden; ideal for romantic soirées. On Sundays a traditional English lunch, flanked by imaginative starters and puddings, is served.

Set lunch £9.50 (excl wine); Sunday lunch £12.50 (excl wine); alc £30 for two.

## The Restaurant

Dolphin Square, Chichester St, SW1 (828 3207)
Pimlico tube
Open: noon–2.30pm Monday–Friday; 7–11.30pm Monday–Saturday (Restaurant); 7.30am–10.30am; noon–3pm and 6–11.30pm Monday–Saturday (Brasserie).

Tucked behind one of the biggest blocks of service flats in Europe, the Dolphin Square Restaurant is quite one of the most romantic places to dine in town. Palm-courtish and reminiscent of a grand ocean liner's dining room, the large room is elegant and the lighting soft. Every night a pianist tinkles through a romantic repertoire and there's jazz on Friday and dancing on Saturday. Owned by Alan L'Hermitte of the ever-popular Mon Plaisir in Covent Garden, this restaurant offers a series of set meals ranging from £9 for one course up to £14 for the menu gastronomique which might include hot soufflé with foie gras, boned frogs' legs poached in mussels with cream, freshly-smoked salmon and escalope of veal stuffed with veal sweetbreads served with wild mushrooms. Desserts are similarly complex but as petits fours come with the coffee we'd recommend opting for their cheese which, as at Mon Plaisir, is one of the best boards in London.

If you stick to house wine (£4.90) two can enjoy an evening here for £35.

The brasserie serves a shorter version of the restaurant's menu plus full English breakfast for £3.50 and continental breakfast for £2.25.

## Romantica Restaurant

12 Moscow Road, W2 (727 7112)
Queensway tube
Open: noon–3pm and 6–11pm daily.

No pussy-footing around here – as the name might indicate, the Romantica is unabashed about its intentions and, by extension, those of its customers. The small room is lit only by candles and wall-lights and decorated in boudoir style with carpets and sheepskins crawling up the wall. The ambiance is helped by whispering waiters who tactfully seat couples apart from the throng. Although a Greek restaurant, the Romantica aims a notch or two higher than kebabs – smoked pork, sesame seed dip, baked red mullet, lamb's liver and sweetbreads, fillets of pork in red wine sauce feature on a menu that should evoke memories of sandy knees at Paleocastritsa. Additional touches of flair include the warming and softening of sweet pastries like baklava and kadeifi – a smashed molar at a time like this could be very distressing. As a clincher, try the sweet orange liqueur filfar – as nice as Cointreau and easier to pronounce if you've had one too many.

About £24 for two.

# Siam

12 St Albans Grove, W8 (937 8765)
High Street Kensington tube
Open: 12.30–2.30pm and 6.15–11.15pm Tuesday–Friday; 6.15–11.15pm Monday
and Saturday; 6–10.30pm Sunday.

This pretty little restaurant was one of London's first Thai restaurants when it opened 14 years ago. Upstairs is a small and fairly
spartan room but downstairs is the lavishly traditional Khantok
Room where you must remove your shoes. A series of alcoves open
into the main dining area and diners sit on cushions, eat at low tables
and are served on bended knee by beautiful, traditionally-dressed
Thai girls. It takes a while to adjust to the dim lighting and low level
but it's most relaxing when you do. The highlight of the evening
meal (set and à la carte) is the Thai classical dance show featuring
the traditional hand dance. The set meal is the best value and unless
you know your way round Thai food, this is what we'd recommend.
The meal changes daily but caters to Western taste in Thai food and
is likely to include prawn crackers, a spicy soup (chicken soup is
excellent with lemon and coriander), perhaps satay, rice, a vegetable dish, a meat and vegetable dish (pork with Chinese cabbage is
particularly good) and a pudding – probably fresh fruit served on
crushed ice.

Set meal £7.80; alc £10, house wine £4.90.

# The Summit Restaurant

St George's Hotel, Langham Place, W1 (580 0111)
Oxford Circus tube
Open: 12.30–2.30pm and 6.30–10.15pm daily.

The idea of romancing somebody in the restaurant of a Trust House
Forte Hotel might not seem altogether likely, but this particular
place has two things going for it. The first is incidental – an under-
current of flirtatiousness generated by the presence of so many
people from the adjacent BBC meeting their forbidden friends
here. The second is more substantial – the impressive views from
the top-floor restaurant some 200 feet up above London, and all that
this might do to one's partner's equilibrium. Be warned that, by
day, the initial impressiveness of the vista quickly fades when you
realise that all the 'good stuff' is east of the west-facing windows.
The Post Office Tower, St Paul's, Westminster, National Westminster Bank building can't really be compensated for by QPR's flood-
lights. At night however, with the sun setting in the west, the office
lights twinkling and M40's sodium glare rising into the sky, a

reasonably funky atmosphere can be generated. Every table has some sort of view and the twilight softens some of the hotel's more boring décor. Even the food may seem better – a pretty good three-course dinner, usually built around something like roast rib of beef from the trolley, or a chef's special like beef Stroganoff or trout meunière. With acceptable hors d'oeuvres – gazpacho, smoked fish, whitebait – pleasant house wine and generous cafetières of coffee, you're in with a fair chance of Heaven on the seventh floor.

Set lunch £10.75 a head; set dinner £11 a head; alc about £35 for two.

*Also Good for When You're in the Mood for Romance:*
L'Arlequin
Bahn Thai
Bell, The
Brinkley's
Café des Amis du Vin
Capital Hotel Restaurant
Caravan Serai
Chalcot's
Chez Victor
Dan's
Feathers Hotel
~~~~~ Duck
Haweli
Joe Allen
Julie's Restaurant
Keat's
Ken Lo's Memories of China
Lafayette Bar
Luba's
Masters
Maxim's de Paris
Mon Plaisir
Monsieur Thompson's
Mont St Michel, Le
Nikita's
Odette's
Oval Tandoori
Peachey's
Phoenicia
Pier 31
Pomegranates
Rules
San Frediano
Sheekey's

South of the Border
Spaghetti Opera
Starr Inn
Thé Dansant, Waldorf Hotel
Tycoon
Village Bistro
Waterside Inn

# 5. When You Want to Talk Business

One of the great pillars of British society is the business lunch – an occasion when people get together to pretend they're working when all they're really doing is eating, while also pretending that they're paying when they're really getting it on expenses. Several professions, notably advertising, journalism, television, the music biz and publishing would not survive without people giving each other lunches. We've tried to suggest venues where anyone working in these dedicated fields might feel at home, since part of the trick of a successful business lunch is being seen pretending to talk business in the right place. Occasionally, it's necessary *not* to be seen or overheard, so we've also selected restaurants where discretion is a by-word and industrial espionage are swearwords. Most of these places take credit cards rather than luncheon vouchers of course, so you can impress your guests with your plastic bandoleer of 'flexible friends'.

# Bertorelli Bros Restaurant

19 Charlotte Street, W1 (636 4174)
Goodge Street tube
Open: noon–2.30pm and 6–10pm Monday–Saturday.

Anyone working west of the City or east of Marble Arch must have been to Bertorelli's for a business lunch at some stage in their career. It's that sort of place – one that acts as a focal point for an entire area. Bertorelli's also cuts across the business spectrum by drawing anyone from dental equipment salesmen to advertising executives, though it still has a strong attraction for publishers, writers and journalists. This is partly due to its literary and artistic associations – George Orwell, Dylan Thomas and Augustus John are all past customers – and partly to do with the unchanging nature of the place. The pale colours, starched white table-linen, wall mirrors, hatstands and the charming, ultra-efficient waitresses in black all suggest an age both Bohemian and civilised.

The unchanging Franco–Italian–English menu is another decisive factor – the two sheets, printed in evocative, school exam-paper purple ink, one offering the day's specials, the other the regular menu, don't go in for surprises, just tried and trusted favourites. Best bets are the pasta and the grills, as sauces can be swamped with tomatoes, though pollo sorpresa, goujonettes of sole and escalope alla Milanese have all won devout followings. Other big favourites are the cream caramel, banana split and, if it's on, terrific bread and butter pudding. If you doubt that this sort of stuff can attract an audience, peer into the big dining-room through the net curtains at about 3pm any day – you'll see a lot of well-fed faces basking in the glow of their flaming sambuccas.

About £25 for two.

# Brasserie Mode

15 Great Castle Street, W1 (580 2125)
Oxford Circus tube
Open: 11.30am–3pm Monday–Friday; bar only 5.30–8.30pm.

The fur-and-Ferrari set of London's rag trade can regularly be found wining, dining and posing in this three-layered brasserie. Formerly a gloomy wine-bar called Shireffs, Brasserie Mode now offers cocktails and wines at a ground floor counter, cheapish snacks at a rear dining-room, and modish meals at a restaurant on the upper level. The gloomy décor has been banished by an attractive combination of black and silver, and the walls are hung with fashion drawings and Parisian photographs, as well as the requisite number of mirrors. Dining upstairs you may expect to find a sort of 'nouvelle fast food' – dishes that are striking for their combinations and visual impact, but which have been largely prepared in advance, leaving only essential cooking to follow. Thus the trois bouchelles du Mode are three little pastry cases, recently filled with spicy chopped beef, scallops and prawns, and artistically served on a baked leaf, tasting rather of Chinese sea-weed. Equally noticeable, and appetising, are the creamy moules boules, and there's the inevitable vegetable terrine among the starters. Main courses follow similar lines – calves' liver in calvados decorated with apple slices, veal fillet in a potato cake and a supreme of salmon in sorrel sauce. Downstairs, cheaper, simpler dishes such as moussaka, moules marinières and steak and kidney pie are served. Wherever you sit, the waitresses strut past you as though they were back on the cat-walk.

About £15 for two downstairs, £30 for two upstairs.

## Café St Pierre

29 Clerkenwell Green, EC1 (251 6606)
Farringdon tube
Open: 7.30am–midnight Monday–Saturday; 11am–3pm Sunday.

The increasingly fashionable Clerkenwell area virtually announced its new-found status with the arrival of the Café St Pierre, an excellent multi-layered operation dealing in breakfasts, wine bar snacks, lunches and serious dinners. Situated on a wide, open corner, the Café features a ground-floor brasserie crammed with tables and rather fragile chairs, and a first-floor restaurant, more elegantly and comfortably furnished. Because of its location – Fleet Street, the City, the Barbican and 'The Guardian' are all close at hand – it's gained a substantial following from the business and journalistic communities.

The brasserie offers substantial snacks in the form of sirloin steak or mussels in mustard sauce, as well as lighter dishes such as omelettes and soups. Upstairs, the restaurant, staffed by cheerful waitresses in Piaf-black, has a long, serious menu and an even longer, even more serious wine list. Main courses might include poached turbot in sorrel sauce, roast grouse in wine sauce with kumquats (a bitter-sweet Japanese fruit) or lamb's kidneys in Pernod and cream. The wine list and menu are helpfully integrated with suggestions for appropriate accompaniments next to every dish. Cooking is of a high standard, although ambition occasionally exceeds ability where fish is concerned. A good value Sunday lunch is also served, featuring the likes of fennel soup, smoked salmon trout in mustard sauce and rib of beef with Yorkshire pudding. Tables come out onto the pavement in summer.

About £8 a head (brasserie); £15 a head (restaurant).

## Chez Victor

45 Wardour Street, W1 (437 6523)
Piccadilly Circus tube
Open: noon–3pm Monday–Friday; 6pm–midnight Monday–Saturday.

On the fringes of Chinatown but still a distinct, 50s Soho artefact, Chez Victor is one of the best places in town for an atmospheric literary lunch. The dull-red décor, lace curtains, bare wooden floors, candles in bottles and plain white napery provide a perfect backdrop to strapping 'cuisine bourgeoise' and stroppy Gallic service. Reassess 'les événements de 68' or discuss your still-unpublished novel over great copper pots of onion soup or lobster bisque. Chew the philosophical fat over calves' liver and bacon, delicious coq au vin, skate in black butter, well-cooked steaks au poivre or classical boeuf bourguignon. There's a short but good wine-list, pots of strong coffee and a tempting range of cognacs and armagnacs. Although it's only just off Shaftesbury Avenue, Chez Victor will still cocoon you on the Left Bank for a couple of highly satisfactory hours. Definitely a place where wearing your cords and smoking Gauloises are compulsory.

About £15 a head.

## Corts Wine Bar

33 Old Bailey, EC4 (236 2101)
St Paul's tube
Open: 11.30am–3pm and 5.30–8pm Monday–Friday.

The name sounds about right for a place so near to the Old Bailey, and one can only guess at the number of barristers and solicitors who return late to the office after lunch with the excuse 'Sorry, I've been in Cort . . .' In fact, the low prices and high quality of Corts make it an ideal lunch venue for all sections of the legal profession from secretary to head of chambers. Despite the rather spartan, shop-front exterior, the large room has a convivial atmosphere – the round tables are good for parties – and a short but well-executed menu. Salads are fresh, varied and plentiful and the roast beef has been both lean and acceptably rare. Simple starters nevertheless show care has been taken – fresh avocado with precise vinaigrette, good home-made potato and leek soup. The hot dish of the day is usually of a high standard – perhaps chicken suprême in a cream and ham sauce. Puddings could do with a break from the cheesecake rut but the wines (and ports) seem reasonable and competitively-priced – I suppose they daren't over-charge with so many lawyers around.

About £8 a head.

## Gay Hussar

2 Greek Street, W1 (437 0973)
Tottenham Court Road tube
Open: 12.30–2.30pm and 5.30–10.45pm Monday–Saturday.

For Close Encounters of the Political Kind (especially Socialist), the Gay Hussar is hard to beat. Safely on the edge of Soho, this Hungarian restaurant has been a discreet haunt of Labour politicians and lobby correspondents for well over twenty-five years now. Considering the often delicate nature of the customers' conversations, the Hussar's red velvet upholstered seating, ranged along both sides of the narrow premises, is a little too 'intimate' for either secrecy or comfort. Still, this doesn't discourage the Foots, Hattersleys and Callaghans from turning up to enjoy Victor Sassie's extensive range of Hungarian food.

It is a cuisine, however, that is no friend to delicate stomachs. Just reading the menu is almost enough to give you indigestion – cold cherry or beetroot soup, smoked breast of goose, Serbian chicken with peppers and tomato, veal goulash with dumplings, brawn with dill and tomatoes, stuffed cabbage with sour cream. But underneath all the riots of colour (like the clientèle, pinks and reds predominate) and flavour, there's some subtle cooking going on. A remarkably good value set lunch is an excellent introduction, and a relatively calm course can be steered via the likes of chicken and lemon soup, quenelles of carp and sweet cheese dumplings. Plentiful coffee, an off-beat wine list and pleasant, efficient service will complete an enjoyable trip down the corridors of power.

Set lunch £8.50 (excl wine); alc about £15 a head.

## George and Vulture

3 Castle Court, EC3 (626 9710)
Bank tube
Open: noon–3pm Monday–Friday.

Wily denizens of the City banks beat their way here most lunchtimes – just follow the pin-stripe crocodile between Cornhill and Lombard Street down to St Michael's Alley. The route suggests furtive pleasures, and the George and Vulture delivers. A wonderfully atmospheric old chop-house, it's housed in a 14th-century pub, with opaque windows, half-panelled walls, faded photographs and a jumble of dining-booths. You may be asked to share a table, but business secrets are safe as the casual air of a public school luncheon disarms all. The food takes the chaps back to their days in the Remove, with liver and bacon, vegetable soup, bubble and squeak, charcoal grills, poached fish and – please headmaster! – treacle tart and lemon meringue. Service is appropriately matronly but don't be surprised if a bun-fight breaks out.

About £18 for two.

## Ken Lo's Memories of China

67/69 Ebury Street, SW1 (730 7734)
Victoria tube
Open: noon–2.30pm and 7–11pm Monday–Saturday.

Apart from the problems of parking (the NCP adjacent to the bus station is the best bet) Mr Lo's restaurant is the perfect solution to the business lunch. There is a comfortable reception lounge and the dining-room is cleverly divided with simple carved wooden screens which give each table a sense of privacy but allow surveillance for competitors. The service is prompt and courteous and if tipped off, the Chinese staff will make sure the meal is served within a specified time limit.

The food on offer has been chosen by owner Kenneth Lo who, via numerous cook books, is a household name synonymous with d-i-y Chinese food. Here his menu is varied, includes several set meals and features all the popular regional dishes (crispy duck, crab with ginger, Szechuan hot double-cooked pork, iron plate sizzled dishes, etc) as well as some elaborate feasts which require prior notice. The most modest set meal, called not entirely appropriately A Simple Family Luncheon, is outstanding value at £7.75 and includes dumplings, soup, two meat dishes, stir-fry vegetables and rice, while The Memorable Dinner (£14.50) or Mini Banquet (£17.50) are more appropriate for an impressive business lunch. The food is served in very large portions and chopsticks are laid as a matter of course. The wine list is international and surprisingly even includes some English wines. Very popular with Chinese businessmen entertaining English clients and with well-heeled OAPs who've obviously done a stint out East and like the occasional sortie with chop suey in a civilized setting.

Set lunch £7.75; dinner from £14.50;
à la carte from £10 a head.

## Leoni's Quo Vadis

28–29 Dean Street, W1 (437 4809)
Leicester Square tube
Open: noon–2.30pm and 6–11.15pm Monday–Saturday.

The whiz-kids and Mr Bigs of the British film industry know exactly 'where they're going' most lunchtimes – to Leoni's. It's not just its prime spot in the heart of the Dean Street–Wardour Street dream industry that attracts them, but also the high-quality food, the discreet and efficient service and the stylish, spacious premises. A comfortable lounge leads through to a thickly-carpeted, delicately-coloured dining room, decked with framed sketches and prints, and finished with crisp, pink napery. The tables are well-separated to allow both privacy and elbow room, qualities the movie mogul needs when he's talking deals and brandishing a two-foot cigar. The standard of decor, and of the waiters' dress, is high, so don't be surprised if you get a 'well just this once' look from the maître d'hotel if you turn up in jeans. The surroundings, in fact, are distinctly un-Italian, and the menu seems to hark back to the days when white tiles and bare walls where just a gleam in Enzo Apicella's eye.

There's no sea bass or carpaccio modishness here, just straightforward Roman and Milanese favourites and a strand of chef's specials to give individuality. Among these, the zuppe Quo Vadis (a clear broth served with egg and croûtons), and the deliciously tender petto di pollo Sophia Loren (chicken breast wrapped with Parma ham, filled with bel paese cheese, breadcrumbed and deep-fried) are tried and trusted, and the waiters have obviously heard all the jokes about Ms Loren's breast, so please refrain. There are big votes too for the Parma ham with avocado, the sturdy Tuscan bean soup, grilled fegato with sage, veal chop and precisely-cooked vegetables. There's also a good three-course set lunch which might include soup or egg mayonnaise, lamb cutlets or trout meunière, a trolley sweet and coffee, which is served in voluminous individual flasks kept warm at your table with their own spirit lamps. A distinctive flourish to a distinctive venue. An experiment introduced at time of going to press is for Leoni's to stay open from 11.30pm–6am serving 'breakfasts' of burgers, club sandwiches and snacks, presumably to catch the late-night smart set from Ronnie's.

Set lunch £9.50 (excl wine); alc about £16 a head.

## Mon Plaisir

21 Monmouth Street, WC2 (836 7243)
Covent Garden tube
Open: noon–2pm and 6–11pm Monday–Friday; 6–11pm Saturday.

Covent Garden's oldest French restaurant is daily packed with regulars who love the hustle and bustle of the place, and the short Routier-type menu. The window is obscured by a profusion of plants and inside the walls are plastered with old French travel posters. The dumb waiter rumbles and the thoroughly Gallic garçons cut a dash past the very closely-packed tables. A back extension has recently been added (this isn't so atmospheric) but apart from that nothing changes.

At lunch a set three-course meal is good value and much favoured by crusty publishers on shoestring expenses, but choosing à la carte is hardly bank-busting. Daily specials are always the best choice but the simplistic French menu has everyone's favourite bistro dish. The omelettes (£1.95), pommes allumettes (70p) and cheese (theirs is one of the best boards in London) are exceptional. Wines from £4.90.

Set three course lunch £6.20; alc £10 a head.

## Le Mont St Michel

282 Uxbridge Road, W12 (749 5412)
Shepherd's Bush tube
Open 12.30–3pm and 7–midnight Monday to Friday; 7pm–midnight Saturday and Sunday.

This family-run place has become a firm favourite over the years and its many regulars, particularly moguls from the nearby Beeb, have watched the couple's children develop from toddlers (often to be found playing with a pet rabbit under the table) to confident youngsters who now serve at table and have taken on their Mum's no-nonsense style. Dad is in the kitchen. During the winter the roof is likely to leak, but the roaring fire more than compensates and in the summer the austerity of the converted shop is lifted by the huge bunches of incongruously-mixed flowers. But it's not exactly comfortable and Le Mont St Michel has the reputation for keeping its diners most of the evening. Still, once you've settled in, it is worth it. The menu is short, rarely changes, the food is always good and it's excellent value. People rave about the mousse of crab or salmon (£1.95), the snails (£2.40), selection of pâtés (£1.95) as they do about the bouillabaisse (£5) and fondue bourguigonne (£6.50) but we always have the same unfaultable meal of shared coquilles St Jacques (£5.20) and a Châteaubriand (£15.65) for two which comes fully-garnished, and crème brulée to finish. Superb. Their house wine is £4.75.

From £15 a head.

## The One Legged Goose

17 Princess Road, St Mark's Square, NW1 (722 9665)
Chalk Farm tube
Open: noon–3pm daily (except Saturday); 7pm–midnight (11pm Sunday) daily.

The rock music business is one of the most pampered of all, so it was a smart move by David Rowles to open his curiously-named restaurant near one of London's largest recording studios. Having worked in one as a staff chef, he was presumably aware of the fat lunches the fat cats awarded themselves. Thus the One Legged Goose's menu reflects the tastes of the music mandarins for various pasta on the one hand (it's fashionable, quick, can be eaten trendily with just a fork, and makes 'cats' fatter), and nostalgic English food on the other ('I miss me muvver's cooking when I'm on tour in Japan'). So here we find the likes of tagliatelle with smoked chicken in pepper sauce and fettucine with clams, side by side with beef and Guinness pie and rack of lamb roasted with honey and orange. For real working-class heroes made good, there's a great poacher's pot (a rabbit cassoulet) while among the desserts there's always a traditional English pudding, perhaps rice or bread and butter. Reflecting the international drinking style of the biz, the Goose offers beers from America, Holland, Italy, Germany and Luxembourg. The two-tiered operation – ground-floor cocktail bar and basement dining-room – is nicely decked out with tiled floor, pastel shades, pink oil-cloths on the tables and, to make the customers feel at home, spotlights and recorded music. Traditional Sunday lunches and summer barbecues on the patio complete the picture.

About £25 for two.

## Pizzeria Amalfi

107 Southampton Row, WC1 (636 5811)
Russell Square/Holborn tubes
Open: noon–3pm and 5.30–11pm Monday–Saturday.

Canny publishers wine and dine their authors at this simple unpretentious one-room restaurant run by two of the (previously longstanding) ex-head waiters of San Frediano. They make a speciality of fresh pasta with a choice of 12 pizza dishes, and the food is well-prepared, fresh, tasy and cheap. Start with freshly-made soup of the day; assorted salami or tuna fish, beans and onion salad and follow with crespoline (ricotta and spinach stuffed pancakes); rolled pasta with ham, onion, tomato and chilli sauce (all from the à la carte) or opt for one of the day's specials which is likely to be a shade less familiar, such as spaghetti al pesto (basil sauce) or green noodles with tuna fish, olives and tomato sauce. Wines from £4.90 a bottle.

From £5 a head for food and wine.

## Le Poulbot

45 Cheapside, EC2 (248 4026)
St Paul's or Bank tube
Open: midday–3pm Monday–Friday.

This was the second Roux brothers restaurant when it opened in 1969, inspired by the great number of business men who lunched at Le Gavroche when it was in Chelsea. Particularly designed for business lunches, each table has privacy provided by high-backed sofas and a series of tall room dividers which link up like a noughts and crosses chart. The dominant colour is burgundy and the dimly-lit basement is rather sombre. The service is good but nowhere near as sharp as at Le Gavroche, and there is no attempt to synchronize the removal of the huge shiny silver domes which cover the main dishes.

The menu changes daily and has all the hallmarks of the Roux excellence. Boudin blanc with a truffle sauce was light and delicious and the médaillons de boeuf Rossini perfectly executed. The cheeseboard is a superb display from Philippe Olivier and is a wiser choice than a dessert as coffee is served with a splendid plate of petits fours secs. Female customers (of which there are very few) are presented with a red rose. Each day a red and a white wine are recommended (Pouilly Fumé 'Les Loges' 1979 £14 and Château De Camensac 'Medoc' £16.80 on a recent visit) and these proved to be the cheapest on the list.

Set meals only; £16.50 a head with service included, so there are no hidden extras.

# Printer's Pie

60 Fleet Street, EC4 (353 8861)
Blackfriars tube
Open: 11.30am–3pm Monday–Saturday; 5.30–11pm Monday–Friday.

Most of Fleet Street's serious eating and drinking goes on behind the closed doors of the many members-only clubs in the area. There is a school of thought which suggests that the reason these premises exist is to protect innocent members of the public from distressing scenes of mass drunkeness and piggery. However, the aforementioned public may gain a glimpse of what life is like in the cellar bars of the Street by dropping in at the bar/restaurant/game reserve known as the Printer's Pie. A ground-floor bar with eating gallery, done in dark woods and red upholstery, tops a basement restaurant with the would-be atmosphere of a gentleman's club. At lunchtimes the place is reasonably pleasant, with a solid, unspectacular English menu offering high quality in the house's mixed grill – a comprehensive plate of chops, sausages, liver and so on; dedicated (who knows why?) to Queen Victoria. Soups and pâtés are generally safe choices too. The cooking in the evening can be a little on the second-hand side and should be avoided for the real pleasure the Pie always provides – the rambling, dislocated conversations of the various demoralised hacks who drape themselves around the bar.

About £22 for two.

# San Frediano

62–64 Fulham Road, SW5 (584 8375)
South Kensington tube
Open: 12.30–2.30pm and 7.15–11.15pm Monday–Saturday.

San Fred is one of the few trattorias (designed by Enzo Apicella) that's managed to transcend the sixties and seventies and still be popular in the eighties. The food is always reliably good and the place efficient and formal without being too smart, but the real secret of its success is the staff. It's still run by the same management who are brilliant at making even first-timers feel as if they've been dining there every night for years. The restaurant comprises two rooms with spotless linen, ceramic tiled floors, comfortable chairs and cream stucco walls.

The food is always the same and always of a high standard; crespoline (spinach and ricotta stuffed pancakes); snails in a creamy garlic sauce; medallions of beef in a red wine sauce and numerous fresh pasta dishes. Their zabaglione is one of the best in town.

San Frediano is popular with the literary crowd – authors being dined by their publishers, actors treating their agents. On Saturdays they're replaced by up-market Chelsea supporters and there are always gals lunching together remembering being wined and dined here in their courting days.

From £10 a head.

## Savoy Grill Room

The Strand, WC2 (836 4343)
Charing Cross tube
Open: 12.30–2.30pm and 6–11.30pm Monday–Friday.

Dining at the Savoy is a memorable experience – the perfect place to sign that million dollar contract. Have a drink first in the American Bar but don't fill up on the irresistible home-made game chips. The Grill Room, at the front of the Hotel, is a large, comfortable wood-panelled room with chandelier lighting, high backed sofas and well-upholstered chairs. The linen is so crisply laundered that the napkins are almost too stiff to use. Service ranks with the best in London (as you'd expect, after all this is the Savoy) and we got the same reverential treatment as David Frost and a couple of well-known politicians on our lunchtime visit.

The menu pretends it's a French restaurant but actually the best things on offer are thoroughly English and roasts and grills are the speciality. Each day there's a special dish at both lunch and dinner. Tuesday is steak and kidney pie (£7), Thursday roast rib of beef with Yorkshire pud (£9.50) and the à la carte varies enormously in price, giving the opportunity to dine well for £12 to £15 a head. The dessert trolley isn't so impressive and we'd recommend their Stilton served with celery. The wine list is impressive with impressive prices.

From £15 a head, but £25 is more realistic, without wine.

## Shireen

270 Uxbridge Rd, W12 (749 9527)
Shepherd's Bush tube
Open: noon–3pm and 6–11.30pm daily.

The Shireen is a stylish Tandoori restaurant whose décor, stunning and simple behind smoked glass windows, was way ahead of its time when it opened five years ago – dark-brown walls and furnishing, subtle lighting and tables placed sufficiently far apart to avoid overhearing everyone's conversation. Plants abound, there is generally a single bloom on each table and service is efficient without being oppressive. The food matches the sophisticated décor and the place is well known to the nearby BBC who use it regularly for business lunches. The menu is long and painstakingly presented and as appetisers we'd particularly recommend kaliji – lamb's liver with spices and onion, cooked and brought to the table in the traditional karahi, and prawn prajapati, a dish of Bengali king prawns marinated and served in the shape of a butterfly. Tandoori dishes are cooked to order, portions are generous, and the vegetable dishes are freshly-prepared. Puddings, too, are way above average. Try sheer khurma, a festive sweet made from fresh milk, vermicelli, dates, nuts and saffron. The Shireen keeps a decent wine list; the house wine is cheap at £3.85.

From £10 a head.

## Sweetings

39 Queen Victoria Street, EC4 (248 3062)
Mansion House tube
Open 11.30am–3pm Monday–Friday.

They certainly got the formula right way back in the 1830s when the Sweeting family opened their oyster bar. Very little has changed since it opened. The functional bare floor-boarded bar and tiny adjoining canteen are packed every day and it takes a fair bit of thrust and parry for non-regulars to get served. In this male stronghold the conversation is noisy and constant and usually City or horse talk, but newcomers do merge in after a few drinks. Everyone heads for their favourite bar (there are three oyster bars which also serve salads, traditional English fish dishes, hearty puddings and savouries and one bar exclusively for sandwiches) and hopes for a bar stool. The turnaround is pretty fast for food, after which you drink à la pub in the middle of the room. Oysters are the finest Colchesters and our favourite main is smoked haddock with poached egg followed by steamed syrup pudding. English food at its best. The staff have been with the company for years and rule their gents with a homely yet firm hand. Drink draught Guinness, blanc de blancs £4.70 or the sparkling version £8.70.

From £5 a head; sandwiches £1.

# The White Tower

1 Percy Street, W1 (836 8141)
Tottenham Court Road/Goodge Street tube
Open: 12.30–2.30pm and 6.30–10.30pm Monday–Friday.

The White Tower was arguably London's first Greek restaurant, opened as it was in 1938. In those days (when Charlotte Street was the centre of Bohemian life – Augustus John had rooms nearby) there weren't hundreds of other places offering taramasalata, moussaka and kebab. These days the White Tower is not generally noted for its food but its original and newer clients flock back for the charm of the place and the superlative style of the manager and his staff. Regulars include press barons like Rupert Murdoch, and a mark of customer affection was displayed when the turnout for the doorman's funeral was almost as big as that for Winston Churchill. The Edwardian house is probably quite unchanged since the restaurant opened and there are two main dining-rooms (and other private rooms for party hire). The linen is thoroughly starched, there are fey paintings of Byron, fish-eye mirrors and fresh flowers on all the closely-packed tables.

The menu makes amusing reading and can only be described as quaint. Many opt for their mezze (£4) which is strictly a starter, but we'd recommend you try the avgolemono soup and avoid the famous pâté Diana which looks and tastes like lard. The Greek cuisine is augmented with international dishes, and these along with the roast meats (particularly good game in season) seem to be the best bets. Scaloppini Zacharof (£7.75) a dish of fried sweetbreads and veal escalope was a success, and amazing value when compared with £6.50 for the moussaka. Finish with delicious light Greek yoghurt and hymettus honey.

From £15 a head for three courses.

*Also Good for When You Want to Talk Business:*
Aykoku-Kaku
Bow Wine Vaults
Brinkley's
Bubb's
Café Pelican
Chez Gerard
Corney & Barrow
L'Escargot
Gardens, The
Grange, The
Masako

Paris House
Pomegranates
School Dinners
Suntory
Tourment d'Amour
Winston's

# 6. When You're Feeling Sporty

Sport and eating out go together like Wimbledon and strawberries and cream. There can be no better preparation for an event dedicated to athleticism and energy than a two-hour catchweight contest with a steak and kidney pudding and a bottle of claret. Indeed some sporting events – rugby internationals, Royal race meetings and Arsenal home games – require their audiences to be well-oiled and well-fed before they can begin. While the abysmal and expensive catering at most sports arenas dictates that any eating should be done outside, the cherry hogs (greyhounds) and certain race-tracks are usually safe to try in their own right. A good rule of thumb, as this is England, is that any place where the attention's on animals rather than human beings will make an effort.

## Ajanta

12 Goldhawk Road, W12 (743 5191)
Shepherds Bush tube
Open: noon–3pm and 6pm–midnight daily.

For the two years that Ajanta has been open it has retained a high standard and is very popular with locals and QPR fans and frequently appears to be a canteen for the nearby BBC. Although it's a long, narrow room with tables arranged in a straight line down both walls like almost every Indian restaurant before the big Westernization (ie Khans, Lal Qila etc) there is no flock, instead the walls are covered with lengths of block-printed traditional fabrics. The staff are friendly and the food is cheap. There are particular dishes on the two-page menu which you'll see on just about every table; their onion bhajia is renowned and their tandoori always seems to be cooked to order. Curries average £2.50 and for those who don't like it too hot their Muglai korma dishes (with almond and cream sauce) are recommended. Vegetarians are well catered for.

Ajanta keep a short wine list and their house wine, £4.60, is something of a pleasant surprise. Carlsberg and Dortmunder Union are on tap.

From £5 a head for food.

## Au Bois St Jean

122 St John's Wood High Street, NW8 (722 0400)
St John's Wood tube
Open: noon–2.30pm Sunday–Friday; 7–11.30pm daily.

Au Bois St Jean couldn't be more convenient for Lord's cricket ground, and its comprehensive opening times make it equally valuable for supper after 'stumps', or for lunch before a Sunday League game. An additional attraction, after a hot day in the sun, is the basement dining room's cool, rustic barn interior. If the French played cricket, their pavilions might look like this. The menu operates on a sensible prix fixe basis for two or three courses, and is marginally cheaper for lunch than dinner. The cooking is imaginative French provincial, so you might start with a fish soup, a hot mushroom mousse, a rough Languedoc pâté with garlic and peppercorns or the very appetising avocat à la Cannoise – avocado filled with crevettes, mushrooms, tomato and a splash of pastis. Of the main courses, the seafood pancake is particularly good, while the rack of lamb with herbs and the boned breast of wood pigeon in a chive, basil and tarragon sauce, have both scored useful half centuries. Close-of-play features good puds like the country-style apple pie 'tarte tatin' and the pancake filled with fresh fruit, cream and cognac. Strong coffee will set you up nicely for another session in the Tavern.

About £26 for two.

## Café Des Sports

294 Fulham Road, SW10 (351 5762)
South Kensington/Earls Court tube
Open: 7–11.15pm Monday–Saturday.

A meal here would be a stylish way to conclude an evening match at nearby Chelsea. Behind discreet black horizontal slat blinds, Café Des Sports looks more like a club than a restaurant but inside it's brightly lit, done out in chic black and white and decorated with superb old French sporting posters and deco touches. The food is surprisingly modestly priced and very good indeed, favouring traditionally popular French dishes such as moules provençales (£1.95), tomato soup with a fiery pistou (£1.50), rump steak (£4.95) and marmite de St Jacques au gingembre (£6.80). The meal begins with smoked salmon on squares of warm toast which, followed by the classic grilled rump steak (two large pieces which covered the plate), pommes allumettes on a side plate (with a doily) and salad, makes a superb meal.

The other choices are varied and prepared with dedication by chef Stephen Nesbitt, who is particulary imaginative with vegetables (a selection of three costs 95p). The cheeseboard is not good but the desserts excellent; crème brûlée being *the* one. Coffee is cona.

A three-course meal for two will see change from £25.

## Carlo's Place

855 Fulham Road, SW6 (736 4507)
Parsons Green tube
Open: noon–3pm and 7–11.30pm Monday–Saturday, closed Sunday lunch.

Up to 50 people can be accommodated in this curious-looking restaurant which makes a feature of the fat gold ceiling pipes which radiate out of a central stove ('all purely decorative' demurred a decorative waitress) and which boasts a vast collection of cuckoo clocks and windows that look like a still from The Day of the Triffids. It's a cheerful place with red and white check table-cloths and a comely waitress who clearly prefers her sporty male clientèle 'fresh' from a match at nearby Fulham. The short menu changes monthly, and is written out in that funny curly writing popular in France and which usually spells disaster here.

The food is very variable but very generous. Mushrooms fried with basil (£3.25) were almost tasteless and very greasy and fresh asparagus (£3.95) either hopelessly overcooked or tinned, but moules marinières (£3.95) were excellent. Canard au gingembre (£6.95) was a fatty specimen with pieces of ginger lobbed in as an afterthought while the house entrecôte (£6.95) was very good. At all costs avoid Carlo's Decadence – a sort of dull cream sponge with chocolate sauce. Their house wine is French and £4.95, and their short list has quite a few finds – a 76 Château Millet was half the price we've seen it on other fashionable lists.

From £10 a head for three courses without wine.

For Saturday afternoon games and Sunday Rugby League, try The Starlight Restaurant, 786 Fulham Road, SW6 a cheap and cheerful Greek-style transport café.

## Chequers Hotel

Lambourn Road, Newbury, Berkshire (0635 43666)
Newbury BR–Paddington
Open: 12.30–2pm and 7–9.30pm daily.

Newbury is one of the few racecourses actually served by its own station and on race days most special trains will unload punters there, leaving them to the whims and prices of large-scale catering. Those who prefer the more personal and leisurely touch might do better to adjourn to Newbury itself where, on the road leading out to that racing holy-of-holies Lambourn, they will find the quiet, old-fashioned Chequers Hotel.

The dining-room here is a plush, comfortable affair with upholstered chairs and floor-to-ceiling curtains. Despite the formality of the setting, the staff are friendly and the food is generally unpretentious, well-cooked and reasonably-priced. The daily set lunch might offer such unimpeachable fare as cream of vegetable soup, steak and kidney pie and cheeseboard, or there might be a roast from the carving trolley. Hints of modernity occur on the à la carte section – a spinach and pasta savoury as starter, or pork escalope flavoured with a lime and orange sauce – and the well-kept sweet trolley, commendably for a hotel dining-room, is packed with freshly-made tarts, gâteaux and pastries. Good house wines will put you in the mood to lose a few bob on Newbury's pretty, open course.

Set lunch £6.50 (excl wine); alc about £11 a head.

# Clinch's Salad House

14 Southgate, Chichester, Sussex (0243 788822)
Chichester BR–Waterloo
Open: 8am–5.30pm Tuesday–Saturday.

One of the highlights of the sporting summer is racing at Goodwood, the beautiful course on the Sussex Downs. It's really worth making a full day of the trip by spending an hour or two in historic Chichester, from where the special buses make the short journey to the track. Lunch, of course, would be an essential element in the proceedings, and Clinch's offers an ideal venue. A terraced house has been converted to provide a large, salad counter on the ground floor and a rather functional, though still attractive, upstairs dining-room. Teams of pleasant, homely ladies staff the counter, helping you to the excellent range of Danish open sandwiches, quiches, pastries and comprehensive salads served in large bowls. A couple of hot dishes are available, perhaps vegetable curry or a superb fisherman's pie, and all the food has that 'freshly prepared for the village show' look about it. This applies particularly to the puddings – delicious lemon cheesecake or chocolate gâteaux. An additional advantage to Clinch's is its licence – good house wine is served in full, half and even dinky quarter-carafes. From here it's a short stroll to the bus station and to your costly appointment with the bookies.

About £8 for two.

# Hung Toa

54 Queensway, W2 (727 6017)
Bayswater tube
Open: noon–11pm daily.

It is essential to arrive early (or pre-order by phone) if you want to try the house speciality of roast meats Cantonese-style. Shiny, chestnut-coloured whole ducks and pieces of pork hang glistening in the window waiting to be dynamically and expertly chopped before your very eyes and all is usually gone by 8pm. If you miss out on the superb roast meats or if you are set for a blow out, their crab with ginger and spring onion is worth getting messy for. The vegetable dishes come crisp and tangy and if you like the mollusc cooked, their oysters are crispy-fried and outstanding value at £5 for a dozen. The restaurant's design is modern and high tech with bare brick walls and not one Chinese lantern, and manages to pack 50-odd into its noisy, busy and functional dining room. And it's very handy for Queensway Ice Rink.

Set meals from £6; alc £8–10.

## Manzils

101 Rosendale Rd, SW21 (761 2031)
Brixton tube
Open: noon–2.30pm and 6–11.45pm daily.

Manzils might look like any run-of-the-mill curry house with its red flock, tables lining the walls, pictures of the Taj Mahal and jingly jangly sitar muzak but it's a real find in desolate Crystal Palace. The staff are particularly nice and helpful and I can't give it a better pedigree than to say one of my best gourmet friends 'takes away' an average twice a week and has never had a rotten meal.

While the athletes from the Palace repair to McDonalds for their high-fibre meal, you can dine exotically on chicken tikka, their garlicky spinach bhaji or excellent hot and slightly sour prawn damsak with lentils. Puddings are restricted to the gulabjumin range but the wine list includes a light German house wine and even stretches to champagne. In fact Manzils is a brilliant place for a reasonably-priced celebratory dinner. Given 24-hours' notice they will lay on one of their stunning regional specialities; lamb or chicken kurzi, a delicious feast for four or more and costing £25 and £22 respectively. Theirs is a fast and efficient take-away.

From £8 a head.

## New Anarkali Tandoori

160 Walton Road, East Molesey, Surrey (979 5072)
Open: noon–3pm and 6–11pm daily.

The nearest racecourses to London are Sandown Park at Esher and Kempton Park at Sunbury-on-Thames. East Molesey lies equidistant between the two and is therefore an ideal venue for eating before or after the meetings. While there's a highly-regarded, expensive, classical French restaurant also in Walton Road (Le Chien qui Fume), the New Anarkali is probably the better prospect for the average punter who just wants to fill up well but reasonably cheaply. Both criteria are met by the New Anarkali, whose food is remarkably well-prepared, extremely nourishing and yet still attractively-priced. You may suspect from the décor – potted plants along both walls, upholstered seats, lemon-coloured table-cloths, no flock wallpaper – that the New Anarkali is a cut above, and the food and the service should certainly confirm this.

Spicy poppadoms and pickles arrive without bidding while you consider a short but distinctive menu. There's a good range of tandoori specials, including a comprehensive 'mix' at just over eight quid. Among the starters however, the king prawn pakoras, in a crisp orange-coloured batter, catch the eye and prove delicious, especially with a splash of tamarind sauce. A recommended main course is the Karachi gosht, a dish of diced chicken or lamb grilled with spices and capsicums in a traditional iron karahi dish, or try the special bhuna talka masala (oven-cooked chicken with spices in a thick sauce of vegetables). Of the curries, the Bangalore phal lamb could be a challenge, since the menu describes it as 'extra hot highly' – just the job for the Boxing Day meeting at Kempton. Special menus of mughlai dishes including a whole khurzi lamb for 3–4 people are available by arrangement. Well worth the trip, even if you're not racing.

About £10 a head.

## The Olde Hatchet

Hatchet Lane, Winkfield, Berkshire (0344 882303)
Off A322 Windsor–Ascot
Open: pub hours; noon–2pm Monday–Friday (restaurant and bar snacks); 7–9pm
Saturday (restaurant); 7–8.30pm (bar snacks)

Ascot is no ordinary racecourse, with even the non-Royal occasions giving off an air of high-class breeding. So it's important to strike the right high-class eating note for your pre-race meals – anything too flashy however would be considered vulgar, while anything too cheap would be considered common. The Olde Hatchet, just a few miles up the road from the course, is a perfect solution. An historic pub, it's been tastefully preserved and offers a welter of exposed beams, white plaster walls, stone floors and a quiet, rural setting (there's even a stable at the back). The food is an apt balance between stylishness and capability, and is available either as bar snacks, or as full meals in a well-appointed but informal restaurant.

The snacks might offer such distinctive items as brochette of monkfish, an authentically-spiced chicken curry, grilled Mediterranean prawns, home made liver pâté or Flemish-style mussels cooked in white wine and turmeric. Some of these dishes also find their way onto the restaurant menu as starters, together with the likes of avocado with prawns and the unusual but successful horse-radish and onion soup. Main courses tend to be more conservative, falling back on classic grills – steaks, lamb cutlets, Dover sole – but there's still a touch of originality about breast of duck in sweet and sour sauce or veal chop in cream and mushroom sauce. Wines are reasonable, but if you've got the time and the courage, try some of the landlord's home-brewed beer.

About £5 a head (bar snacks); £10 a head (restaurant).

## Oval Tandoori Restaurant

64 Brixton Road, SW9 (582 1415)
Oval tube
Open: noon–2.30pm and 6–11.45pm Monday–Friday; noon–11.45pm Saturday.

The success of the two-year-old Oval Tandoori is proof that the ubiquitous curry house is almost a thing of the past. Inspired by sophisticated Indian restaurants such as the Khyber and Khans in Westbourne Grove, the Oval takes pride in preparing its curries to authentic recipes – 'each dish has its own subtle blend of flavours and spices, mixed and processed with almost alchemical skill' is no idle boast from the restaurant's menu.

To complement the food, many of the best aspects of the days of the Raj feature here; warm scented towels are presented at the end of the meal and the layout of the restaurant allows for privacy and comfort.

The food is a perfect example of how subtle and distinctive Indian food can be, and it doesn't leave the mouth on fire. Tandoori is cooked to order and arrives moist and tender, and much is made of presenting dishes sizzling straight from the cooker. A three-course meal averages £12 but most diners make do for far less. The fast and efficient take-away service is renowned locally.

Come to think of it, this is one of two parts of town (Regents Park is the other) where second rate Indian grub just isn't on; we've heard that the man who can handle three Shredded Wheat loves it.

From £12 a head.

## The Paddock Grill

Walthamstow Stadium, Chingford Road, E4 (527 7277)
Walthamstow Central tube, then bus
Open: Tuesday, Saturday and every other Thursday, 7.15pm.–10.15pm.

For a vibrant sporting night out with a difference, you'd be pushed to beat greyhound racing at Walthamstow Stadium. The arena itself is a dazzling sight – a huge white tower at one end lit by a thousand rolling numbers as bets and odds are displayed; a central area of fairy lights and fountains; blue and pink neon light displays; and three modern but distinctively different eating areas, all safely enclosed from the elements. On one side of the track is a pie and mash bar, while opposite it, in the grandstand, there's a fixed menu steak bar (The Stowaway) overlooking the finish, and the à la carte Paddock Grill overlooking the start and the home straight. The Grill is arranged as half-a-dozen tiers, each with an eating counter and comfortable seating for up to three hundred people. Considering the scale of the operation, the waitress service is amazingly efficient and the food, though limited in range, is cooked proficiently to order.

The menu offers a complete range of simple grills – steaks, lamb cutlets, liver, gammon steaks, plaice, Dover sole – flanked by prawn cocktail/avocado style starters and cheesecake/gâteau style puddings, although there is a range of ice-creams available. Special dish of the day might be tender grilled scallops with bacon. With the constant parade of races (from 7.45pm to about 10.15pm at fifteen or sixteen-minute intervals), the swirl of waitresses and bet-collectors (they place your wagers for you and collect any winnings), and the screams of excited punters, it certainly shouldn't be a dull evening. Reservations are essential, especially for Saturday nights when they're often booked up to two months in advance.

Admission £1.70; meals about £12 a head.

## Richmond Rendezvous

1 Wakefield Road, Richmond, Surrey (940 6869)
Richmond tube
Open: noon–2pm; 6–11pm daily.

Very handy for the Snooker Club but a fair stroll (everything is) from the ice rink, this comfortable Chinese restaurant is quite the best in Richmond. Situated bang opposite Richmond bus terminal, the restaurant is housed in a quaint, shanty-town-style long low building. Inside, the place is a-bustle with extremely efficient Chinese staff quite used to its predominately middle-class clientele who prefer eating a pre-ordered set meal (for two to six people, at £8.50 a head) with a spoon and fork to being adventurous with chopsticks. A la carte the menu ranges over all the popular Peking dishes and if variety is required it is essential to go in a group of four or more and share the dishes as they average £3.50 each. Portions are large and unless you have a particular favourite their crispy duck served with spring onion, the 'plum jam' and pancakes is more than enough for a substantial meal for two (£8, half duck) preceded by either barbecued spare ribs (£2.90) or dried scallops and seaweed (£2.70). Finish with crunchy toffee apples (£1.60) which will be dunked in cold water at your table. Incidentally, banquet parties can be arranged at £10 a head.

From £10 a head.

## Romano's

30 Clifton Road, W9 (286 2266)
Warwick Avenue tube
Open: noon–2.30pm and 6–11pm Monday–Saturday.

People heading westwards from Lord's after stumps have been drawn can safely fall upon the hospitality of this friendly neighbourhood trattoria. The white plaster décor is relieved by some dark wooden panelling and shuttering, which, together with a few beams, can give it a longboat-like appearance – well the cooking's certainly ship-shape. The usual tratt starters might be enlivened by items from the daily specials blackboard – stuffed aubergines or fresh artichokes with vinaigrette perhaps – while the main courses mostly offer a straight bat – escalope Milanese, calves' liver with sage, piccatine al limone. More ambitious flourishes however, bring you excellent pollo Cavour (chicken breast rolled with ham around garlic butter), the rich sogliola Vecchia Romagna (Dover sole in a bisque de homard, brandy and mushroom sauce) and tender scallopine alla Luisa (fillet of veal with brandy, cream and mushrooms). Again, the daily specials might offer more exotic choices – even lobsters have put in an appearance. Fresh seasonal fruits are usually offered as alternatives to the stodge trolley – strawberries and cream after a long day in the pavilion. Perfect! Some tables outside too on the hotter days.

About £12 a head.

## Sheppards

1 Prince of Wales Terrace, off Kensington High Street, W8 (937 6222)
Kensington High Street tube
Open: noon–11.30pm Monday–Friday.

Opposite the Park and a quick jog from the Albert Hall, this pretty, pale-pink and pale-blue basement restaurant is presided over by still very glamorous ex-model Claire Sheppard. 65 can be accommodated in the L-shaped room and there's an adjoining bar for knocking back cocktails first. The menu is English with French overtones and will appeal to those who like honest, plain cooking, nicely presented. Smoked salmon pâté, hot broccoli mousse and a home-made soup are typical starters and rack of lamb, steak and kidney pie and salmon trout in cream and chive sauce are popular main dishes. Bakewell or treacle tart, chocolate mousse cake or sorbet follow.

They serve an excellent value two course lunch which costs £3.80; à la carte £10 a head. A set tea is served during the afternoon for £2.25.

## The White Swan

Riverside, Twickenham (892 2166)
Twickenham BR – Waterloo
Open: pub hours.

Before the mayhem of a Twickenham rugby international, you may like a few hours of good food, good beer and quiet contemplation. You should be able to enjoy them all at this almost rural riverside pub just five minutes walk from the bustling town centre. There's an eclectic array of jumble and furniture inside, plus one or two locals with hairy dogs – these can be ignored in favour of choice home-made snacks of a warming nature. Soups, stews and casseroles are usually available – the hot-pot is especially good – as well as above average pâtés, cheeses and salads, and not many pubs have been known to serve tzatziki, the Greek yoghurt and cucumber dip. There's a small garden on the river bank for use during the cricket season.

About £7 for two.

## Woodlands

402a High Road, Wembley, Middlesex (902 9869)
Wembley Central BR–Euston
Open: noon–3pm and 6–11pm daily.

Trying to eat before a Wembley football game is not an easy experience – too often it comes down to grabbing a hamburger on the move or queuing in a packed pub for a linesman's lunch. If you do wish to make an occasion of going there however, Woodlands is a good bet. For one thing, the premises are en route from Wembley Central station to the stadium itself and so couldn't be more convenient. The restaurant is also smartly-appointed – red-brick floor, air-conditioning, modern prints on walls – and the food, South Indian vegetarian, will make a pleasant change from hot dogs or fish and chips.

Football fans suspicious of Indian vegetarian food ('wot no meat?') will be reassured by the fact that the portions here are huge, and that the dishes have, to a certain extent, been Anglicised. Thus the delicious and filling mixed uthappam is described as a 'lentil pizza, topped with tomatoes, onions and coconut' and the vegetable cutlets bring the offer of tomato ketchup rather than exotic Indian pickles. Assorted snacks include samosas, fried lentil fritters (pakodas), masala dosa (pancakes stuffed with potatoes, onions and nuts) and warming mixed vegetable curry. Three good value set meals (thalis) are offered, embracing savouries, breads, vegetable curries, rice, pickles and dessert, and these are probably the best idea since it's terribly easy to over-order.

There are two large tables in the centre of the room, fitted with revolving trays, for group eating (team lunches?), good wines and lagers are available, and the recorded music is more likely to feature George Benson than Ravi Shankar.

About £8 a head.

## Yesterday

12 Leopold Rd, SW19 (946 4300)
Wimbledon Park tube
Open: 12.30–2.30pm and 7.30–11.15pm Tuesday–Friday; 12.30–2.30pm Sunday.

Escape the queues for strawberry teas and head for this other sanctuary of English tradition, where John Freeman offers dishes based on traditional English fare dating back to the fourteenth century. The menu is a crash course on the culinary proclivities of our forebears, with a series of anecdotal titbits – did you know that tomatoes were once called love apples? The restaurant has been very tastefully arty-craftily designed with brown bare brick walls, oak refectory tables, candle-light (even on a bright day) and a collection of suitable period pictures. The kitchen is hidden at the back of the converted shop behind a splendid old screen.

Some of the dishes sound better than they taste and subtlety is often lost by over cooking or by the sheer enormousness of the portion – the steak and kidney pie is recommended to those with a hearty appetite. All meat and fish are bought locally every day so they often run out of certain items – baked mackerel in watercress is usually one of the first to go. Finish with peaches in brandy, home-made negrita ice-cream or the filling apple Grassmere – a variation on apple charlotte with breadcrumbs. There are no English wines but just about every other country's. The French house wine is £5.20.

From £10 a head; lunchtime menu averages £5 a head.

## Yew Tree Restaurant

98 High Street, Epsom, Surrey (78 25505)
Epsom BR–Victoria or Waterloo
Open: noon–2.30pm and 6.30–11pm Monday–Saturday.

Racing at Epsom is an all-embracing sporting occasion, with the crowd on the Downs cutting across the class barriers. This handy little restaurant in the centre of the town – you can't miss the fairy-lit yew tree which gives it the name – seems to reflect this broadness of appeal by catering for a variety of pockets and tastes. The surroundings – wood-panelled, oak-beamed 'tea-shop' style interior, hung with horse-brasses – are perfect for all contingencies, from quick lunch to long, celebratory dinner.

A cosmopolitan menu ranges all over Europe for its cheerful dishes – whitebait, ravioli, onion soup are among the starters, while grilled lamb cutlets, calves' liver and bacon, salmon steak with parsley butter and saltimbocca alla Romana feature among the main dishes. Experimentalists might wish to try the beef Mexicana (strips of fillet sautéd in a tequila and red pepper sauce), though the sauce can disappoint compared to the meat. A good value set lunch might offer roast lamb, flanked by egg mayonnaise and crème caramel. A modest but useful venue.

Set lunch £4.50 a head (excl. wine); alc about £10 a head.

## Young's

19 Canonbury Lane, N1 (226 9791)
Highbury & Islington tube
Open: noon–2.30pm and 6pm–midnight daily (until 11pm Sunday).

Football fans heading for Arsenal (surely some mistake here?) may like to have their pre-match meal at this smart Cantonese and Peking restaurant, possibly named in honour of a former centre-half. Big Willie would probably enjoy the extensive list of dishes available here, all cooked to a high standard and served in surroundings more reminiscent of a wine bar or Charlie Nicholas's kitchen – smoked glass mirrors, Hessian wall-covering and comfortable modern chairs. For groups of two or more (eleven and a substitute?) there are reasonably-priced, fairly comprehensive set meals. If you're choosing individually the warming sweet and sour soup and the delicious prawns on sesame toast are recommended. Equally fine are the steamed chicken in lemon sauce with huge Chinese mushrooms and the fried beef in oyster sauce. The spare ribs in plum sauce are good, but can be a bit light on meat, and besides it's worth leaving room for Young's spectacular toffee bananas which arrive looking like a plate of little footballs. Drink beer, good French house wine or tea. From here it's a short walk across Highbury Fields to the ground and 'Char-Lee'.

About £18 for two.

*Also Good for When You're Feeling Sporty:*
House on the Bridge (Ascot Races)
Lord's Carver (Lord's Cricket)
Partners 23 (Epsom Races)
San Frediano (Chelsea FC)
Tickell Arms (Newmarket Races)
Waterside Inn (Royal Ascot)

# 7. When You're Out and About

When you are out sight-seeing, visiting street markets, art galleries and museums or devoting a whole day to shopping, you will need sustenance of an informal and fast-ish kind. We include recommendable restaurants and cafés inside the tourist institutions but also offer alternatives with a particular bent towards places that are cheap, large, don't require booking and where the food is fuel rather than three star, but good. Where shopping is concerned we list places that are convenient but just off the main drag, so you will be hard pushed to find an 'ordinary' fast food eaterie in these pages.

## Antiquarius

15 Flood Street, SW3 (351 5353)
Sloane Square tube
Open: 10am–6pm Monday–Saturday.

Right at the back of this huge covered antique market that dominates the Flood Street corner of the King's Road is a small and
cheerful café. The restaurant, primarily aimed at the market traders, has achieved a wider reputation with local office workers and
canny regulars to the market. The menu is not ambitious and the
food is wholesome, prepared fresh daily and cheap. Nothing costs
more than £2 a dish and there are usually specials each day such as a
chicken lash-up or a goulash. Cheaper fillers like bangers and mash,
ratatouille, shepherd's pie, cold meats, salads and good sandwiches
go like hot cakes and often run out. It's a small modest place; you
queue for service and if there's no seat you can take away. Not
licensed.

From £2 for food.

## The Ark

35 Kensington High Street, W8 (937 4294)
High Street Kensington tube
Open: noon–2.30pm and 7–11.20pm Monday–Saturday.

High Street Kensington is one of our most stylish shopping streets,
so it's no good suggesting any old burger bar for a meal break.
Instead, try the Ark, set back from the main road in Kensington
Court, and with a lot more style than its reasonable prices might
indicate. The large heavy wooden entrance doors suggest a classy
venue and indeed the Ark is high on atmosphere – starched white
table-cloths, lots of panelling, period prints and mirrors and orange
wall-lights give the ground-floor room a cosy feel (the basement
room is more starkly lit and modern).
   The food is less involved than the décor but just as tasteful.
Simple bistro dishes predominate – escargots, onion soup, smoked
haddock quiche and artichoke vinaigrette will probably appear
among the hors d'oeuvres. Main courses offer gigot d'agneau,
ballotine of chicken breast in lemon sauce, foie de veau provençale
(liver with tomatoes and garlic) and perhaps raie au beurre noir
(skate in a sharp butter and vinegar sauce) from the menu du jour.
Puddings include such classics as chocolate and orange mousse and
crème brûlée. The cooking is generally of a high standard. Indeed

97

the only problem you might expect is negotiating the tightly-arranged tables with your shopping bags.

About £22 for two.

## Bamboo Kuning

114 Seymour Place, W1 (723 2926)
Baker Street tube
Open: noon–3pm and 6pm–midnight.

After a visit to Madame Tussaud's or the London Planetarium, enjoy a quick one-courser upstairs or go down to the larger basement room for a leisurely meal at this authentic and very reasonably priced Malaysian, Indonesian and Singaporean restaurant. A set four-course meal for two with a bottle of house wine is excellent value at £16 but choosing à la carte should present no problems because each dish is thoroughly explained and none costs more than £2.50. Try satay, the traditional Malay kebab, as a shared starter, and share a selection of dishes such as Nasi Goreng – special fried rice with shredded chicken and shrimps; Bamboo Kuning Kambing, steamed lamb fried with chef's special sauce; Udang Goreng, deep-fried prawns with Gado Gado, the popular Indonesian salad served with peanut sauce. Desserts are weird and shouldn't be missed. A word of warning; unless you like it very hot, avoid anything called a sambal; it will be heavy on chilli.

From £5 a head for food.

## Bar du Musée

17 Nelson Road, SE10 (858 4710)
Greenwich BR–Charing Cross
Open: noon–3pm and 6.30–11pm Monday–Saturday; noon–2pm and 7–10.30pm Sunday.

Greenwich has a host of attractions for the visitor – bookshops, parks, a theatre and of course the Maritime Museum, from which this dark, cosy, wood-panelled wine-bar gets its name. Interestingly furnished and pleasantly staffed, its selection of smashing home-cooked food makes it a good port of call. A changing menu can offer simple fillers like soups, cottage pie or sausage and mash, home-made spicy hamburgers or warming beef and mushroom casserole, together with the slightly more ambitious (for a wine bar) chicken Kiev or veal escalope stuffed with ham. Further attractions include wholesome puddings (sherry trifle, apple crumble) and Rombouts filter coffee. There's also a highly reasonable wine list and, in keeping with the maritime context, one or two good ports. Classical music adds to the classy atmosphere. Stools at the bar and half-bottles of the house wine also make it agreeable for the lone diner. Eat in the pretty garden during the summer.

About £16 for two.

## Bloom's

90 Whitechapel High Street, E1 (247 6001)
Whitechapel tube
Open: 11.30am–9.30pm Sunday–Thursday; 11am–2.30pm Friday.

An almost ritual follow-up to a Sunday morning browse around the raucous East End markets of Petticoat Lane is lunch at Bloom's, a long-established Jewish restaurant which operates under strict kosher supervision. The long, rather functional, garishly-lit premises are nevertheless crammed with an atmospheric bustle of traders, punters and orthodox Jews, which, together with the hectic service, certainly makes an event of eating there.

Some of the food, unfortunately, may not live up to the atmosphere, so careful choosing is usually necessary to avoid disappointment. The hot soups with dumplings (kreplach, kneidlach) and the chopped liver with egg are generally reliable, and the hot salt beef with fresh slices of caraway bread arrives in huge tender portions. Potato cake latkes are crisp too, though other vegetables, tsimmes (chopped carrots in sweet sauce) for example, can be soggy. Veal and chicken schnitzels and the sweet and sour cabbage should prove reliable alternatives, but a soup, salt-beef and a delicious lockshen pudding (cinnamon-flavoured noodles) will be more than enough for a cheery meal. There's a take-away counter too if you can't stand the bustle. Drink lemon tea (no milk or dairy products allowed), or Israeli wine. Beware of closures for Jewish holidays and festivals.

About £9 a head.

## Caffe Mamma

24 Hill Street, Richmond (940 1625)
Richmond tube
Open: noon–2.30pm and 6.30–midnight Monday–Friday; noon–midnight Saturday and Sunday.

The perfect place to stoke up after a walk in the park, Caffe Mamma specializes in regional pasta dishes and the pasta is made almost to order on the premises. Nothing costs more than £3, everything is home-made and portions are gargantuan. Aside from 18 pasta dishes, there's a daily home-made soup, six salads and a selection of water ices, ice-creams, cakes (including birthday cake) and fresh fruit salad with marsala. The most expensive wine is a Frascati at £5; even champagne is only £6.95. Decent coffee is on tap from an espresso machine. The decoration of the restaurant certainly deserves an award for originality and is designed to echo the view across a Naples back street, even down to hanging a line of washing inside the restaurant!

From £3 a head.

## Camden Brasserie

216 Camden High Street, NW1 (482 2114)
Camden Town tube
Open: noon–3pm and 6.30–11.30pm Tuesday–Saturday; noon–2pm Sunday.

Bang in the middle of the pulsating Camden Town action, this very popular and extremely well-executed brasserie is the perfect place to relax after a shopping spree in the markets or a canalside walk. The close proximity of the TVam building and Capital Radio down the road also makes the place very handy for media types, so it is now essential to book a table well in advance at any time of day.

Black and white photos of the markets hang on the whitewashed stretches of brick wall, functional maroon oilskins topped with white paper cloths cover the tables and the whole exercise looks and feels like its French counterpart.

A short menu ranges from home-made soups (95p), pasta of the day (£1.90 starter, £3.70 main) and a chef's salad to serious stuff like rib of beef for two (£12) and steak teriyaki (£5.70), but is supplemented by a blackboard of plats du jour. On Saturday and Sunday they do a special brunch menu which features seasonal French classics such as moules marinières (£2.25 for a starter, £4 main) and smoked salmon and scrambled egg (£2.95) for those with a delicate disposition. Don't forget, it's a brasserie so there is no minimum charge.

From £5 for food.

## Carriages

43 Buckingham Palace Road, SW1 (834 8871)
Victoria tube
Open: for food 11.30am–10.30pm Monday–Saturday; restaurant 12.30–2.30pm and 7.30–11pm Monday–Friday.

Carriages couldn't be handier for visits to ogle Buckingham Palace, situated as it is opposite the Queen's carriage house. The place is large and on two floors, both with distinct characters; upstairs is open all day for food, licensed at the appropriate times and run as a wine bar, while downstairs is a more formal restaurant with a prix fixe two- or three-course meal at £7.25/£8.75. The bar menu is another example of how the brasserie influence is upon us and how innovative wine bar food is at last becoming. Quiche and limp salad is out and delicious filling snacks like croque madame (three French-fried ham and cheese sandwiches topped with poached egg) with a large bowl of spinach and bacon salad is in. They make their own soda bread and proper puddings like bread and butter and chocolate mousse tart. All food is prepared to order and the standard is pretty good for the moderate prices. Décor, though, is a little odd at first glance – a series of low brick walls, tall wrought iron work and false plain wood ceiling, but this actually breaks up the room and gives a little privacy quite successfully.

Around £5 for food.

## Chicago Rib Shack

1 Raphael Street, Knightsbridge Green, SW7 (581 5595)
Knightsbridge tube
Open: 11.45am–11.30pm Monday–Saturday; noon–10.30pm Sunday.

Escape from the crazy world of Knightsbridge to another weird world just off the main drag. 200 can be seated in this ex-Beejam freezer factory, now almost taken over by a curious collection of pigs and chickens which take up every spare bit of wall and shelf space. It's a totally American experience here ('have a nice day, how are you all') and the food is the result of owner Bob Payton's search for the perfect rib. They come as a rack and the best accompaniments are Hillary's onion loaf – an amazing crispy construction – coleslaw and crispy stuffed potato skins. At lunch (until 5pm) you can eat unlimited numbers of chicken wings for £2.25 or an all-in rib meal for £3.15. Cheesecake, pecan pie or ice cream follow. After a long dispute Payton has landed a full licence so it is possible to call in for a drink; cocktails all sorts, US beers and Californian house wines. Happy hours are between 11.45am–12.45pm and 5.30–7pm Monday to Saturday, when all drinks are half-price and champagne £7.50 a bottle. Incidentally, the spectacular mahogany bar was taken from a Glasgow pub – by the SAS presumably.

From £5 a head.

# The Crêperie

56 South Molton Street, W1 (629 4794)
Bond Street tube
Open: 10am–midnight.

Parent of the Bar Crêperie in Covent Garden (see Eating Outside section) and with an almost identical menu, the place is ideal for speedy and cheap sustenance after the shock of South Molton Street prices. During the summer tables are set outside in the alley which leads off South Molton Street and when there's a breeze sitting here can be like eating in a wind tunnel. Inside the restaurant (which is at the end of the alley) it's all hustle and bustle and queuing for a table is quite common at peak times. The crêpes are cooked to order, should be eaten fast – they turn rubbery and bland when cold – and look like a fat square brown envelope. There are 24 savoury and 12 sweet fillings to choose from; the savoury crêpes are surprisingly filling and the thin crisp sweet ones are addictive. Cider or house wine £4.95.

From £5 a head.

# L S Grunts

12 Maiden Lane WC2 (379 7722)
Covent Garden tube
Open: noon–11.30pm Monday–Saturday; noon–10pm Sunday.

Set back in a little courtyard, the outside of L S Grunts gives the impression of a far larger and more glamorous restaurant than the reality especially when you have to squeeze past the owner's (?) Porsche. Queuing is the norm and there's a no-bookings system so small parties generally end up sharing a table. It's a noisy and hectic place with far too many tables packed far too closely, and it's curiously decorated with a 34-foot-long mural of the Chicago skyline and a continuous self-advertising video. The menu is short and based around the deep-sided Chicago pizza which is cooked to order and generally shared by two or more, and which makes a tasty, filling and cheap meal. Light eaters can dip into the old-fashioned bath tub called The Shower Room which is a help yourself salad bar. Cheesecake, brownies and ice cream follow.

With a cocktail and/or house wine from £5 a head.

# ICA

Nash House, The Mall, SW1 (930 0493)
Piccadilly tube
Open: noon–8pm Tuesday–Sunday.

Jill Parkinson is the latest chef to take over the eating facilities at the Institute of Contemporary Arts. A private caterer of some repute, Jill is attempting to provide a varied and daily-changing menu of generous portions of wholesome food. The emphasis is on value for money and the menu caters for those wanting a cuppa and a cake, a bowl of homely soup, salad or a three-course meal. Vegetables au gratin, a doorstep wedge of sausage and bacon pie, taramasalata and fish pie are typical and all are under £2. Of the main dishes any curry (made by a Thai chef) is particularly recommended but it's the puddings that steal the show. Sherry trifle bears no relation to a nursery version and is packed with fresh fruit, nuts and made with chocolate cake while the fruit brûlée topped with caramel is addictive. The rather awkward 'space' for eating is vastly improved by moving the servery to the far end (there is no waitress service) and placing tables along both sides. Otherwise take your food to the popular upstairs bar or ante room between restaurant and bar. There are ambitions to change the area structurally and that may have happened by the time this book appears in print. House wine £3.95.

Food from £1.10 to £6 for three courses.
Admission only with membership (£10) or day ticket (50p).

# Jules Bar

85 Jermyn Street, SW1 (930 4700)
Green Park tube
Open: noon–2.30pm and 6–10.30pm Monday–Saturday.

Shopping in Jermyn Street, what? Popping into a chum's place in St James's? Then if one's in need of a snifter and a spell with the nose-bag one should jolly well beetle along to Jules Bar. Spiffing sort of place really. Has a very clubby atmosphere, what with the old oak-panelling, RAF fighter plane prints, red leatherette chairs and a lounge lizard tinkling at the piano. Decent line in cocktails too. And in that rather cosy, saucily-lit back room one can canoodle with one's popsy, or indeed one's sugar-daddy, over tip-top snacks. They've got a couple of continental numbers among the starters – taramawhatsit and a sort of Froggy liver pâté – but one would much rather have the old smoked salmon or potted Stilton. No foreign infidels in the main courses though! Prime Scotch steaks, Dover soles, sausages and mash (over four quid though!), lobster soup, roast lamb, beef casserole, club sandwiches with chicken and bacon – all jolly good stuff too. They even have a bully beef hash with fried egg, though I suppose the Yanks will claim that as one of theirs. Between you and me, Buffy and I don't just go for the nosh and the pukka atmosphere – they have these rather pleasant young girls you see, dressed up in men's clothes, trousers, black tie and waistcoat! Getting a crab sandwich from one of these certainly puts the wind back in one's sails. Jolly nice place all round – but watch for the stiffly-priced brandies.

About £13 a head.

## Lemonia

154 Regent's Park Road, NW1 (586 7454)
Chalk Farm tube
Open: 6pm–midnight Monday–Saturday.

After an afternoon among the wildlife of Regent's Park Zoo, adjourn to the nearby Lemonia for a restoring Greek meal. To call Lemonia a kebab house would be a bit like calling Snowdon's aviary a bird-cage, since in terms of décor – paintings, tapestries, lots of hanging floral baskets and some unusual photographs – it's much more than that. In the summer, the best place to eat in what is otherwise a packed honeycomb of rooms and basement levels, is the ground-floor conservatory at the rear. This has a sliding roof for warm evenings, and you usually have to get there early to bag a seat in it. If you fail, the food will more than compensate for disappointment. Unexpected starters include trahana, a Cypriot soup of wheat and milk, generally served in winter, and the garides, chilled prawns dressed with lemon and oil. Thereafter, try stuffed seasonal vegetables, stifado (beef casserole), or the tender sweetbreads in wine. If you're feeling unadventurous, there's a good range of charcoal grills from kebabs and lamb cutlets to spring chicken, while the perfect supper is provided by the meze – the selection of dishes – at £4.90 each for a minimum of two persons. It's not as gargantuan as that at the Rodos (see page 48) but makes up for that with subtle cooking and diversity of flavours. If you're visiting the Zoo on a Sunday when Lemonia is closed, try Mustoe Bistro (see page 170) across the road, which is open for both lunch and dinner.

About £25 for two.

## Monsieur Thompson's Restaurant

29 Kensington Park Road, W11 (727 9957)
Ladbroke Grove tube
Open: 12.30–2.30pm and 7.30–10.30pm Monday–Saturday.

The now ten-year-old Monsieur Thompson's is a charming establishment which succeeds on the two most essential points to a restaurant; the food is reliably good and the atmosphere and decoration are easy on the eye – and the whole experience is easy on the wallet. The French menu is kept short, changes seasonally and is always augmented by daily specials. At lunch they offer an all inclusive daily-changing set menu (£8 two courses, £10 three) which is particularly popular on Saturdays, and in the evening it's à la carte. The chef's specialities are fish and pâtisserie and he's always got a good eye for presentation and making the most of contrasting and complementary colours. The restaurant is on two floors; upstairs is pleasantly light and breezy, decorated in opulent country style with hessian walls, bare floor boards, red and white check table cloths, lovely huge old mirrors and a two-foot Marilyn Monroe doll incongruously sat on the window ledge. Downstairs is slightly more cosy and in the evening both rooms are candle-lit. You can rely on being served an innovative, light and delicious meal which, considering the quality of ingredients and care that has gone into the food's preparation, is good value for money. House wine £4.95.

Set meals from £8; à la carte from £12 a head.

## Rhodes Kebab House

112 Lisson Grove, NW1 (724 1450)
Marylebone tube
Open: noon–11pm Monday–Saturday.

Church Street Market is one of the most comprehensive in London – at the Edgware Road end, the Thursday–Saturday stalls offer everything from fresh fruit to cut-price Domestos, while at the Lisson Grove end, the shops, stalls and Alfie's Antique Market deal in all manner of bric-à-brac, furniture and old books. Despite its popularity, there isn't much in the area in the way of restaurants, but this modest little kebab house just down Lisson Grove is a good enough place for a fill-up after the fray. Simply furnished – rubber plants, tourist-board posters, mosaics and a depiction of the Colossus at Rhodes (or is it Sting at Wembley?) – it offers a standard range of Greek kebabs and grills, all freshly-cooked and served with generous salads. Best bets are the huge kleftico (roast lamb), the mixed kebab (pork and lamb) with salad or the pastourma (spiced sausages). The usual dips and sticky cakes flank the main courses.

Worth noting on the drinks side are the Castello Minos, a full-bodied, fruity Cretan red wine, and the orange-flavoured liqueur, filfar. The couple who run the place are extremely friendly and chatty.

About £6 a head.

## Royal Academy Restaurant

Burlington House, Piccadilly, W1
Green Park tube
Open: 10.30am–5pm daily.

Visitors to the Royal Academy should have little trouble finding a decent place to eat, since the gallery's own restaurant is one of the best value operations in the area, and well worth a visit in its own right. Situated down a twisting corridor to the left of the main foyer, the restaurant is stylishly spacious, neatly furnished and features arched windows, delicate pastel colours, high ceilings and an exotic Pre-Raphaelite mural running round part of the room. A self-service, cafeteria-style counter dispenses hot savoury snacks in the order of baked potatoes with cheese and onion, ham and celery au gratin, creamed leek soup or cheese and noodle hot-pot. There's also a more substantial dish at lunchtimes – perhaps stuffed loin of lamb with vegetables. In addition, the salad and cold buffet selections are very good (quiches, cold meats, pâtés, cheeses) as are the desserts and pastries. Carafes of decent wine are available and there's also an adjacent bar. After lunch, tea with cakes and sandwiches is served throughout the afternoon in the quiet and restful atmosphere befitting an art gallery.

About £6 a head.

## Serendipity

The Mall, Camden Passage, N1 (359 1932)
Angel tube
Open: 11am–1am (last orders midnight) Tuesday–Saturday; noon–10.30pm (last orders 10pm) Sunday.

Sitting on top of a large arcade of antique shops on the fringe of Camden Passage antiques market, Serendipity couldn't be more convenient for drinks, snacks, fast meals and rejuvenative cocktails after a visit to this or the nearby Chapel Street market. It's a sizeable place which makes a feature of the large glass skylight. Potted plants, stained glass windows and marble tables give it a light and airy quality and the menu is sensibly short and fast, featuring a range of substantial salads, pies, burgers and pasta with nothing over

£4.35 (rosemary grilled lamb chops) and most dishes under £3. Though owned by the people who also run the highly revered, and now eleven-year-old Fredericks just up the Passage, Serendipity has no pretensions to haute cuisine. The place is light-hearted, reasonably-priced and essentially a fast food haven. They offer a full range of cocktails and house wines start at £3.50. Serendipity also has a wine bar licence so it's not essential to eat.

From £5 a head for a light meal and drink.

## The Village Bistro

38 Highgate High Street, N6 (340 5165)
Highgate tube
Open: noon–2.45pm and 6–11.30pm Monday–Saturday.

Highgate has a lot to offer the browsing visitor – spectacular views across London, a host of antique and old book shops, Kenwood House and its summer Saturday concerts and even the famous cemetery are all worthy of attention. How apt then that the Village Bistro should reflect the surrounding neighbourhood by being small, pretty and tasteful. A converted cottage on the main street, the bistro is so tiny it can barely fit tables and diners in at the same time. Despite the crush however, the staff work wonders on the two-floored premises in turning out an excellent and imaginative range of French specialities. On the standing menu, there's a delicious deep-fried, bread-crumbed Emmental with tartare sauce, crêpes de volaille, chicken liver pâté and poire avocat Trianon – baked avocado with seafood, glazed with Hollandaise sauce. Plats du jour might include vichyssoise or marinated mackerel. Main courses include such old bistro favourites as goulash and a meat fondue (beef, chicken and veal in a bouillon with sauces), while pan-fried specials could be trout with almonds, chicken breast in egg and parmesan, or veal cutlet in tarragon and cream sauce, with watercress, chives and sorrel. Simple sorbets or rich crêpes de fraises might be among the puddings. The 11.30pm last orders are ideal for post-Kenwood suppers, although the premises can get a bit sultry on hot summer nights.

About £28 for two.

## Winston's

24 Coptic Street, WC1 (580 3422)
Tottenham Court Road tube
Open: 11.30am–3pm and 5.30–11pm Monday–Saturday.

After enjoying the historical pleasures of the British Museum, what more patriotic venue could there be than nearby Winston's? A tasteful tribute to the belligerent Prime Minister, it's a combination of wine bar (on the ground floor) and Edwardian club dining-room (on the first floor). Both are impeccably furnished – oil paintings, mahogany booths, stained glass windows, Churchillian memorabilia – and both offer reliable, in some cases inventive, English food. The likes of lamb and apricot pie, calves' liver with blackcurrants, whole baby salmon and Blenheim beef casserole have all been robustly successful. Less demanding appetites can enjoy the good range of salads (avocado and mango with lime dressing) or the starters/supper snacks (salmon, spinach and pear tart with lemon yoghourt, goulash soup). Puddings are usually in the style of chocolate and crème de menthe mousse, fruit compôte or rhubarb and blackberry pie. After enjoying this British fare and the gentility of the morning-suited head-waiters, you'll feel much less keen about giving back the Elgin Marbles.

About £25 for two.


*Also Good for When You're Out and About:*
Astrix (King's Road)
Cathay Restaurant (King's Road)
Chaopraya (Oxford St/St Christopher's Place)
Green and Pleasant (Covent Garden)
Hung Toa (Queensway)
Juicy Lucy (Regent Street)
Luba's (Knightsbridge)
Mandeer (Tottenham Ct Rd/Oxford St)
Melange (Covent Garden)
Metro, Le (Knightsbridge)
Olde Hatchet, The (Windsor Safari Park)
One Legged Goose (London Zoo)
Richmond Rendezvous (Richmond and Park)
Royal Horseguards Hotel (Whitehall/Trafalgar Sq)
Shampers (Regent St)
Slinky's (Whitehall)
Solopasta (Camden Passage/Chapel Street Market)
Surprise (Oxford St/Berwick Street Market)
Tuttons (Covent Garden)
Vasco & Piero's Pavilion (Oxford Street)

# 8. When You Don't Want to Cook Sunday Lunch

Judging by the difficulty we had in deciding which restaurants to include in this section, the traditional British Sunday lunch has never been more popular. While traditional British restaurants like the Hungry Horse in South Kensington and Rules in Covent Garden do it all the time, restaurants of all cuisines, all over town serve a set three-course roast Sunday lunch which would be hard to undercut at home. These lunches can be a quickie before or after market visiting, such as Chalk and Cheese opposite Dingwalls in Chalk Farm, a comfortable and leisurely affair as at Masters in Queensgate or a family affair at Lucky's in Ealing where they lay on an entertainer for the children and serve them with free kiddiburgers.

There are also numerous alternatives to satisfying pangs for Mum's cooking or solving the problem of a hangover or empty cupboard. Chinatown is alive and well on Sundays; there are stylish elegant tratts such as the Rossetti in Swiss Cottage which will serve your favourite Italian meal. Or you can relax ethnic-style in some-

where such as the dimly-lit Indonesian and Singaporean Bunga Raya in Bayswater.
*(See Index for places also open Sunday evenings)*

## Mrs Beeton's

58 Hill Rise, Richmond (940 9561)
Richmond tube
Open: 10am–5pm and 6–11pm Tuesday–Saturday; 10am–5pm Sunday and Monday.

This place is based on a brilliant idea. A rotation of different chefs (mostly female) take over the restaurant for a lunch or evening session and prepare all the food on offer for their session. Everything on sale is entirely home-made and you can be assured of large portions of good homely cooking served fast and very fairly priced. The place is very popular with locals who pop in for a slice of cake and a coffee, and on Sundays people flock in after a walk in the Park for a bowl of soup or one of the day's specials which tend to be under £3. A Sunday lunch visit there might offer a choice of starters such as smoked mackerel pâté (with home-made bread and butter), crustless leek and cheese flan and broccoli and bacon flan (all 95p). The three main dishes when we visited were chilli con carne, beef Naranja (beef braised in white wine and oranges) and a very good coq au vin (£2.95) and all came with crunchy wild rice. The undisputed highlight though was the pudding; 15 different and gorgeous-looking and -tasting gâteaux, 80p. Lemon walnut meringue, fresh fruit pavlova, butterscotch gâteau and the aptly-named squidgy rum gâteau were divine. The place is small and cramped and more like a provincial coffee bar than a restaurant so it isn't a place to linger; the small upstairs ante room with three tables is nicest. In the basement there's a small antique shop through which you have to traipse to get to the loo. Booking is advised for evening meals.

From £5 a head.
Not licensed, pub almost next door or take your own.

## Bunga Raya

107 Westbourne Grove, W2 (229 6180)
Bayswater tube
Open: noon–3pm and 6–11.30pm daily.

This large Malaysian restaurant has served consistently good food since it opened. The initially rather stark room has been softened by the pretty, brightly-coloured Chinese kites that decorate the walls, and the huge upside-down parasol which acts as a central lampshade. It's run with friendly concern by a young Malaysian couple and it's possible to see into the amazingly small kitchen where the delicious, tasty and spicy food is prepared.

Bunga Raya will do all the choosing for you and serve a many-course meal including a bottle of wine and liqueur for two for £21.50 but choosing à la carte shouldn't present too many problems. Their satay, served with pounded rice blocks, chunks of cucumber and onion and a vast bowl of the peanutty dip, is a popular starter (£2) as is the freshly-made sliced spring roll (£1.10). Good choices for a main dish include Ikan Pang Gang Pecel (£3.80) a whole grilled flat fish coated with a tasty tomato-based thick sauce; a hot Rendang (£2.70), beef curry or crispy Ayam Goreng (£2.50), chicken cooked in coconut. Eat rice or noodles and perhaps a vegetable dish such as Syur Lemak (£1.90), fresh vegetables in a creamy coconut sauce. If you are sharing dishes, take a little of each and eat separately with the rice; the flavours are very distinctive and should not be mixed. French house wine £4.50.

From £5 a head alc; set meal with wine £23.50 for two.

## Bunny's

7 Pond Street, NW3 (435 1541)
Hampstead tube
Open: 7–11pm Tuesday–Sunday; noon–3pm Sunday.

For anyone nursing a Sunday morning hangover, Bunny's may be a good bet since it's a dark, windowless basement restaurant that's candle-lit even in daytime. The pink table-linen and muted colours are also easy on the eye, though the half-price children's menu (£3.30) means there's usually a few Tamsins and Sebastians screeching around you. To their credit, the staff try to seat family parties in the remoter corners and alcoves of the room. Although it's a French restaurant during the week (stuffed quail, escargots in Pernod, gigot d'agneau), Bunny's offers a traditional English Sunday lunch with Gallic starters – perhaps onion soup, garlic bread or a smoked trout pâté. The choice of roasts embraces beef, pork and lamb, all served with generous supplies of well-cooked, appropriate vegetables. Puddings from the trolley are pastry-based and might include apple crumble, fruit pies or coffee cakes. Service is brisk and friendly, and there's usually a tasteful turn at the piano or classical music to help the atmosphere. Depending how you approach these things, you can work up an appetite/walk it all off, before/after your meal on the Heath nearby.

Set lunch £13.10 for two (excl wine).

# Le Caprice

Arlington House, Arlington Street, SW1 (629 2239)
Green Park tube
Open: 12.30–2.30pm Monday–Friday; 7pm–midnight Monday–Saturday;
noon–3pm Sunday.

Now firmly established as one of the best ways to see off a boring
Sunday, Le Caprice's à la carte brunch is a seductive mixture of chic
setting, attractive food and star-spotting – there's always the
chance that one of David Bailey's 60s portraits which adorn the wall
will appear in the flesh, looking fifteen years younger, rather than
fifteen years *older*, than they did in the photo. The wide-ranging
menu offers simple snacks like bagels with smoked salmon and
cream cheese, scrambled eggs and bacon, or crisp Caesar salad,
together with modish main dishes – lamb sausages with onion
marmalade; chopped veal steak; salmon fishcakes in sorrel sauce.
Traditionalists can stick to country-house favourites like smoked
haddock with poached egg. It's all brilliantly conceived and executed (the staff are particularly efficient) – and if you get your
head behind a pitcher of Bloody Marys or a jug of Buck's Fizz, you
needn't wake up till Monday.

About £25 for two.

# Chalcot's

49 Chalcot Road, NW1 (722 1956)
Chalk Farm tube
Open: 12.30–2.30pm Tuesday–Friday; 7.30–10.45pm Tuesday–Saturday;
12.30–2.30pm Sunday.

One of a breed of North London neighbourhood restaurants which
often pass unnoticed by people outside the immediate area, Chalcot's certainly deserves a wider audience, especially for its excellent
Sunday lunches. Chef Colin Thompson offers considerable depar-
tures from the tyranny of roast beef and two veg – a prix fixe,
three-course lunch for £7.85 with three delicious alternatives in each
section. Start with a plate of three pâtés, a vegetable soup or fruit,
follow with a main course featuring meat, poultry or fish – filet de
boeuf en croûte: supreme of chicken in a cream and mustard sauce;
poached salmon trout with Hollandaise – all beautifully cooked
and presented. Classic French puds like crème brulée and chocolate
mousse. The narrow, bare-brick wall gives off a slightly bleak
day-time atmosphere, so go back at nights to explore the adventurous main card by candle-light.

Set lunch £15.70 for two (excl wine); alc about £30 for two.

112

# Chalk and Cheese

14 Chalk Farm Road, NW1 (267 9620)
Camden Town/Chalk Farm tube
Open: noon–2.30pm and 6.30–11pm Tuesday–Saturday; noon–3pm Sunday.

This modestly-priced, pleasant, family-run two-floor restaurant offers a bistro-style French-ish menu. On Sundays they serve a traditional three-course Sunday lunch at £5.50, half-price for children. There's generally a home-made soup and pâté but otherwise starters are pretty basic, such as egg mayonnaise and fresh orange juice. The main course affords a varied choice but roast leg of pork with apple sauce and stuffing, chicken in red wine sauce, grilled trout and a vegetarian dish of the day are always available. All main dishes come with three vegetables. Puddings are for those with a healthy appetite; bread and butter pudding, sherry trifle and apple and almond flan. Homely rather than sophisticated; one of the best value set Sunday lunches in town.

Set Sunday lunch £5.50; alc from £8.

# Chez Gerard

8 Charlotte Street, W1 (636 4975)
Goodge Street tube
Open: 12.30–2.30pm and 6.30–10.45pm daily (except Saturday lunch).

Bustling and busy during the week, the Charlotte Street area (Fitzrovia to the locals) can be a bit of a bleak wasteland on Sundays. All the more commendable then that Chez Gerard stays open with its good charcoal-grilled specialities filling in nicely for the Sunday roast. They only open the lower level of the restaurant – dimly-lit, polished wooden floor, smart banquette seating – but this tends to concentrate the service which can be a bit vague (and terse) on a hectic week-day. Main dishes include côtellettes d'agneau, brochettes and steaks, all accompanied by grilled tomatoes and huge bowls of delicious frites. Start with a warming onion soup, pâté, charcuterie or, if they're on, moules marinières. Finish with excellent cheeses and a rich chocolate mousse. The house claret is always reliable. An agreeable consequence of the relaxed Sunday atmosphere is that the rather sexy T-shirted waitresses don't mind you practising your French on them.

About £24 for two.

## Drake's

2a Pond Place, SW3 (584 4555)
South Kensington tube
Open: 12.30–2.15pm and 7.30–11.30pm Monday–Saturday; 12.30–2.45pm and
7.30–10.30pm Sunday.

The phrase 'traditional English Sunday lunch' sometimes has a
rather functional ring about it, conjuring up images of simple roasts
in gravy with over-cooked vegetables. How pleasant then to find a
restaurant dealing in imaginative English dishes, most of which can
double up as Sunday lunch substitutes. Of course you may fancy the
idea of baked sea-bass with fennel or veal escalope stuffed with
grapes and chestnuts, but if the roast meat 'munchies' have got you,
fear not. Drake's, you see, deals in a short range of spit-roasted
dishes, from loin of pork with apricots and roast lamb with braised
onion, to fresh duck with a choice of sauces, apple or wild honey
with thyme. In addition the menu might offer Norfolk turkey with
chipolatas or the splendidly tender noisettes of lamb, served on
croûtons with a sharp mustard and sesame sauce. Sandwich these
with baked stuffed mushrooms, dressed crab or salmon in aspic for
starters, and chocolate truffle cake, treacle and orange tart or
cream-filled brandy snaps for dessert, and you have a Sunday lunch
to defy any English winter. The robustness of the food is matched by
the décor – bare floors, brick walls hung with tapestries and high-
class ducks flying up the wall. Of course choosing individually rather
than set-price wallops the cost up, but the quality's worth the extra
expense.

About £35 for two.

## Filling Station

304 Kentish Town Road, NW5 (267 6410)
Kentish Town tube
Open: 9am–5pm and 7–11pm Monday–Saturday; 10am–4pm Sunday.

Two years ago ex-student Diana Gentle and a small group of her
friends took the plunge and designed and opened the Filling Station. The look is fifties but the spirit eighties and the place has
carved quite a niche for itself by providing wholesome and cheap
food in a relaxed atmosphere. There is a weekly-changing menu
with daily specials and you can expect to find lasagne, ratatouille,
shepherd's pie with salad and potatoes followed by chocolate fudge
cake, trifle and apple pie, and all main dishes will be under £2,
puddings under £1. They squeeze their own fruit juice and make
milk shakes but are not licensed. On Sunday they offer a choice of

mega breakfasts – a traditional English blow out for £2.75; American Diner of corned beef hash, pancakes and syrup; Edwardian Express of scrambled egg, mushrooms, buttered muffins (both £2.50) and the Continental of croissant, orange juice and coffee at £1.75. You can breakfast here during the week on bacon, sausage and toast for £1.20, croissant and jam 65p.

From £3 a head for food.

## Golden Duck

6 Hollywood Road, SW10 (352 3500)
Earls Court tube
Open: 7pm–midnight daily, 1–3pm Saturday and Sunday.

No need to head for Soho for a Chinese feast of a Sunday lunch, why not do it in comfort in the somewhat eclectically done-out Golden Duck? The Duck was something of a pioneer when it opened in the sixties and was the first London Chinese restaurant to successfully marry a pleasant Westernized décor with competently-prepared Peking food. Though the Duck indirectly bred the stylish and elegant I Ching, Tai Pan, Zen, Paper Tiger and Red Pepper (sadly recently closed) its décor was very sixties with a beautiful yin-yang window and psychedelic, predominantly red, colour-scheme and saloon-style swinging doors. Nothing has changed and you sit in a time warp to enjoy the reliably good food. (as we went to press the Chef moved to the excellent new South East Asian Non-Ya, 73 Old Brompton Road, SW7 (584 4323); from £8 a head). Golden Duck was the first restaurant to serve Szechuan food which is still a speciality (a set Szechuan meal is available) but the wide-ranging menu is very clear and explicit and if you have any doubts there are various 'leave it to us' meals available (including a vegetarian version).

From £8 a head for food.

## Jake's Restaurant

14 Hollywood Road, SW10 (352 8692)
Earls Court tube
Open: 12.30–2.30pm daily, 7.30–11.45pm Monday–Saturday.

In a small road packed with more than its fair share of good restaurants (Brinkleys and The Golden Duck in particular) Jake's holds its head up high and serves generous portions of wholesome, Frenchified English food at modest prices. The ground floor with its cocktail bar overlooks a small terrace garden while downstairs it's more of a bunfight.

On Sundays the shortish menu is reduced and they offer a choice of traditional Sunday lunch dishes. Eggs benedict and Jake's blini – smoked salmon, sour cream and Danish caviare on a muffin are perfect runners in to roast beef with Yorkshire and a wonderful home-made steak, kidney and mushroom pie. Home-made puddings or cheese follow. They allow children to share a portion or go half-price and Sunday lunch works out at £10 a head including house wine.

From £18 for two.

## Leonardo's

397 King's Road, SW3 (352 4146)
Sloane Square/South Kensington tube
Open: 12.15–2.45pm and 7.30–11.15pm Monday–Saturday; 12.15–2.30pm Sunday.

Tucked away in an unprepossessing and untrendy row of Worlds End shops, the windows hung with drab yellow curtains, Leonardo's does not look inviting. Inside it's a different matter altogether; the tiled floor, pale yellow colour scheme, ladderback chairs and drawings from Da Vinci's notebook add up to a very pleasant scene. A stupendous cold table dominates the room and the regional menu is overwhelmingly long and some of the dishes over-ambitious. The spaghetti da Vinci baked in a paper case with a garlicky shellfish sauce is quite a novelty but as a general rule we'd advise choosing the simpler dishes. Desserts are from the trolley. Clientele can be fashionable, and Barry Sheene who lives nearby and whose photo is on the wall has been known to visit.

Food from £8 a head. House wine under £4.

## Lord's Carver Restaurant

Ladbroke Westmoreland Hotel, Lodge Road, NW8 (722 7722)
St John's Wood tube
Open: 12.30–2.30pm and 6–10pm daily.

One of the best ways of dealing with a Sunday lunch out, especially if you're en famille, is to hit a carvery. This one, overlooking the Nursery End of Lord's Cricket Ground, is reckoned to be one of the best. The large first-floor room is packed with tables of all sizes, and the copper-plating on the pillars adds a further garish note to what is not the quietest of eating experiences – the presence of a large number of children, some in the high chairs provided by the hotel, and a constant bustle of people heading for the carvery counters, make it rather like eating in an airport departure lounge. Nevertheless, the fixed price deal is a reasonably good one – £9.95 for three courses (£5.50 for children under ten) – since the self-service element generally means you can get as much meat and vegetables as you can eat.

The starters in the deal are fairly negligible – soup, melon, prawn cocktail, pâté – but good for what they are, and it's really not worth paying the extra for more 'exotic' hors d'oeuvres like Parma ham with melon. The tiled carvery counters offer a good range of high-quality roasts from beef, rare and well-done, lamb, pork and, as this is St John's Wood, salt-beef. Kitchen assistants actually do the carving, so the trick is just to keep holding your plate out till you think you've got enough, though second helpings are encouraged. If you're not into straight roasts, there's usually another 'speciality', such as chicken casserole, available. Puds are the predictable but passable sherry trifle and gâteaux stodge, though somewhat surprisingly, the cheese-board isn't plastic wrapped and portions are plentiful. With some vicious mark-ups on the wines and service not included, a family of four won't get away for less than forty quid – so you could obviously eat cheaper at home, but then that's not the point, is it?

About £28 for two.

## Maroush

21 Edgware Road, W2 (723 0773/0571)
Marble Arch tube
Open: noon–5am daily

Bored with traditional English Sunday lunch? A Lebanese meze meal (a series of hot and cold snacks) couldn't be more different and is never boring. At Maroush there is no set meze meal but there is a huge list of Lebanese hors d'oeuvres to choose from. Eating this way also means you can eat lightly or really gorge yourself and the more of you in the party, the more variety you can enjoy and the cheaper the meal will work out. All Lebanese meals automatically start with a dish of chilled undressed and uncut salad (half a cos lettuce, baby cucumber, carrots, radishes, pepper, etc) and olives and these are eaten throughout the meal and account for the £1 cover charge. All the dishes range from £1.25 to £2.50 and come garnished with huge sprays of parsley. You can evolve a vegetarian or a meat meal. Our favourites include the traditional salad of chopped parsley, tomato, onion and cracked wheat called tabbouleh; garlicky chicken wings and lemony livers; hummus; grilled and pounded aubergines; falafel (deep fried balls of chick peas, broad beans and vegetables) and triangular pastries filled with spinach, onions, pine kernels and lemon juice. All these dishes are shared and treated as dips using ball-shaped pitta bread as a shovel. Follow with a delicious honey-drenched baklava-style pastry stuffed with pistachio nuts. Drink the traditional aniseed Arak (£14.50

enough for two glasses each for four) or their excellent house wine at £4.

From £5 a head.

## Masters

190 Queen's Gate, SW7 (581 5666)
South Kensington tube
Open: noon–3pm and 5.30–11pm in bar; 5.30pm–1am Monday to Saturday (last orders midnight); noon–5pm (last orders 4pm) Sunday lunch.

Masters is the perfect place for a long, late Sunday lunch. Tucked between two hotels it's a huge place with a comfortable cocktail/wine bar upstairs and delightful white-painted wood-panelled basement dining room with adjoining Piano Bar. The main restaurant is large but somehow the mixture of two simulated log fires, walls packed with paintings, tall green plants all over the place and a rose on each table make it appear cosy. The à la carte is Italian but their three-course Sunday lunch features the traditional English roast at an all-in £7.95.

There's a choice of six Italian starters including bresaola, a salad of mozzarella, avocado, tomatoes and cucumber and a substantial minced meat, aubergine, tomato and mozzarella dish. There is a choice of roast lamb, beef and pork but everyone seems to go for the beef which comes with Yorkshire pudding and is a generous, thickly-sliced portion. To follow there's a delicious selection of nursery-style puddings or a limited selection of Italian cheese. The Italian waiters are wonderfully tolerant of young children. Go before 2.30pm and you'll almost have the place to yourself, otherwise book.

Set meal £7.95, children half price; alc £15 a head.

## Mumtaz

4–10 Park Road, NW1 (723 0549)
Baker Street tube
Open: noon–2.30pm and 6–11.30pm (11pm Sunday) daily.

An increasing number of Indian restaurants are offering buffet lunches and dinners at the weekends. The Mumtaz, a beautifully-appointed, air-conditioned 'palace' on the edge of Regent's Park, serves a very good value Sunday buffet for £6.95 per person. A long table sports a wide cross-section of the high-class restaurant menu, from meat and vegetable curries to tandoori chicken and prawns. The food is kept hot on spirit burners and replenished at regular intervals, along with all the poppadoms, pickles and nan breads you require. It's self-service so you can help yourself to as much as you want, and they don't seem to mind second helpings – thirds we're not sure about. For vegetarians they do a splendid thali, encompassing curries, rice, raita (yoghourt dip), dal (lentils), nan and poppadoms. Walk it all off in the park afterwards.

Set lunch £12.90 for two (excl drink); alc about £20 for two.

## Pollyanna's

2 Battersea Rise, SW11 (228 0316)
Clapham Junction BR–Victoria
Open: 7pm–midnight daily; 1–3pm Sunday.

After a brisk Sunday morning game of frisbee on Clapham Common, you can retire to the north-west corner of the greenery and a pleasant, informal restaurant called Pollyanna's. During the week, the multi-levelled, panelled-pine, gingham-clothed houseboat-like premises deal in highly-regarded, imaginative Franco–English dishes – venison in red wine with a redcurrant and game sauce and bananas, calves' liver with pears in a Poire William sauce, fillets of monkfish on a bed of spinach with Grand Marnier sauce and orange segments, and the vegetarian stir-fried fruit and nut casserole with tofu, all feature regularly. Come Sundays however, it's back to basics, with a good value Sunday lunch built around traditional English roasts (beef, lamb, pork, turkey) and steak and kidney pie or deep-fried goujons of sole. The roasts arrive cooked precisely to order, accompanied by plentiful vegetables, but the steak and kidney pie has been known to bring a rather blackened gravy with it. Starters are basic – curried pea soup, taramasalata, prawn cocktail, smooth duck liver mousse – and puddings tend to be delicious but sloppy – chocolate pudding and custard, coffee and brazil-nut ice cream with hot chocolate sauce, banana rumble featuring ice-cream, Cointreau and honey. The spartan seating/heating make it best for jolly group dining, though the evening menu (last orders midnight, nb) deserves intimate attention, as do the extensive, serious wine list (complete with tasting notes) and the classic range of armagnacs, cognacs and calvados.

Set Sunday lunch £6.95 a head (excl wine); alc about £30 for two.

## The Rossetti

Ordnance Hill, NW8 (722 7141)
St John's Wood tube
Open: 12.30–2.30pm and 7–11pm daily.

Piling into the pub on a Sunday lunchtime is as much a part of the routine as the lunch itself. Here, you can enjoy both under one roof, since the Rossetti is both a Fuller's pub (on the ground floor) and a smart Italian restaurant (on the upper floor). The modern, stylishly-decorated complex also boasts a lounge bar bivouac to get you through that difficult climb from pub to restaurant. The trattoria, with its tiled floors and cream walls is a light, airy sort of place, especially pleasant on a summer day when the large windows are opened to accommodate breezes. No special menu is offered on a Sunday, but that particular relaxed atmosphere is generated by the sight of well-heeled Italian families in their church-going best. Choose then from a familiar trattoria card – tuna and beans, sea-food salads, pasta to start, with petto di pollo 'found' (rolled chicken breast filled with garlic butter) or the chef's special veal escalope (in cream and mushroom sauce) as a main course. There's the usual load of sleep-inducing stodge on the trolley, but as it's Sunday, you can nod off at home instead of at the office.

About £30 for two.

## Spy's

79 Castellain Road, W9 (286 4801)
Maida Vale tube
Open: noon–2.30pm Monday–Friday; 7–11pm Monday–Saturday; 12.30–2pm Sunday.

Anyone requiring a no-nonsense traditional English Sunday lunch could do a lot worse than head here. A small but pleasantly-furnished neighbourhood restaurant, Spy's (dedicated to the cartoonist and featuring his work) offers three courses for £7.50, all based around the usual Sunday roasts – beef, lamb, pork or chicken. Served with all the essential trimmings (Yorkshire pudding, apple sauce, crackling etc), the roasts are flanked by reliable soups and pâtés (perhaps chicken liver and brandy) and mouth-watering English puddings in the apple crumble and custard mould. 'Really nice' sixties/early seventies music will compound the Sunday afternoon languor. During the week their menu embraces imaginative bistro dishes like veal and apricot casserole, lamb on a skewer with peppers, onions and tomato, and escalopes of pork in a piquant cream sauce with capers and gherkins. They also include a statutory vegetarian dish every day – but who wants to know about that on Sundays?

Set lunch £15 for two (excl wine); alc about £24 for two.

# Surprise

12 Great Marlborough Street, W1 (434 2666)
Oxford Circus tube
Open: noon–3pm daily; 6–11.15pm Monday–Saturday.

For anyone fancying an authentic American brunch, the Surprise's is as good as any in town. For an all-in price of £6.15, you get three belt-straining courses. Start with blueberry muffins and hot biscuits or baked grapefruit with dark rum, then choose from the classic American breakfast dishes waffles and maple syrup, eggs Benedict and the huge corned beef hash. Weight-watchers can go for the excellent salad bar while die-hard patriots can have an English roast lunch instead. The long, airport lounge-style room is brightened by art gallery posters and sports photos, while imported Michelob beer adds to the illumination. Service is out of the 'Have a Nice Day' charm school which may grate a bit on a hung-over Sunday morning.

Brunch £12.30 (excl wine); alc about £20 for two.

*Also Good for Sunday Lunch:*
Bell, The
Busabong
Café St Pierre
Chuen Cheng Ku
Fakhraldine
Feathers Hotel
Holland's Wine Bar
Hungry Horse
Lucky's
Manzil's
Mustoe Bistro
Nineteen
One Hampstead Lane
One Legged Goose
Perfumed Conservatory
Phoenicia
Porter's
Read's
Rudland & Stubbs
Salvador's El Bodegon
Texas Lone Star Saloon
Tilley's Eats
Toscannini
Tourment d'Amour
Waterside Inn
Yesterday

# 9. When You Want Entertainment

There are times when a meal out doesn't provide enough of an occasion; when you want more than just food and drink. There are also times when it is essential to have a bit of distraction to help conversation along or perhaps cover up the fact that conversation is not coming easily – first dates and obligatory meals with client or relatives are perfect examples. Our selection caters to your every need, whim or mood and the choice is enhanced by the fact that the food is good too. We cover Thai dancing and boxing, cockney singalongs with live turns, background piano music, jazz, dancing and theatre and even Smarty Arty!

## The Archduke

Concert Hall Approach, South Bank, SE1 (928 9370)
Waterloo tube
Open: noon–2.15pm and 6–10.40pm Monday–Friday; 6pm–midnight Saturday.

Although The Archduke draws a large proportion of its clientele from South Bank culture-vultures, its enterprising policy of providing live music every night gives it an additional identity after the early evening rush has subsided. Based in a cleverly-converted set of railway arches (hence the rumble of trains overhead) The Archduke operates as both a wine bar (at ground level) and informal restaurant (on an upper gallery). The spacious, airy, brightly-furnished rooms are ideal for enjoying the piano-based jazz music and singing, on offer from 8.30–11pm every night. The wine bar (open 11am–3pm weekdays and 5.30–11pm every evening except Sunday) deals mainly in light buffet snacks and salads. The restaurant has a more substantial menu, which in the evenings is structured around a novel list of sausages – several varieties of banger from Greek sheftalia, through Auvergne fumée and venison sausage to good old British porkers. Alternatives to the sausage régime might come in the form of leek mousse, a pork, onion and gherkin terrine, stuffed peppers or oriental pork with Chinese cabbage and red peppers, all at reasonable prices and with an attractive wine list too. Tasteful music, good food, fine wines – 'Underneath the Arches' was never like this.

About £8 a head.

## Bates

11 Henrietta Street, WC2 (240 7600)
Covent Garden tube
Open: 1–3pm and 5.30–11.30pm Monday–Saturday.

One of the Garden's most attractive and relaxed restaurants features English food with the emphasis on using wild foods such as dandelion leaves, nettle, sorrel, coltsfoot and lambs lettuce. The chef has spurned his classic training in both English and French food (he was most recently sous chef at the Savoy), his menu changes constantly and he hopes to evolve a new English cuisine based exclusively on naturally reared and grown produce.

Scallops wrapped in spinach; whole salmon trout wrapped in puff pastry and served with a warm cucumber sauce are some of the more adventurous items in his repertoire, but plain classic dishes such as Dover sole, chargrilled veal with Stilton butter and stuffed baked apple also feature.

Most nights a pianist plays from 9pm and on Thursday and Saturday he's joined by a sax player and singer and the whole place dissolves into a good old sing-along. There's a great sense of fun and occasion here and Hallowe'en and other English festivals are given suitable treatment by the staff.

£12 a head.

## Busabong Thai Restaurant

331 Fulham Road, SW10 (352 4742)
South Kensington tube
Open: 12.30pm–midnight daily.

Upstairs at the nine-year-old, delightful and atmospheric Busabong you can enjoy a night out with a difference. For if you book a meal in their spectacular Khan Tok Room (where shoes have to be removed and you dine sitting on cushions) you can get indigestion watching Thai boxing, classical dancing and sword fight shows or take to the floor yourself (to dance) on Saturday night. You can opt to choose from a devastatingly long (over 100 dishes) menu or take pot luck with a many-dish set meal at £15 a head.

Quieter meals can be enjoyed in the lavishly-decorated ground floor Morakot Room where Thai fast food noodles are kept ready in a cabinet and where you can eat your fill for under £3. Choosing à la carte will average £8 a head and there is a wide choice for vegetarians. Don't miss the potent Thai cocktails.

Set meals £15 a head; alc from £3 for one course meals;
£8 for three courses.

## Café Pelican

45 St Martin's Lane, WC2 (379 0309)
Leicester Square tube
Open: 9am–2am daily.

The owners of this new café, salon and restaurant in the heart of theatre-land have set out to recreate a proper Parisian brasserie in the style of Le Coupole. The long and narrow premises (previously an LEB showroom) lend themselves perfectly to the two tier operation and the long bar is a pleasant place to prop (despite too few and fixed bar stools) and enjoy a bar snack (a choice of baguette sandwiches from 75p, various assiettes – ham, pâté etc, salads and hot plats du jour such as grilled steak and chips £4.50) while there are tables along the opposite wall and a large restaurant (seating for 160) at the back.

The mood is twenties and with the exception of naff-ish imitation plants which let the side down, the style and atmosphere are just right. The food is prepared by Gerard Mosiniak (late of La Grenouille, Abingdon Road, W8) and his nouvelle-style cooking is imaginative and of a consistently high standard. All main dishes are prepared to order and, despite the large number of covers, so far there have been no lapses in quality.

Pheasant in puff pastry with wild mushrooms (£2.50) is a generous starter and with a salad makes a perfect light meal as does the traditionally-prepared fish soup with rouille (£2.20). Main dishes are both rich and innovative – mixed fish steamed and creamed in a julienne of peppers (£7.50) and breast of duck marinated in truffle juice and cooked pink £7.40) – and plain, such as the French classic of grilled beef steak (£5.75). Breakfast is served and so are children's portions, and a menu promotionnel, three courses with a glass of wine, is £7.50.

At the back of the restaurant is a piano and most nights a jazz pianist – different artistes alternate – plays appropriate twenties jazz music, the rest of the time atmospheric Piaf and other French favourites croon in the background.

Set meal £7.50; snacks from £2; alc from £10.

## La Fava

143 Goldhawk Road, W12 (740 0844)
Shepherd's Bush tube
Open: noon–3pm and 6.30–11pm Monday–Saturday.

Now six months old, La Fava has carved quite a niche for itself as a friendly, warm, cosy and very reasonably-priced Italian neighbourhood café/restaurant. Set back from busy Goldhawk Road, the nicest seats are tucked upstairs where the roar of the open barbecue soon blots out all thoughts of Shepherd's Bush. The restaurant is comfortably and unpretentiously done out with navy and white gingham oilskin cloths and 'artist's impressions' of ballet and theatrical costumes decorate the white washed walls. The menu is short and hand-written and the food astoundingly cheap. As well as all your favourite Italian specials (antipasto £1.85, minestrone 65p, pasta £1.95, escalopes around £3 and chicken dishes under £3) the menu features huge hunks of steak, chops, fish and prawns which will be barbecued before your very eyes. All the main dishes come garnished with delicious made-to-order thick chips and tinned petit pois and any choice is guaranteed to satisfy even the heartiest eater. Cassata, home made crème caramel and wonderfully alcoholic zabaglione follow.

125

Most evenings and definitely at the end of the week, the owner's love of guitar (tapes play continually through lunch and dinner) gets the better of him and he treats his captive audience to a wide ranging repertoire, including flamenco. As you hit the next bottle (house wine is a modest £3.45) it's pretty easy to forget all about England and 'tele port' to a little Italian village . . .

From £6 a head for food.

## The Footstool Restaurant

St John's, Smith Square, SW1 (222 2779)
Westminster tube
Open: 11.30am–3pm Monday–Friday; 5.30–11pm on concert evenings.

St John's, Smith Square is one of London's most attractive venues for classical and choral concerts. It's a striking baroque building with ornate pillars and towers, and now the crypt of this former church has been imaginatively converted to provide a companion restaurant, The Footstool. The large, subterranean room – arched, bare-brick pillars lit by spotlights, draped with greenery, packed with tables – offers buffet dishes and concert suppers (£4.75 for two courses and coffee) for those evenings when there are recitals in the concert hall above. And throughout the week, it serves distinctive, waitress-service lunches for wandering MPs or BBC World Service personnel.

A typical lunchtime menu might offer green pea soup, tuna mousse, barbecued spare ribs or deep-fried mushrooms filled with Stilton as starters. Main courses could be lamb sweetbreads in a tomato and mushroom sauce, sweet and sour pork, sirloin steak or poached mackerel with gooseberry sauce. While for the most part the music and the food are kept separate, the Thursday lunchtime recitals (held fortnightly at 1.15pm) actually take place in the restaurant, allowing guests a highly entertaining lunch. The food reverts to the buffet operation – cold meat, game or vegetable pies, pâtés, cheeses, smoked mackerel, home-made soups, spicy sausage casserole, cheesecakes – while the recitals usually take the form of light-hearted classical and modern songs, laced with poems and readings.

There's a good wine list, complete with 'overtures' and 'finales' for sherries and ports, to help the atmosphere along, though take a tip and stock up at 1.10pm as they close the bar during the performance.

Concert suppers £4.75 (excl wine); alc £5 a head (buffet), £12 a head (restaurant).

## Gallery Restaurant

Camden Palace, 1a Camden High Street, NW1 (387 0428)
Mornington Crescent tube
Open: 9pm–3am Tuesday–Saturday (last orders 1.30am).

If you decide to eat at the late night hop spot's restaurant, admission is free to the Palace. It's not a restaurant for a quiet tête-à-tête and though the deco surroundings of mirrored walls, chrome railings and skyscraper lighting is soothing enough, the pulsating noise from the dance floor below means conversation has to be snatched. The menu is international fast food with dishes such as avocado and bacon salad, snails and garlic bread, spaghetti bolognaise, various salads, steaks and burgers, with a few more sophisticated dishes like escalope of veal in a cream and mushroom sauce.

The food is very reasonably priced (three courses under £10 a head but one-course meals are less than half that) and way above the normal standard of club food. The restaurant is situated at the very top of the Palace (the stairs appear to be going to heaven) and you can sit back and watch the dancing before slipping down to work off the meal. A traditional English breakfast is also served in the restaurant and costs £3.85.

From £5 a head.

## Geno Washington's

212 West End Lane, NW6 (431 2891)
West Hampstead tube
Open: 7pm–2am (last orders 1.30am) Tuesday–Sunday.

It's not often that professional singers run restaurants and its even less common for them to use the restaurant to perform in. But here, in collaboration with the premises' previous restaurateur – it was Elle Chéri – and his French wife, sixties soul hero Geno Washington has succeeded in offering good bistro fare and a live turn. Every night (but please book and check), Geno does two mini concerts accompanied by a guitarist in the long narrow basement (upstairs is run as a wine bar). It's comfortably if eclectically done out – there is a strange seaside grotto at the far end – and the food is excellent value. A set meal at £5.95 features, steak, boeuf bourguignon or escalope de veau cordon bleu or there is a short, modest and competently prepared à la carte selection. The whole set-up is relaxed, informal and could turn into a night of surprises if Geno picks on you to try out his other passion, magic.

From £8 a head if choosing the set meal; alc from £10.

# Haweli; The House of Indian Haute Cuisine

15–17 Hill Rise, Richmond (940 3002)
Richmond tube
Open: noon–2.30pm and 6–11.30pm Monday–Friday; 6–11.45pm Saturday and Sunday.

Beautifully and comfortably decorated in pale apricot and white, a quarry-tiled floor and the large room made more intimate by several pillars and tall swaying plants, Haweli is typical of the new fashion in smart, cocktail-serving Indian restaurants. Here they go to some trouble to explain the importance of particular herbs and spicing in their regional menu and are a far cry from the curry house of yore. Most evenings one or two Indian musicians complete with a variety of beautifully carved and resonant instruments squat on a small recessed 'stage' and give diners a background concert of popular Indian music. On Sundays, the entire evening is devoted to a more serious entertainment when the musical repertoire is poetic, includes traditional folk songs and the audience of diners is predominately local Indian gentry.

Despite the floor show and the luxury of the setting, the Haweli is moderately priced with meat dishes under £3 and all vegetable dishes under £2. Their tandoori is cooked (as it should be) to order; the chicken tandoori will arrive succulent and tasty as opposed to the more familiar dry and orange meat widely served. House specialities include the perfect dish for those who don't like hot food; Lamb Pasanda Nawabi which is cooked in cream with yoghurt and ground nuts. Haweli offer a small selection of Indian sweets, including the popular gulab jaman and lychees as well as the increasingly familiar kulfi – a refreshingly mild home-made ice-cream with pistachio and almonds.

From £8 for food.

# Jorgen's Weinstube

22 Harcourt Street, W1 (402 5925)
Edgware Road tube
Open: noon–3pm and 5.30–11pm Monday–Friday; 6–11pm Saturday.

This pleasant wine bar cum bistro on two floors (ground and basement) has two attractions – cheap but wholesome German food and a sedate backcloth of classical music, which on Tuesday and Friday nights extends to the appearance of a classical violinist. This makes a pleasurable, restful change to the loud thump of Steely George or Boy Dan that wine bars normally inflict on their customers. The small, candle-lit basement is the best spot to enjoy the entertainment and the choice range of Teutonic scoff. Start with the delicious cheese and pork strudel, or the pork liver pâté with port and brandy on rye. Follow up, if you've room, with Bremer huhnerragout, a chicken and lemon casserole with onions, mushrooms and asparagus. Other specialities include jager schnitzel (shallow-fried veal with rich mushroom sauce and cauliflower cheese), bratwurst (pork sausages with herbs) and of course, sauerkraut (hot white cabbage). Most of the wines are familiar German but there are two dry Frenchies for those who can't take the sweetness or fruitiness. If you just want to drink and listen to der musik, try a plate of continental niblets – they knock salt and vinegar crisps into a cocked hat.

About £16 for two.

## Jun

58–59 Great Marlborough Street, W1 (437 7268)
Oxford Circus tube
Open: noon–2.30pm Monday–Friday; 6pm–1am Monday–Saturday.

You can have little complaint about the entertainment here since, to a large extent, you provide it yourself. 'Karaoke' is the Japanese word for it, which basically means a 'singalong' – only being a modern, brightly furnished Japanese restaurant, Jun conducts the singalong in a modern, brightly furnished Japanese way. At the far end of the room is a small stage, flanked by every item of contemporary home entertainment you could think of – video, television set, huge sound system with echo chamber, microphones and to complete the picture, a video camera trained on the stage which then projects pictures of the singers onto the TV set behind, incidentally allowing people to bring along their own tapes and record themselves. If you fear that standing up 'naked' is too much of an ordeal, be assured that the restaurant has a wide range of cassettes which feature only the backing tracks to assorted Japanese and European standards. So you can croon away ('Misty', 'Nowhere Man', many other Beatles numbers) with a full orchestra, not to mention the echo chamber, supporting you, and with lyric sheets provided. It's ideal for party entertainment, when the rock star or the ham in you becomes to much to contain, and it's equally entertaining watching the contrasting attitudes of British and Japanese – the one jokey and sheepish, the other deadly serious and self-confident. Almost as an incidental, Jun's food is in fact of an excellent quality. There are no tempura or table-cooked dishes, but there's a great range of appetisers (23 in all) of which the gyoza (steamed meat dumplings with garlic), the satsuma age (deep-fried fish cakes) and the yasai itame (pan-fried mixed vegetables with pork slices) are all very good. Among the main courses, the kaki fry (deep-fried, breadcrumbed oysters) are wonderful, and the kushi katsu (deep fried pork and vegetables on a skewer) is also recommended. Two set meals are offered which may be a good way to concentrate on the singing – altogether now, 'Hello Jun Gotta New Datsun?'

Set meals £15 and £18 a head; alc £16 a head.

## King's Head

115 Upper Street, N1 (226 1916)
Angel tube
Open: pub hours. Dinner 6.45pm, show 7.45pm Monday–Saturday.

One of London's liveliest and most successful fringe theatre venues, the King's Head has a long track-record of distinguished productions – 'Kennedy's Children', 'Spokesong' and 'Mr Cinders' to name but three. The chance to see such plays, preceded by a three-course dinner, is a considerable attraction in itself but the clincher is that if you dine first, you get the best seats.

The back room where the productions take place is a rather cramped affair with a barely-raised stage. Long communal tables and simple wooden chairs form the furnishings, so a good view and a seat that doesn't wobble are essential.

Happily, the meal in this deal isn't negligible – three good, home-made courses might offer a packed vegetable soup, cod baked with grapefruit and vegetables and fruit, cream and ginger. Communal pots of coffee are included in the price, but reasonable house wine (at £4.50 a bottle) isn't.

Service, complete with pretty patterned crockery, is much more pleasant than the pub's slightly louche atmosphere might suggest. The bar staff's insistence on charging you in 'old' money terms (pounds, shillings and pence) will wind you up, but given a decent play, it's a good night out. Above-average bar meals can be taken through for the pub's regular lunchtime productions, and there's live music most nights – after the show has finished of course.

About £9.50 a head (including show, excluding wine).

## Palookaville

13A James Street, WC2 (240 5857)
Covent Garden tube
Open: noon–3pm and 5.30pm–1.30am (last orders 12.15).

There's live jazz every night at the basement American-style restaurant and wine bar which serves cosmopolitan food with French specialities. It's run by Jacques Rochon, son of the family who run the 23-year-old and very successful Chez Solange in St Martins Lane, and the décor is modern. Naive paintings and trendy waitresses provide the decoration.

The food has had its ups and downs but as we go to press it has been reliable for some months after a very bad patch. They cater for everything from a light snack to a full meal and there is a choice of being in the wine bar or restaurant. Food in the wine bar (seating for up to 120) includes Chicago-style pizza, frankfurters, Caesar salad and brochettes for around £2 a dish. The restaurant has a more ambitious menu. On Saturday lunchtimes and between 5.30 and 7.30pm they serve a three-course meal plus coffee for £5.50, and each day there are 'specials' which tend to be French, such as ratatouille (£1.25), moules marinières (£1.95) and raie au beurre noir (£3.85). A la carte is certainly varied and you take pot luck with dishes such as Rai's Szechuan soup and Viennese escalope. French dishes are likely to be the most successful. Finish with a home-made sorbet.

From £8 a head; house wines from £4.45.

---

## Pier 31

31 Cheyne Walk, SW3 (352 5006/352 4989)
Sloane Square tube
Open 11am–3pm and 5.30–11pm (food until 8pm) bar; noon–2.30pm and
7–11.30pm Monday to Saturday.

Re-launched after a previous life as Mister Smith's with the same young aristocratic owner Henry Smith, Pier 31 is hotly tipped by us to be Chelsea's most fashionable spot by the time we are in print. New part owners include the Tai Pan team of Patrick Lichfield and Edward Lim and the large crescent shaped premises has been stylishly re-vamped with a stunning black marble floor, black venetian blinds, a deco influence and pretty lighting, some of which is upturned and mounted on mock pillars. The view across the Thames (it's bang opposite Albert Bridge) is obscured by the restaurant's landmark, a life size dolphin, but attention is kept inside the restaurant by its superb food and the tinkling of Pier 31's resident pianist.

The bar itself distinctly divides the bar area and restaurant and its the bar where the pianist resides. Here tipplers can enjoy Pier 31's housewine at £4.95, champagne at £14 and during lunch and until 8pm sample some of London's best executed bar snacks such as proper sealed toasted sandwiches, steak sandwiches, veal croquettes with a tasty dip and omlettes. The Japanese chef has devised a brilliantly varied and orientally influenced menu with the emphasis on simplicity and top quality ingredients. His sashimi, duck yakiton and beef teriyaki will have you believing Pier 31 is a Japanese restaurant while his fish soup with saffron rouille and croutons and noisettes of lamb in a tarragon sauce prove chef Makita (Mosquito to his friends) Homma is equally at home with European dishes. There are grills too; seafood lovers shouldn't miss Eddy's Pacific Prawns – soy dipped and barbecued in the shell. Finish with cheese, an ice cream or sorbet.

Bar snacks from £3, à la carte from £12 a head.

## Pizza Express

10 Dean Street, W1 (439 8722)
Tottenham Court Road tube
Open: 11.30am–1.30am daily.

Of course the best jazz venue in London is Ronnie Scott's club, but most punters take the view that the food there can be as dubious as the patron's jokes. So if you want to make a complete evening of listening to high-quality jazz, two restaurants in Peter Boizot's extensive chain fit the bill. The Pizza Express in Dean Street has the standard style on the ground-floor (tiled floor, red wooden chairs, greenery, and prominent pizza oven), with a cramped cellar restaurant for live jazz. The Pizza on the Park (11 Knightsbridge, SW1 235 5550) has an almost identical set-up but with a more spacious basement room, and a slightly more stylish atmosphere. The music (available 9pm–1am Tuesday–Sunday at Dean Street, 8pm–12.30am Monday–Saturday at the Park) is a good class mixture of English stalwarts and visiting American stars.

The food, of course, is a straight-ahead range of nicely-cooked pizzas with a variety of toppings and, in the jazz rooms, a variety of apt names. Favourite dressings include the American Hot (pepperoni sausage, mozzarella, tomato and peppers), the Neptune (tuna, anchovies, olives, capers, onion and tomato) and the comprehensive Four Seasons. Italian wines and beers make up the drinks, of which you'll probably need quite a lot given those sweaty basements. Admission charges vary depending on the act, but are usually around £4–£5.

About £12 a head (incl admission charge).

## Pratts Restaurant and Brasserie

Camden Lock, Commercial Place, NW1 (485 9987/6044)
Camden Town/Chalk Farm tube
Open: brasserie 9am–midnight daily; restaurant 12.30–2.30pm and
7.30pm–midnight Tuesday–Saturday.

The entertainment on offer at Pratts is pretty diverse; one night you
could find chamber music and the next a one-man show but the
overriding theme is to feature young musicians and performers. Set
above the Lock's workshops and overlooking the entire Lock and
canal, Pratts has a spectacular location and is a delightful barn-like
room complete with beams. Whitewashed with little decoration the
brasserie is the smaller space and offers a modest and varied menu
ranging from breakfast any time of the day (from £1.50), various
substantial salads (£3), soup, saucisson and rarebit as well as main
dishes such as fillet steak (£7.50), breast of duck with a fruit sauce
(£6.50) and burgers (from £4.50). Tea (scones with jam and clotted
cream £1.20) is also served.

The restaurant goes in for rather elaborate nouvelle cuisine-
inspired food of a variable standard; the plainer, less intricate dishes
proving more successful.

Brasserie, from £2 a head for food; restaurant £10–£15.

## School Dinners

34 Baker Street W1 (486 2724)
Bond Street tube
Open: noon–3pm and 7pm–midnight Monday–Friday (£5 membership)

'Entertainment' is perhaps the wrong word to use here – it's more
like 'titillation'. The subterranean premises, done out as a facsimile
library and study, offers a concept called 'School Dinners', the
principle feature of which is young waitresses wearing skimpy
school uniforms and suspenders. Each table is allotted a waitress
who remains at your side (occasionally on your knee) to top up
drinks, to fetch your food and, if you step out of line in any way, to
administer a jokey but very public caning.

All this seems to be a very big hit (forgive the pun) with the
grinning male diners who pack the place, though I'd imagine any
woman guests might take a different view of the proceedings. A
vestige of the original concept (school-type food) remains with a
blackboard menu offering such evocative delights as roast pork with
crackling and apple sauce, and mince pie and custard. For the most
part though, the food is up-market international stuff, well-cooked
but highly-priced (around eight quid for a mixed grill!). It's fun and

entertainment in a leering, Benny Hill sort of way, and there are plainly some men who regard it as a valid venue to entertain business friends but, despite the offer, you wouldn't want your photograph taken here for £5 – £10 *not* to have it taken maybe . . . A further branch has now opened in Barnards Inn, Holborn, and has been publicly blessed with Royal Patronage by Prince Andrew.

About £23 a head.

## Spaghetti Opera at Terrazza-Est

125 Chancery Lane, WC2 (242 2601)
Chancery Lane tube
Open: noon–3pm and 6–11.30pm Monday–Friday.

If you've ever suffered at the hands of singing Italian waiters, you can get your revenge here by watching *them* suffer in silence as the 'professionals' take over. The management of Terrazza-Est, an otherwise standard trattoria in the Mario and Franco chain (now owned by Kennedy Brookes), came up with the idea of having live opera to accompany evening meals. The singing is provided by aspiring operatic students wanting convivial practice, and the enterprise works wonderfully. An elegant upstairs room has been provided – high ceilings, whitewashed walls hung with oil paintings, subdued lighting – and between 7.30 and 11pm each weekday night, a couple of formally-attired singers, with piano accompaniment, perform high-quality extracts from such lyrical luminaries as Verdi, Rossini, Cole Porter and Gershwin. Conversations hush politely during the singing, but the eating and drinking and the scurrying of the white tunic-clad waiters goes on, creating an informal and enjoyable atmosphere, which the singers seem to relish as much as the 'audience'.

To complement the unstuffy nature of the evening, the restaurant provides two unpretentious set menus – one offering simply a pasta (spaghetti bolognese, tagliatelle, linguine alle vongole), a mixed salad and a half-bottle of house wine, the other offering three courses with coffee. Choices on this might be tuna and bean salad, stracciatella soup or the rather pungent-tasting mozzarella in carrozza (deep-fried cheese with anchovies and garlic). Simple but good quality main courses are veal escalopes in a sherry, mushroom and cream sauce, grilled trout with butter and almonds or a chicken escalope with garlic, herbs and tomato. Given the efficiency of the operation and the excellence of the singing, you won't begrudge the 15% service charge.

Set menus £5 (incl wine); £6.50 (excl wine).

## Thé Dansant, Waldorf Hotel

Aldwych, WC2 (836 2400)
Holborn tube
Open: 3.30pm–6.30pm Friday and Sunday.

As the country returns to Victorian values, the leisured classes have come out of the cupboard again in a big way. A sign of the times has been the return, and huge popularity of, 'thé dansants' at several of London's top hotels. The Waldorf operates one of the best every Friday and Sunday afternoons, offering a full, traditional English tea – dainty sandwiches, scones and cream, pastries, bridge rolls – together with music from the Palm Court Quartet.

You can either watch passively from the fringes of the elegant, chandeliered and mirrored room as the 'band' trips its way through pre-war favourite melodies, or you can take your partner down onto the floor for a gentle waltz and pretend that you're Torvill and Dean off-duty. If you can overcome the embarrassment factor, it's a pleasant and stylish way to kill time between the pubs closing and opening again. Reservations and smart dress are required.

£8.25 a head.

## Tycoon

43 Kensington High Street, W8 (937 9795)
Kensington High Street tube
Open: noon–3pm and 6.30pm–midnight daily.

Living up to its name, Tycoon is a lavish basement restaurant done out in dark wood with gross OTT chandeliers, photos of latterday tycoons, mirrors and featuring a tacky little rock pool complete with splashing water. There seems to be an Arab connection somewhere along the line and the place has a night club smack to it. As the evening progresses a pianist of the old school will probably invite 'the ladies' to choose a melody or two and you can settle into an old-fashioned sort of evening. The food is French and very good almost without exception. Their oysters (£6.95) are the finest Colchester No 1's but their fish pâté (£2.90) is not successful. If you're feeling adventurous, slices of brill with a raspberry sauce (£4.25) is a curious mixture but a very successful one. Fish is definitely a strong point here and the slices of monkfish with a red peppercorn sauce (£5.75) and turbot with a champagne sauce (£8.25) are highly recommended. Meat lovers could do no better than to share the Châteaubriand (£18) which comes fully garnished and is cooked to perfection. Desserts are limited to sorbets, crêpe suzette and cheese. Perfect for the time when you feel like getting dressed up and wallowing in schmaltz.

From £20 a head.

*Also Good for Entertainment:*
Apicella '81
Chez Louisette
L'Estanquet
Fatso's Pasta Joint
Flanagan's
Langan's Brasserie
One Hampstead Lane
Paddock Grill, Walthamstow Stadium
Porters
Restaurant, The
Siam
Verrey's

# 10. When You're Out in a Gang

While the first consideration when you're out in a gang is space, several other factors come into play. Are the staff tolerant of rowdy behaviour? Is a party atmosphere encouraged or will it be like the Last Supper? Is the menu evenly-priced so as to avoid those unseemly rows over who ordered a £7 main course and only chipped in a fiver? While the larger Indian and Chinese restaurants are obvious choices for group eating, the staff tend to be less enamoured of the excesses of stag-night or hen-party celebrations than say, a Greek or Italian restaurant. If you can get organised in time, it's worth trying for special menus at discount prices.

## Aarti Restaurant

14 Hanway Street, W1 (631 4119)
Tottenham Court Road tube
Open: noon–3pm and 6–10.30pm Monday–Friday; noon–10.30pm Saturday.

If eating in a gang sometimes seems largely a choice between kebabs, curries or chicken chow meins, why not consider a vegetarian meal instead? This well-appointed but oddly decorated (Aladdin's Cave?) Southern Indian restaurant is tucked away off Oxford Street/Tottenham Court Road in a vegetarian enclave which also features the Mandeer. A branch of the favourably-regarded Chaat House in Leicester, the Aarti is obviously in a state of growth (they've acquired the premises next door) but already caters happily for parties on the existing premises. An additional advantage of the Aarti is the provision of complete, self-contained meals on trays (thalis), thereby minimising confusion and argument as to who ordered what and how much it was. Rigidly vegetarian (they apparently won't even allow eggs on the premises) the Aarti offers two particularly outstanding meals. The special mix chaat (£2.10) is billed as if it were a 'starter', but the collection of hot vegetable-filled samosas, dahivara (dal dumplings in yoghurt with sweet and mint chutney), hot aloo choley (spiced chick peas) and spicy potatoes, will probably finish you off for the evening. Meanwhile, the aptly-named marharaja thali (£6.95) is a feast – three vegetables, puries (wheat pancakes), lentil curry, rice, raita (yoghurt), poppadoms, chutneys, salad and a sweet. Bet you can't eat more than one . . .

About £9 a head.

## Anemos

34 Charlotte Street, W1 (636 2289)
Goodge Street tube
Open: noon–2.45pm and 6–10.30pm Monday–Saturday.

This is the perfect place for eating out in a gang, for Anemos is known for its ability to create an instant party mood complete with cavorting waiters who will join in with the background Greek music and dance to order. It's a long, narrow restaurant with a few relatively private tables, some of which go outside on warm days, but a long trestle table to suit almost any size of party can be arranged. The food is typical popular Greek fare; taramasalata, hummus, kebabs, moussaka and shredded wheat-style honey-soaked pastries and turkish delight served with the coffee to follow.

Retsina at £4.95 a bottle is a good deal. At lunchtime it's popular with young account execs from nearby adland.

From £5 a head for food.

## Bouzy Rouge

221 King's Road, SW3 (351 1607)
Sloane Square tube
Open pub hours; off licence 11am–9pm Monday–Saturday; noon–2pm and 7–9pm Sunday.

This basement wine bar with its long bar and several distinct sections with alcove seating, and live music on Saturday evenings and at least one other night a week, is the perfect place for a night out in a gang. Despite being on the King's Road it isn't a trendy place or particularly favoured by any clique, and has an easy atmosphere. Below its own off licence it has a decent wine list with wines under £4. They devote a cold cabinet (at the far end of the long narrow room) to a variety of cold meats, quiche, salad, taramasalata, pâté and cheese, and prepare a rotation of international hot fillers such as lasagne, macaroni cheese, etc daily. These are rarely more than £2 a dish. During the summer visitors have access to a small yard/garden.

Food from £2.

## Chez Louisette

102 Baker Street, W1 (935 2529)
Baker Street tube
Open: 11.30am–3pm and 5.30pm–midnight Monday–Friday; 7pm–midnight Saturday.

Touring parties from Madame Tussaud's often take refuge in this discreet but fairly large basement wine bar at the top end of Baker Street. The atmospherically Gallic décor – posters, photographs, oil-cloths on tables, general dinginess – is augmented by the higgledy-piggledy arrangement of furniture, with tables easily pulled together for larger groups. A short but choice menu offers the likes of garlic bread, vegetable soups, salads, pâtés and cheeses, together with well-cooked steaks, frankfurters and hot specials along the lines of lasagne or country beef and vegetable stew. Finish with fruit pies or tarts. The wine list is a bit predictable but reasonably-priced, and you could always try their reliable Rioja if you're in an anti-French mood. Chez Louisette's location means that it attracts a young cosmopolitan crowd, and the fact that you can linger till midnight gives the continental drift a further push. The occasional live music – a singer at a piano, or a guitarist – will probably help the party mood.

About £7 a head.

## Chicago Pizza Pie Factory

17 Hanover Square, W1 (629 2669)
Oxford Circus tube
Open: 11.45am–11.30pm Monday–Saturday; 1–11pm Sunday.

There's a queuing system at this large and noisy basement restaurant which belts out continuous video shows of American baseball, football and basketball and can seat 275. The restaurant specializes in deep dish Chicago-style pizzas covered with cheese, tomato and a choice of sausage, pepperoni, mushrooms, green peppers, onions and anchovies. It's the perfect place to eat in a gang because you share the pizzas (small ones feed two to three, the large ones four to five) and the rest of the menu is pretty limited so there won't be the usual disputes over who had what. It's cheap too; from £4.15 (for two) to £8 (for three to four) is the pizza price range. Cheesecakes are their pudding speciality (the chocolate version is as addictive as their pecan pie) and these automatically come with two forks. Cocktails, US beers and a cheap housewine.

From £5 a head.

## Cinecitta Roma

74 Welbeck Street, W1 (935 2794 for party bookings)
Bond Street tube
Open: 6pm–1.30am Monday–Thursday; 6pm–2am Friday and Saturday.

Beneath the Vecchia Milano restaurant, yet another in the reliable Spaghetti House chain, is a companion self-service café which also doubles as a disco. The operation is a serious one, with a good sound-system, spacious raised dance-floor, and one or two spectacular decorative effects, including an Italian coastline mural dotted with lights. There's also an intimate section representing the interior of a luxury train. In the circumstances it may seem incongruous to have a self-service food counter, but it's certainly a more efficient way of getting your meal. It also cuts down all that dithering over ordering when you're out in a gang. Despite the functional system the food is reasonably good, just a shorter and cheaper selection of the Italian stuff served upstairs at the Vecchia. It's mainly pastas – spaghetti bolognaise, lasagne – with a few meats and chicken dishes added – perhaps polpettine (meatballs) or pollo alla cacciatore. Drinks are also served from the counter and there's the usual palatable Spaghetti House carafes for what the wine buffs call 'quaffing'. After the food, it's up onto the dance floor. There's an entrance charge of about £2 Monday–Thursday, which goes up to £3 on Fridays and Saturdays when there's a more convivial atmosphere with Italian students and Scandinavian housewives on shopping trips well to the fore.

About £10 a head.

## Efes

80 Great Titchfield Street, W1 (636 1953)
Great Portland Street tube
Open: 11.30am–11.30pm Monday–Saturday.

Anywhere within a stagger of Broadcasting House has to be well-prepared for the sudden arrival of BBC personnel on an end of programme 'wind down'. Efes, a bright bustling Turkish kebab house, handles these sort of intruders with skill and charm, so ordinary human beings stand a fair chance of being treated equally well. The room isn't particularly big, but pillars, arches, mirrors and crammed-together tables give it a larger capacity than first seems likely. The packing of customers also guarantees a party atmosphere, into which you'll be welcomed raucously. The principal diet here is kebabs and grills (take-away too), albeit of a Turkish breed. Antep koftesi is tender minced lamb, rather like the Greek sheftalia, while the karisik izgara is the equivalent of a mixed grill. Slightly more subtle is the pilic siste, rolled breast of chicken, grilled with peppers on a skewer. Various hot sauces and salads accompany these. Muska burek, pastry filled with soft cheese and parsley, or arranot gigeri (fried, diced lamb's liver) are slightly different starters to the usual Mediterranean dips or stuffed vine leaves. Potent Buzbag wine will keep the party spirit going.

About £9 a head.

## Fatso's Pasta Joint

13 Old Compton Street, W1 (437 1503)
Leicester Square tube
Open: noon–midnight Monday–Thursday, noon–1am Friday and Saturday.

Fatso's, in the heart of Soho, is the perfect place for a cheap and filling West End meal. Pasta is the speciality and it's served in lively high-tech surroundings complete with computer table games in the ante room.

Fatso's make no claims to perfection in their product and though there is always plenty of the pasta it's unlikely to be al dente, but their sauces are tasty. Accompany the meal with a salad or opt for a pizza. As we write this review Fatso's are operating an 'eat-as-much-pasta-as-you-can' for £2.25 which we hope they will keep on as a permanent feature of the restaurant (Monday to Thursdays only). On Mondays all cocktails cost £1 and on Fridays and Saturdays a magician does a turn at midnight.

Under £5 a head, house wine £4.50, cocktails around £2.

## Flanagan's

100 Baker Street, W1 (935 0287)
Open: noon–2.30pm and 7–11pm daily.

Behind the narrow, pseudo-Dickensian frontage lurks a spacious, authentically-furnished Cockney fun-palace with seating for over a hundred in a variety of booths (up to eight persons) or at long, open tables (for larger hordes). Wherever you sit, there is little privacy – escape might be a better word – from the Flanagan's communal experience. This is roughly akin to having a meal with Chas and Dave, Joe Brown and the Bruvvers and Arthur Mullard rolled into one. A pearly-waistcoated, bowler-hatted pianist thumps through all the old singalong favourites and everyone is expected to join in – even the napkins double-up as song-sheets. The food is typically English 'fare' – tripe and onions, Irish stew, steak, oyster and kidney pudding – with lots of extremely tenuous references to W. G. Grace, Mrs Beeton, Lord Nelson and the like. If you're in the mood for a knees-up, it's all great fun and the food, somewhat surprisingly for a 'tourist-trap', is not just an after-thought.

About £20 for two.

## Henry J Bean's But His Friends All Call Him Hank Bar and Grill

Abingdon Road, W8 (no phone)
Kensington High Street tube
Open: 11.30am–11pm daily.

Despite having the longest and most ridiculous name in the business, Henry J Bean's is the perfect place for one of those rowdy nights out. It's also a brilliant place to take children and forget them – there's a separate section equipped with a beautiful 1947 Wurlitzer juke box and several pin ball machines.

Previously the Abingdon pub, the premises are leased to Chicagoan Bob Payton (of The Chicago Rib Shack and The Chicago Pizza Pie Factory) and he's given it his usual larger than life stamp. Parts of the ceiling and walls are papered with Chicago newsprint and an eclectic selection of ephemera is gradually covering all wall space. The bar still offers all Charringtons and some of the Bass range (in two pint jugs for sharing) plus cocktails and the food is restricted to three starters, four mains and three desserts, and is collected by the customer from a serving hatch when your number is called over the tannoy.

Deep fried potato skins with sour cream and chive dip (£1.75) are a perfect munch with drinks, while their smokehouse burger (£3.35) is a delicious version of that ubiquitous food. Best of all though are the desserts; pecan pie or chocolate cheesecake (£1.45) are addictive. Another branch of Henry J Bean's, complete with huge garden, has now opened on the site of the Six Bells pub, opposite the Fire Station in the King's Road.

## Joy King Lau

3 Leicester Street, WC2 (437 1132)
Leicester Square tube
Open (for tim sum only) 11am–5.30pm and then till 11.30pm for the rest of the menu Monday–Saturday, 10pm Sunday.

Ironically, this place on the edge of Chinatown is equally good for dining alone (particularly for its tim sum) and for eating in a gang. Stylishly decorated in dark brown with comfortable modern rattan chairs and mirrors the entire length of the dining rooms, it sensibly covers its tables with easy-clean glass tops. The staff are some of the most efficient and courteous in Chinatown and their menus are explicit enough for first timers to tim sum or those not very familiar with Chinese food. An ideal 'gang' meal would be during tim sum hours. Here you choose from a special menu and the delicious and contrasting steamed and deep fried dumplings arrive fast in sets of three and most cost 75p a set. King prawn dumpling is crispy and deep fried while the incongruously named mixed vegetable dumpling (there are actually no vegetables in this but lean slices of pork), and chicken buns, delicious puffy stuffed balls, all arrive in the rustic steaming-baskets. Sweet confections include curious but addictive mixtures such as water chestnut paste, coconut paste and fresh cream peanut broth. The traditional accompaniment is China tea and depending on your greed, this sort of meal would be unlikely to cost more than £4 a head. Incidentally, if downstairs is full, there's another replica room above.

Tim sum meals from £3 a head; à la carte from £4.

# Kuo Yuan

217 High Road, NW10 (459 2297)
Willesden Green tube
Open: 6pm–11pm daily; noon–2.30pm Saturday and Sunday.

This long-established Peking restaurant on busy Willesden High Road is well worth a trip up from central London if you've got an occasion to celebrate with friends. Although the premises aren't exactly large, they're compactly furnished and a couple of the circular tables are capable of taking parties up to ten. While you're unlikely to be accommodated if you turn up on spec, a few days' notice and a rough estimate of how much you wish to spend a head (say £10) will allow the manager to prepare a veritable feast for you and your party. Sharing the meal is helped by a revolving tray placed in the centre of the table, though whether you'll want to share as the sumptuous dishes are laid before you is another matter. A typical party menu might run to eight or nine courses, embracing (deep breath) various hors d'oeuvres (sesame prawn toast, seaweed) crab and sweetcorn soup, Chinese dumplings, aromatic Peking duck with pancakes, sweet and sour pork on crispy rice, chicken and almond in bean sauce, quick-fried prawns, seasonal vegetables and finally toffee apples. Like the Apaches, the dishes just keep a' coming. If you're prepared to spend a little more and leave the choosing of the meal to the manager, exotic items not usually on the menu can turn up in front of you.

About £10 a head upwards.

# Mandra Kebab House

31 Windmill Street, W1 (636 9014)
Goodge Street tube
Open: noon–3pm and 6pm–1am Monday–Saturday.

Behind the gaudily-painted windows inviting you to celebrate your anniversary here, lurks a Greek fun palace which has been known to accommodate thirty-one drunken journalists at half an hour's notice. The cavernous basement where the main catering takes place features lines of packed tables, a small bar decked with Anthony Quinn look-alikes, and an area set aside for dancing and general tomfoolery. Both of these activities are encouraged, especially the dancing, with waiters and waitresses frequently laying plates aside to join in and demonstrate how it should be done. The food – mainly charcoal-grilled kebabs, sheftalia, sausages and the spit-roasted kleftico – is all priced at around £3.50, so it's the ideal stuff to avoid those unseemly rows over bills which all too often blight group eating – 'I'm sorry, but Gavin's escalope was two pounds more than my chicken actually, *and* he had a salad'. If you're in a less pressurised set-up, you might take time over the afelia à la Cypriote (pork in red wine, coriander seeds, with roast potatoes and rice), the moussaka in individual bowls, the roast quail, or indeed something the menu describes as 'red muler' (red mullet, I hope). If you give the Mandra more than half an hour's drunken notice, they'll do a party menu for a pre-arranged price.

About £20 for two.

## Nineteen

19 Mossop Street, SW3 (589 4971)
Sloane Square tube
Open: noon–3pm and 7–11.45pm daily, closed Saturday lunch.

This is where young Sloanes have been congregating for years to feed on wholesome, freshly-prepared international food served by candle-light at scrubbed pine tables.

The menu changes frequently but expect the likes of onion soup gratinée, whitebait, corn on the cob, ambitious goulashes and fussy fish dishes followed by thoroughly traditional English puddings such as crumbles, syllabubs and tarts. During the week they serve a two-course set lunch with coffee at £4.25 and on Sundays a traditional roast with two vegetables for £3.50. Eating à la carte and drinking a bottle of their good plonk averages £8 a head.

Set lunch £4.25; Sunday lunch £3.50; à la carte from £8 with wine.

## Parsons

311 Fulham Road, SW10 (352 0651)
South Kensington tube
Open: noon–12.30am daily

Parsons no longer has the same cachet it held in the early seventies when it was the hang-out of anyone who was anything (or knew someone who was something) on the hip scene. Despite a nasty 'fat fire' in the kitchen which gutted the place, the owners have achieved a replica of Parsons' original look so the restaurant hasn't really changed since it opened some 15 years ago. Amid palm trees, mirrored walls and wooden tables that are mostly either too low, too high or wobbly, they serve vast portions of spaghetti, steaks, burgers, cauliflower cheese, various popular Mexican dishes, salads all sorts with a choice of dressings and a range of ice-creams and American-style puddings for dessert. Loud taped rock music and second generation trendies still keep up appearances and queues still form but Parsons is no longer a fashionable haunt. The perfect dish for gang eating is their spaghetti. It comes with a variety of sauces and a second helping is available free to anyone who makes it through the gargantuan first portion.

Food averages £5 a head.

## Porters

17 Henrietta Street, WC2 (836 6466)
Covent Garden tube
Open: noon–3pm and 5.30–11.30pm (10.30pm Sunday) daily.

Porters, as in Covent Garden market, you understand – and if you don't you soon will when you arrive in this large, bustling, warehouse-like restaurant decked out with rugged wooden tables and all manner of market signs and memorabilia. A sort of console-cum-reception deals briskly with queues and large groups though it's often just a matter of swanning in as though you've booked. There's usually live jazz-rock music in the evenings to add to the heaving atmosphere. Despite all this, the food – basically robust English pies – is more than an afterthought. Steak and mushroom, turkey and chestnut, and Billingsgate pies (cod and haddock in dill sauce) catch the eye, all accompanied by baked potato or chips. Vegetarians are catered for (just) with the Porters Pie, filled with vegetables in a light curry sauce and topped with wholemeal pastry. All the pies are priced roughly the same except for steak, oyster and clam which is about 60p more – so watch for the flash Harry in your group who orders one. Puddings are predictably but deliciously bulldog British – steamed syrup sponge, treacle tart, jam rolypoly and wonderful bread and butter pudding. The waitresses seem temperamentally equipped to deal with drunks and loud groups (a wide range of real ales is offered), though in its quieter moments, Porters gives thought to kids – cheaper Sunday lunches and high chairs are available. Otherwise it's one for the office party or stag night.

About £10 a head.

## Rasa Sayang

10 Frith Street, W1 (734 8720)
Leicester Square tube
Open: noon–3pm Monday–Saturday; 6pm–10.45pm Monday–Thursday;
6pm–11.45pm Friday and Saturday.

As an alternative to sharing an Indian or Chinese meal, why not consider a Malaysian evening at this smartly-furnished, spacious restaurant in Soho. The Habitat-style tables and chairs are easily

146

arranged for group eating, though if you're really serious and there are enough of you, the basement dining room, with its own bar and grotto-like disco, can be hired for a private buffet. Otherwise enjoy the delights of Rasa Sayang's extensive and varied Malaysian and Singaporean menu. Essential starters are the satays, skewers of beef or chicken, served with cucumber, rice cakes and a deliciously savoury peanut gravy. Traditionalists will also enjoy the lumpia – crispy spring rolls. Most of the food is strongly-flavoured, sometimes with garlic, often with chilli or peanut sauce and occasionally, like the lightly-fried prawns (udang), with hot sambal sauce. Other ideal 'party' dishes include boneless, crispy spare ribs of pork, katio kentar (chicken pieces in coconut gravy) and ikan taucho (deep-fried fish cutlets in savoury black-bean sauce). The most soothing of the sweets, and your tongue will probably need it, is kolak pisang, a sweet confection of banana slices in coconut milk with brown sugar. If two of you want to be anti-social (and greedy), there's a spectacular set meal at £23 all in, to include two starters, five main courses, wine and liqueurs. Deals this good could break up the party!

About £12 a head.

## Smithy's Wine Bar

28–32 Britannia Street, WC1 (278 5659)
King's Cross tube
Open: 11.30am–3pm and 5.30–7.30pm Monday–Friday.

Converted from an old stable and warehouse, Smithy's is a spacious lunchtime haunt, and its whitewashed walls, stone floor, and jumble of long wooden tables, banquettes, church pews and barrels provide a knockabout decor for larger parties. Food is sensibly limited to charcoal grills (T-bone steaks, pork and lamb chops) and hot specials like moussaka, lasagne or beef Stroganoff, so costs are kept pretty even. To go with these, there are half-a-dozen bowls of salads from which you help yourself. For the weight-watching, choosing from the cold buffet – cheeses, pâtés, smoked fish – may be more appropriate. Puddings are restricted to cheesecakes and gâteaux, but it's worth having a hunk of Stilton instead because it's relatively cheap, and also allows you to enjoy some of Smithy's smashing ports. There's a good selection of wines too – but then there should be, as Smithy's is a part of the adjoining wine warehouse. There are also one or two large, private cubicles for the more organised office party.

About £8 a head.

## The Standard

23 Westbourne Grove, W2 (727 4818)
Bayswater tube
Open: noon–3pm and 6pm–midnight daily.

Set in a clutch of Indian restaurants (Khan's, The Khyber) The
Standard gets the 'gang' vote, because of its cheapness, because of
its good quality food, and because the staff are pretty brisk about
getting punters in, fed and out, so you can usually get a table even if
there's a queue. The old place has been spruced up a bit, with pale
yellow colours on the deflocked walls and tablecloths, smart Venetian blinds masking prying eyes and a fancy spiral staircase at the
front of the room. The menu, though, remains a classic blend of
tandoori specialities, meat curries, and a selection of vegetarian
dishes. Of the tandooris, the prawn sheek kebab (prawn mince,
onions, spices) roasted on a skewer, may seem sacrilegious, but it's
delicious nonetheless. The best chicken dish is probably the Jaipuri
(chicken in yoghurt, mildly spiced, served with boiled egg), while
mutton moghalai (lamb pieces and egg cooked in cream, spices and
nuts) is a favourite among the meat courses. The vegetarian thali
meal is also reasonable value. Drink lager of course, but don't get
cheeky with the waiters, or they'll have you out quicker than you
can say 'Bombay Express'.

About £8 a head.

## Villa Carlotta

39 Charlotte Street, W1 (636 6011)
Goodge Street tube
Open: noon–3pm Monday–Friday; 6–11pm Monday–Saturday.

Part of yet another Tavola Calda/Spaghetti House operation
(there's a self-service section adjacent) Villa Carlotta is nevertheless a distinctly top-of-the-range example of the chain's capabilities.
The ground-floor dining-room is crammed with plants and wooden
tables in standard style, but upstairs, in the so-called 'Giardino della
Villa', there's a large, beautifully airy spread of rooms capable of
handling well-behaved groups. The vines and plants hanging from
the rafters, the large windows opening onto Charlotte Street, and
the tasteful Italian menu make the Giardino an ideal venue for a
summer party. On your way in, you may notice the restaurant's own
pasta makers at work, so it'll come as no surprise to see the stuff
looming large on the menu. The speciality is linguine (yellow
noodles) served with a wide range of sauces – from Genovese
(cream sauce with pine kernels) to 'al pesto' (cream cheese,

flavoured with Parmesan and basil). Stuffed tomatoes feature in a safe list of antipasti, while main courses boast the deliciously light piccatine al limone (veal slices with lemon, butter and parsley), the reliable roast chicken with rosemary and garlic and perhaps one of their excellent daily specials like fresh salmon salad. The zuppa Inglese (chocolate-flavoured trifle) should not be missed. Good litre carafes of house wine provide ideal party plonk.

About £12 a head.

*Also Good for Group Eating:*
Agra
Ajanta
Astrix
Bamboo Kuning
Bar Crêperie
Bunga Raya
Café Pacifico
Café Pelican
Caffe Mamma
Calabash
Carriages
Chelsea Pot, The
Chicago Rib Shack
Chuen Cheng Ku
Costa's Grill
Crystal Palace
Diamond, The
Fakhraldine
Famiglia, La
Gallery Restaurant
Geno Washington's
Han Kuk Ko Kwan
Hard Rock Café
Ho Ho
Hung Toa
Joe Allen
Jun
Kolossi Grill
Langan's Brasserie
Little Italy
Maroush
Manzil's
No. 1
Old Rangoon
Ooblies

Paddock Grill, Walthamstow Stadium
Palookaville
Pasta Connection
Peppermint Park
Phoenicia
Pollyanna's
Pucci Pizza Vino
Richmond Rendezvous
San Frediano
Serendipity
Siam
Sidi Bou Said
Soho Brasserie
Sunrise
Tuttons
Widow Applebaum's
Woodlands
Zen

## 11. When You're Out Alone

It's important here to distinguish the different styles of eating alone – sometimes you're alone because you've chosen to be, other times you're alone by necessity and just occasionally you're alone but hoping you won't be for long. Most restaurants have an ambiguous attitude to the solitary diner – it's easy enough to accommodate you and they're usually happy to oblige, but you always get the impression that they're watching that empty space opposite you and calculating how much it's costing them. This, and the fact that it has a lower self-consciousness factor, makes eating at bars, counters or brasseries by far the best option for single people. You can nuzzle into your fashionable magazine, smoke foreign cigarettes, cultivate an air of mystery and still growl at anybody trying to take the stool next to you – unless you fancy them of course . . .

## Astrix

329 King's Road, SW3 (352 3891)
Sloane Square tube and bus to Worlds End
Open: noon–midnight daily.

Astrix, named in honour of the little Gallic cartoon hero, was London's first French crêperie aping the traditional Normandy galette (savoury) and crêpe (sweet). That was ten years ago and now there are crêperies all over town which, like Astrix, serve endless combinations of fillings. The crêpe arrives folded like a fat envelope and it's wise to eat the thing fast before it has a chance to cool down and get rubbery. It's wise too to choose a moist filling; a combination with cheese, ratatouille or a cream mixture are best of all. The traditional Breton cider is on sale and makes a delicious, cheap and surprisingly potent accompaniment (approximately £2 a bottle). Sweet crêpes work even better, so much so that we once watched a couple munch their way through the classic lemon juice with sugar, black cherries with ice cream and finally an outrageous apple, calvados, cream and ice-cream concoction. The pancakes start at £1.50.

From £3 a head.

## Bar des Amis

11–14 Hanover Place, WC2 (379 3444)
Covent Garden tube
Open: 11.30am–3pm and 5.30–midnight Monday–Saturday.

The basement bar of this excellent three-tiered operation is a perfect place for solitary diners, always provided you can get a stool. Peak times are generally 1–2pm and 6–7pm when the small, gloomily atmospheric room with its yellowing, low ceiling does a fair imitation of the Black Hole of Calcutta. If you can avoid these times, or better still, get there before them, seat yourself at the 'thrust' bar and shout your orders to the playful French patron – you can tell when he's not preoccupied because he starts doing 'trimphone' impersonations. The menu is a terrific blend of cheap Gallic café snacks and choice but reasonably-priced bistro dishes. On the snack side, the soups are outstanding and served as they are in large tureens, you can always offer some around if you want to make new friends. Other winners are the frisée aux lardons (lettuce and bacon salad), the plate of five cheeses, the charcuterie and the croque monsieur. Main dishes are listed on the blackboard and are simply versions of specials being served in the two restaurants upstairs. So you might find monkfish aux coquilles St Jacques, pork and lentil casserole or braised venison with vegetables, while on the standing carte, there's always the delicious boudin noir (French black pudding). The sheer volume of business sometimes overstretches the kitchen, but any complaints are promptly and politely dealt with. You're unlikely to come across problems with the wines as the place is part of a wine shipping chain. Fine armagnacs and good coffee will also make you feel at one with the throng around you. Thirsty opera-goers might like to note that the bar sounds an intermission bell, so you don't miss the show, or your drink.

About £9 a head.

## Blushes

52 King's Road, SW3 (589 6640)
Sloane Square tube
Open: 11.30am–midnight Monday–Saturday; noon–10.30pm Sunday.

An inappropriate name for as brazen a singles bar as you could wish to strut across, Blushes is a short walk from Sloane Square and attracts a young, fashionable, posing crowd who keep one eye on the mirrors and the other on the action. Before the cry of 'sexism' goes up, this comment applies to both male and female customers. If you're alone, the trick is to stride in, being careful not to pull the wrong glass door or slip on the polished floor, and step confidently up to the raised level at the back where the bar is situated, and order yourself a cocktail. Conversation is virtually impossible above the thump of the stereo, so you may have to get by on body language. In the circumstances, food is almost an afterthought, but there's a reasonable range of wine bar stodge – good thick soups, standard pâtés and cheeses, chilli con carne, spare ribs, burgers and steaks. There's a quieter, more spacious eating area downstairs (via a spiral staircase) but then that's not really where you want to be. A few tables are pulled onto the front patio in the summer to enhance the operation – so make sure you park your Porsche Cabriolet right outside.

About £10 a head.

## Boltons

198 Fulham Road, SW10 (352 0251)
South Kensington tube
Open: 11am to 11pm Monday–Saturday; 11am–10.30pm Sunday.

Wine bars are the ideal place to eat or drink alone (particularly for women) because they often have bars lined with bar stools. Boltons is no exception and has the added advantages of being a very pleasant place, handy for the busy middle part of the Fulham Road, which serves superb food *and* has a good wine list. Run by the wine importers who also own the stylish Ebury Wine Bar and Draycotts in South Kensington, it's pleasantly designed with wooden shutters that block out Fulham Road, pretty Edwardian-style wall lamps and etched mirrors. Tables are marble slabs mounted on old sewing machine legs and the overall look of the place is light and airy and particularly pretty in the evening when the main lights are dimmed. They serve the best wine bar food in town, with daily specials plus regular dishes. Stilton and walnut tart, plateau de fromage (about eight cheeses in perfect condition), terrine maison with onion chutney and an authentic fish soup served with rouille and croûtons are all highly recommended. Delicious breads too, and between 11am and noon and 3–5.30pm Boltons serve tartine, brioche and croissant with home-made jam, patisserie, madeira and other cakes and home-made ice cream. Dishes average £2 each and house wine is £3.95 a bottle with several very fairly-priced better quality wines at around £6.

£5 a head for a snack meal, sharing a bottle of wine.

## Bow Wine Vaults

10 Bow Churchyard, EC4 (248 1121)
St Paul's/Mansion House tube
Open: 12.15–2.15pm (restaurant); 11.30am–3pm and 5–7pm (bar) Monday–Friday.

Being alone in the City at lunchtime can be a forbidding experience – all those people with other people to meet for lunch and there you are on your ownsome. Take refuge in the delightful, atmospheric cellar restaurant of the Bow Wine Vaults tucked away in a narrow court behind Bow Church. The premises operate as a wine store and wine bar (old fashioned décor, few seats, cheeses and sandwiches) on the ground floor, but the cosy, painted-brick basement has a fully-fledged serious restaurant. The solitary diner is welcomed by the sight of a long, tall counter, attractively topped with white linen, and once seated there you can enjoy your own company and the house's excellent food. Imaginative starters have included a thick and warming creamed haddock and spinach soup, avocado filled with prawns and black caviar, moules marinières and a tasty apple and Stilton fritter. Main courses usually continue the strand of Franco–English flair with the likes of pigeon and mushroom pie laced with armagnac, wild duck casserole with walnuts and apricots and roast poussin with a Dijon mustard and chervil sauce. Simpler tastes are catered for by a range of prime Scotch steaks. While the alcoves and private booths are usually bursting with lunch parties, an additional sign that the single diner is not discriminated against is the generous number of decent wines offered by the glass. Finish off with baked apples and mincemeat flamed in calvados, cheese and port – now try to get off your stool.

About £12 a head.

## Braganza

16 Frith Street, W1 (437 5412)
Open: noon–2.30pm and 6.15–11.15pm Monday–Saturday.

Part of the Wheeler's chain of fish restaurants (now owned by Kennedy Brookes) the Braganza boasts a smart, eleven-seater marble-topped oyster bar on the ground floor. This is a perfect location for an elegant solo meal. Of course, you're not compelled to eat oysters, but the Braganza at least offers them cooked in sauces (mornay, florentine, Americaine) for those too squeamish to take them raw. In addition, the bar has its own stylish menu serving the likes of whitebait, smoked fish pâté, excellent fresh salmon fishcakes, grilled prawns and fish pie. As wine is served by the glass, and several good half-bottles are available, the solitary diner is not discriminated against when it comes to drinking. Given the elegance of the surroundings it also seems a particularly suitable place for ladies to eat alone without being pestered.

About £10 (for one).

## La Brasserie

272 Brompton Road, SW3 (584 1668)
South Kensington/Knightsbridge tube
Open: 8am–midnight Tuesday–Friday; 8am–11.30pm Monday; 10am–midnight Saturday; 11am–11.30pm Sunday.

The day's newspapers provided on rods by the management give the perfect cover for lone diners at one of London's first and still most authentic and attractive brasseries. Breakfast is served in the morning, and for the rest of the day a wide-ranging menu includes moules marinières, boudin noir, blanquette de veau, andouillette grillée, pot au feu and tranche de gigot with flageolets. Daily specials are chalked up on the board behind the long bar (where you can eat – ideal for loners) and it's the sort of place where you think you're going to get off lightly and end up paying £15 a head. It's a large busy place with waiters formally dressed in long white aprons but despite the authentic garb, service can be slow. The décor is thirties with lots of mirrorwork and during the summer a few tables are parked on the deep pavement overlooking Conrans and the beautiful Michelin building.

From £8 a head.

## Crystal Palace

10 Hogarth Road, SW5 (370 0754)
Earls Court tube
Open: noon–2.30pm and 6–11.30pm daily.

Situated in a small alley off Hogarth Road, Crystal Palace is one of the new wave of Chinese restaurants. Behind split bamboo blinds the restaurant is on two floors and plainly but stylishly decorated in cream and black with wooden floors and bentwood chairs. It's a cosy place, and the friendly staff make it an ideal venue for eating alone. There's seating for 30 downstairs and 40 in the upstairs room, which is available for private hire.

The menu is explicit and features both Szechuan (hot and spicy) and the more familiar Peking food. Choosing à la carte averages £2.25 for poultry, £2.50 for meat and £3 for seafood but best value can be had from the Leave-It-To-Us feasts (alas for two or more). The Szechuan feast features the famous Bang Bang chicken (sesame chicken salad) and hot Ganshow prawns, while the Peking version includes the popular crispy aromatic duck. A cheap and delicious meal for one might consist of hot and sour or Wanton soup (£1.10); lemon chicken (£2.25) or beef shreds in black bean sauce (£2.40), steamed rice (80p) and toffee apple with sesame seeds (£1.05). The house wine costs £4.50.

From £5 a head.

## Daniels

8 Bridge Court, EC4 (353 1863)
Blackfriars tube
Open: 11am–3pm and 5–8pm Monday–Friday.

Daniels, in a small quiet alley behind Fleet Street, is a small and friendly wine bar (previously a Lyons store house) done out in green and white and decorated with photos of ex-footballer owner Billy Jennings on the field. There's a long bar for propping, plus a few tables, and the menu is written up on a blackboard. Although in the heart of the Print it's not a cliquey place and almost anyone would feel at home here. The menu is international with cheap fillers such as lasagne and chilli for under £3; pies with crinkly chips or baked potato (£3.50) which is strictly nursery fare – unsophisticated, filling grub. It's not a place to go out of your way to for the food, but it is cheap and a useful bolt hole when you can't face the likes of El Vinos. The wine list is long and international and house wines start at £3.90.

From £3.00 for food.

## Dôme

38–39 Hampstead High Street, NW3 (435 4240)
Hampstead tube
Open: 9am–11pm (10.30pm Sunday) daily.

You would have thought that the last thing Hampstead needed was another 'tea-room', but the Dôme has succeeded spectacularly by offering the locals both the leisurely atmosphere they're used to and the French image they aspire to. The Dôme's extensive, modern brasserie-style operation is a particular boon to single Hampsteads at a loose end during the day – novelists, poets, lecturers on vacation and the like. Continental breakfasts (and continental papers) are provided from 9am, and you can either perch on the bar stools or enjoy friendly waitress service at the bent-wood, French café-style chairs and tables.

After breakfast, an enterprising snack menu is served throughout the day and into the night – individual fondues, charcuterie, croque monsieur, hot dogs, salade Niçoise, melted brie with toasted almonds and apple, and these are all perfect dishes for the solitary diner. Apart from the bespoke list of beverages – hot chocolate with whipped cream, citron pressé, espresso coffee – there's a short but varied, reasonably-priced wine list (house wines by the glass) and attractive cocktails. The Dôme is highly hospitable to the single customer (women should feel no unease), though if you do strike up a conversation, you could wind up sharing a raclette – this is the house's Swiss speciality (look for the electric cheese-melting machine) consisting of a layer of melted cheese, laced with salami, ham, new potatoes and pickles. There's a small sun-terrace on the first floor for summer days when the Dôme's ice-cream specials will be particularly attractive.

About £5 a head.

## Holland's Wine Bar

6 Portland Road, W11 (229 3130)
Holland Park tube
Open: 11am–3pm and 5.30–11pm Monday–Saturday; noon–2.30pm and 7–10.30pm Sunday (food orders: 12.30–2.30pm and 7–10pm).

Most wine bars still deal in clichés like quiche and chilli con carne so it's a pleasure to report that at Holland's the catering is imaginative and well-organised. This makes it less attractive to the single-minded, gold-chained, shark-toothed studs who normally prowl wine-bars, and thus more hospitable to the solitary female or male diners who just want a meal and a drink without being pestered or aggravated, respectively. This is not to say that Holland's is entirely chaste – at lunchtimes it's full of young girls seeing middle-aged men who certainly aren't their fathers, and at any time the closely-packed tables and convivial atmosphere make chance meetings likely. In the evenings, the dining is restricted to the upper gallery and the large rear conservatory (smashing in summer), so any chance meeting, if you're seeking it, is more probable downstairs. However, if food is your main concern you'll be delighted by the daily-changing menu of good hot meals – calves' liver in red wine sauce, roast Shetland lamb, scrambled egg and smoked salmon – as well as the reliable salads (turkey, glazed ham, roast beef) and the quick snacks (soups, filled baked potatoes, garlic mushrooms). The puddings (fruit fools, crumbles and cheesecakes) and the coffee are good too. Service, by teams of ever-so-polite young ladies, is outstanding.

About £16 for two.

## Kentucky Fried Chicken

659–679 Old Kent Road, SE15 (639 3033)
Open: 11am–midnight daily.

The ultimate in dining alone is a take-away meal, and this is the ultimate take-away. It's London's only drive-thru, a £500,000 investment from KFC. You can eat inside the building (we're loath to call it a restaurant) but if you're in a hurry or really want to eat alone you drive onto the circuit, choose from the large and easy-to-read menu, order into a big microphone and by the time you've got to the hatch, your meal will be ready for collection. You then have the choice of scooting off home (they are packed in relatively heat-retaining packs) or parking in a side street or in their special car park. Inside the 'eat-in facilities' it's finger lickin' all the way (ie they have no cutlery). The menu is short and cheap; children's special of chicken, chips and a drink 98p and from £1.67 for two pieces of chicken and chips up to £4.83 for the family value packs of eight pieces of chicken, four portions of chips and four rolls. Zizz it up with coleslaw and barbecue beans both 30p. Not licensed.

From £2 for food and a non-alcoholic drink.

## Lafayette Bar

32 King Street, SW1 (930 1131)
Piccadilly Circus tube
Open: noon–3pm and 5.30–11pm Monday–Friday.

Situated beneath the restaurant of the same name, this is a devilishly attractive cocktail bar for the single-minded drinker and diner. The small, windowless basement room is oak-panelled, candlelit and hung with saucy modern prints, all of which gives it a stylishly flirtatious atmosphere. The dozen or so tables are usually filled with lunchtime parties or early evening 'happy hour-ers' (in fact four hours, from 5.30–9.30pm). So install yourself at the bar, nibble olives and peanuts and just wait for that glamorous Italian model of your fantasy to seat him/herself on the stool next to you. The cocktails (around £1.70) embrace most of the favourites, but if you want to shed your inhibitions quickly, try one of barman Errol's own creations for about £3 a go – a De La Rosa Smack (framboise, gin and green Chartreuse) or the stupendous Ring (nine different rums and liqueurs) should do the trick. To eat, there's a short but choice selection of snacks – smoked salmon and scrambled eggs, steak sandwich, chilli con carne and tortillas, spare ribs or poached eggs on crab meat in a Hollandaise sauce – all freshly-prepared in the restaurant's kitchen. Lafayette's central location – just off Pall Mall/Lower Regent Street – also makes it an ideal early-evening rendezvous before a night in the West End.

About £7 a head.

## La Nassa

438 King's Road, SW10 (351 4118)
Sloane Square/South Kensington tube
Open: noon–2.45pm and 7–11.45pm daily.

There's an atmosphere of expectation and joie de vivre at this sister restaurant to the nearby La Famiglia, both of which are run by the ebullient Alvaro. It's much favoured by Chelsea-ites and the show-biz fraternity, many of whom have left a signed photo. It is not a place to dine alone in the evening, but at lunchtime you could end up having a jolly time. Women, either alone or in a group, are given a 10% discount at lunch. The menu is vast and features several home made pasta dishes, bulked up with daily specials. The food has a variable reputation but the menu does feature everyone's favourite Italian dish. Bresaola (£2.55) the tasty smoked beef, and zuppa pavese (£1.40) clear soup with egg and toast, are safe bets as are any of the plainly prepared meat dishes such as calves' liver sautéd in butter and sage (£4.25) and charcoal grilled saddle of lamb (£3.95). Pasta as a main course (£2.95) makes a good lunch dish; the tortelloni (stuffed with cheese and spinach with a tomato sauce) is recommended.

From £5 a head; £10 is more likely.

## Rumours on the Park

41 Mackennal Street, NW8 (722 5009)
St John's Wood tube
Open: 11.30am–3pm and 5.30–11pm Monday–Saturday; noon–2.30pm and
7–10.30pm Sunday.

This is a companion cocktail bar to the brash singles establishment
in Covent Garden, and while here the décor and atmosphere are
less obviously geared toward dating, there's little doubt that that's
what most of the young customers, single or otherwise, have got in
mind. The large open room (it was formerly a pub) has a central
mahogany bar with stools and a polished wooden floor, while along
the wall there are comfortable sofas and low-slung 'coffee tables'.
Wherever you sit, you can get a good view of what's occurring.
Unless, ironically, you want to eat. The main room, you see, is for
drinking and posing only, and at £3 each outside Happy Hours
(lunchtimes, early evenings), the cocktails are cheaper to pose with
than to drink. The small 'bistro' in the back room sports only
half-a-dozen tables, and serves simple but good quality snacks in the
line of ½lb burgers, sirloin steak, steak and kidney pie, avocado and
tuna salad, chocolate mousse and so on. It's pleasantly furnished –
watch for the 'wow, man!' 70s mural to go with the 'wow, man!' 70s
music – but not really where you want to be. It does have its
compensations for male customers however, because the room is on
the flight path to the ladies' loo. So if you sit there munching for
half-an-hour, you'll get a parade of all the female pulchritude in the
place. No such reciprocal arrangement exists for the ladies . . .

About £10 a head, with cocktail.

## Russkies

6 Wellington Terrace, Bayswater Road, W2 (229 9128)
Notting Hill Gate tube
Open: noon–3pm and 5.30–11pm Monday–Friday; 7–11pm Saturday; 7–10.30pm
Sunday.

Named in honour (?) of the Soviet Embassy opposite, this basement
wine bar (mind the spiral staircase) generally has a sedate, 'mature'
atmosphere ideal for easy-going solitary drinkers. The main room is
tastefully and cosily furnished, with the exception of the dished,
wooden bar-stools which look, and can feel, like medieval torture
instruments. A small new extension has more space but less atmosphere, and is useful for group eating. Reflecting the old-fashioned
style, the home-prepared food tends to go for safety rather than
adventure, which is no bad thing in the days of the pina colada

160

cheesecake. Here, you're in lasagne, moussaka, vegetable soup, grilled trout and apple sponge country, and very reliable it is too. The cheeses are usually well-kept and there are decent ports and a couple of English wines to show any visiting Russkies a true taste of the decadent West.

About £7 a head.

## Shampers

4 Kingly Street, W1 (437 1692)
Oxford Circus tube
Open: 11.30am–2.45pm Monday–Saturday; 5.30–10.45pm Monday–Friday.

Shampers is that rare phenomenon, a wine bar serving good food. Part of a small chain owned by New Zealander Don Hewitson, (The Cork and Bottle, Cranbourn Street, Bubbles in North Audley Street and Methuselah's in Victoria Street are the others) Shampers reflects the house style with a smashing range of hot and cold snacks complementing a choice range of wines. The premises are small, gloomily Gallic but atmospheric, with a large bar and display counter looking out over a row of tightly-packed but comfortable tables and chairs. A basement room is useful for larger parties. Any 'meetings' (there's a youthful crowd of publishing people and shop assistants) will take place, albeit discreetly, on the upper floor.

Hot dishes change daily but usually offer the likes of stuffed beef with mushroom and brandy sauce, roast chicken with lemon and tarragon mayonnaise, or savoury vegetable gratin. Pâtés, inventive terrines (chicken and leek), good cheeses and delicious puds such as lemon cheesecake or chocolate mousse gâteau complete the picture. Packed at lunchtimes, Shampers is considerably more leisurely, and seductive, in the evenings.

About £8 a head.

## Sheekeys

28–32 St Martin's Court, WC2 (240 2565)
Leicester Square tube
Open: 12.30–3pm and 5.30–11.30pm Monday–Saturday.

Sheekeys, which dates back to 1896 and claims to be London's oldest fish restaurant, is full of old-world charm. Dine in style in the cosy and comfortable restaurant whose walls are covered with signed photos of theatricals, but if you're alone opt for the oyster bar. They don't take bookings here and the turnover is brisk. It's a delightful room, the oysters are snapped open to order and you can flirt with several people at once in the deco tile decorated mirror which extends the length of the bar.

Aside from oysters there's a short bar menu of daily specials or you can choose from the plain dishes (stewed eels with mash; poached smoked haddock, turbot, their own fish cakes and grilled lobster) or their other specials which are more fussily prepared. There is a limited selection of meat dishes. House wines from £5.

Half a dozen oysters under £5, or from £8 a head for food.

## Tuttons

11–12 Russell Street, WC2 (836 1167)
Covent Garden tube
Open: noon to 11.30pm daily.

This place was amongst the first restaurants to open at the beginning of the Covent Garden explosion. Run as a brasserie (there's no set charge or necessity to eat a full meal) Tuttons has a prime site on the edge of the piazza overlooking the new tourist mecca, the Market. In the summer tables go out on the cobbles and it's a good place to watch the world walk by. Inside there is a large pleasant main room with a small annexe, and an equally large space downstairs in the basement. It gets very busy and booking is only permissible in the rather soulless basement. No longer run by its originator Paul Tutton (he sold out after a long wages dispute but still runs his original restaurant South Of The Border), the current owners continue to use glamorous waitresses, aim for a fast turnover and uphold the brasserie menu. Food is wholesome and portions and prices fair. Home-made soup (£1), a huge salad (£3.20) made with spinach, mushroom, bacon and sour cream dressing; steak and kidney pie (£3.80) and crème brûlée (£1.50) are typical examples of the menu.

Around the corner in Russell Street a small area is devoted to counter service cold food. House wine £4.90.

From £3 a head for food.

## The Widow Applebaum's Deli and Bagel Academy

46 South Molton Street, W1 (629 4696)
Bond Street tube
Open: 10am–10pm Monday–Friday and 9am–6pm Saturday.

For going on nine years this strangely-named place with its curious façade has been dispensing a pleasantly down-to-earth antidote to the frenzy of South Molton Street. There is no such widow, but the place is run by a large, extremely friendly and pleasant lady (with her husband) and although she is not American the food is. The menu caters for all appetites, with portions on the gargantuan side. They serve burgers and ham and eggs, but most notable is the range of US sandwiches including BLT, a very good ruebens (salt beef, cheese, sauerkraut on brown toast) and lox (smoked salmon) with cream cheese on a bagel. Other tasty snacks include potato latkes (crisp potato pancakes) and less complex sandwiches like salt beef or hot pastrami. Unlike its logo outside, the premises are plainly decorated with bare floorboards, vast mirrors, hanging plants and photo blow ups of American high rise buildings. Upstairs there's a cocktail bar where you can drink without eating.

From £3 a head for food.

*Also Good for When You're Alone:*
Ajimura
Antiquarius
Bamboo Kuning
Bar du Musée
Café Pacifico
Café St Pierre
Chez Solange Wine Bar
Coffee Shop, YWCA
Costa's Grill
Crêperie, The
Diwana Bhel Poori House
L'Estanquet
Gamin, Le
Huff's
Joy King Lau
Lucky's
Manzi's
Melange
Metro, Le
Neal's Yard Tea Rooms
Pizzeria Amalfi
Raw Deal
Soho Brasserie
Sweeting's
Texas Lone Star Saloon

# 12. When You're Out with Parents

Taking your parents out for a meal usually presents you with one of the world's most insoluble problems – how do you get your mother to enjoy someone else's cooking? Additional hazards in this social minefield are a parental desire always to see what it is they're eating (ie, no foreign muck with sauces), to get a good cup of tea (forget the wine list) and yet to find somewhere sufficiently stylish for them to brag about when they get home ('But we've got a Berni Inn in Scunthorpe'). Generally speaking, English food is favourite, though you may tempt them to an ethnic restaurant provided they've been on holiday to the country concerned without getting food poisoning. It's as well also to head for places with homely, civil service – a cocky Italian waiter who brandishes his big pepper mill at mother could cause a lot of trouble.

# Aunties

126 Cleveland Street, W1 (387 3226)
Great Portland Street tube
Open: 12.30–1.45pm Monday–Friday; 7.30–9.45pm Monday–Saturday.

The Victorian parlour décor – drapes, scatter cushions, oil-lamps – and cosy atmosphere of Aunties should be thoroughly reassuring to any parents over forty, and let's face it, most of them are. They will not suffer a racy time at Aunties, but they'll leave well-fed and well-filled. Traditional English pies form the basis of a three-course, fixed price menu, with a variety of fillings from beef and onions to breast of wood pigeon with sultanas. Either side of these, expect to find solid soups and good pâtés as starters, with old favourites like sherry trifle or bread and butter pudding bringing up the rear. The tightly-packed tables are a little prohibitive to the exchange of intimacies, but then again when did you ever tell your parents anything about your private life?

About £22 for two.

# Christian's Restaurant

1 Station Parade, Burlington Lane, Chiswick, W4 (995 0382)
Chiswick BR
Open: 7.30–10.15pm (last orders) Tuesday–Saturday.

Christian's strikes just the right balance between homeliness and sophistication. Pale grey French ticking lines the walls, powder blue and white check cloths and napkins are crisply laundered, flowers from nearby gardens adorn the tables, home-made jams and chutneys are for sale from a central table, but the one-room restaurant is dominated by Christian and his kitchen. You can watch him cooking everything to order and the sort of French food he prepares is the sort you'd probably prepare for a dinner party. Seasonal, wholesome and very fresh produce are Christian's hallmarks and snails with garlic butter served on vegetables in red wine, kidneys flambéd in cognac and finished with cream and herbs or casseroled chicken with honey and ginger are typical dishes from the monthly-changing menu. There's no cheese but a limited selection of home-made desserts. French house wine £4.

£10 a head.

## The English House

3 Milner Street, SW3 (584 3002)
Sloane Square tube
Open: 12.30–2.30pm and 7.30–11.30pm Monday–Saturday.

On entering The English House your parents' first impression may be that you have mistakenly brought them to a private house – Buckingham Palace for example? The tiny dining-room is drenched in luxuriant carpets, curtains and wallpaper and hung with mirrors and chandeliers, while the tables boast silver salvers and tall, flickering candles. Upstairs, the lounge is just that – sofas, armchairs, reading lamps – it's enough to make you put your smoking jacket on.

The opulence of the surroundings is matched by the menu – a serious, scholarly attempt to bring to life the 'Court and country recipes' of England. The recipes are culled from various sources and may include the likes of chilled crab and orange soup, braised beef with oysters, Cornish chicken pie and assorted fruit fools, all served with great solemnity. The atmosphere can be suffocatingly formal, so it's a good place to take parents if you're getting married/ divorced/or leaving the country, and want to impress them for one last time. Lunches may be cheaper than dinners, but whatever the prices, the quality of the food usually lives up to them.

About £25 a head.

## L'Epicure

28 Frith Street, W1 (437 2829)
Leicester Square tube
Open: noon–2.30pm Monday–Friday; 6–11.15pm Monday–Saturday.

Screened by thick net curtains from Soho's more carnal excesses, L'Epicure clings faithfully to the world of gentility and style our parents always claim they knew. The fiery jet that burns above the door tells you not that they have struck oil, but that most of the cooking is done over lamps – indeed the faint smell of spirit from these, together with the hotel lounge interior and formal service, are powerfully evocative of the fifties. While the menu does now boast the occasional nod to changing fashion (deep-fried camembert with tomato salad), most of it is set in the days when cream sauces were not only acceptable but demanded. So, among the starters, there are snails, frogs' legs, oeufs en cocotte, while main courses include such classics as sole meunière, entrecôte Diane and crêpes de volaille (diced chicken breasts in cream and mushroom sauce in two pancakes). Flourishes are provided by the likes of guinea-fowl, sautéd in butter and flamed with yellow Chartreuse, or wild duck with black cherries. Having ordered, just get mum and dad to sit back and enjoy the lamp show.

About £30 for two.

## The Fountain

Fortnum and Mason, 181 Piccadilly, W1 (734 8040)
Piccadilly Circus tube
Open: 9.30am–11.30pm Monday–Saturday.

Fortnum and Mason's Fountain is a charming and civilised way to entertain the folks. The cosy ground floor restaurant (entrance in Jermyn Street) has soothing upholstery and carpets, bright chandeliers and efficient waitresses in traditional black and white uniforms. The menu is equally reassuring, offering such immutable British fodder as Welsh rarebit, steak and kidney pudding (F&M's own, of course) and the neglected but still cherished ice-cream sundae. Other hot dishes might include lamb cutlets or minute steaks, while there's a comprehensive range of sandwiches and salads, including the patrician 'sea-shore' with crab and prawns. The only hint of the 1980s is the appearance of an item called a lobsterburger, otherwise it's 50s gentility all the way. One of the best sundaes is the lyrically-named Dusty Road featuring coffee and chocolate ice-cream, whipped cream and macaroons.

About £6 a head.

## The George Inn

77 Borough High Street, SE1 (407 2056)
Borough tube
Open: 12.30–2.30pm and 6.30–9pm Monday–Saturday.

Most of London's historical pubs have fallen into the hands of one large catering chain or another, with the ironic result that bland, anonymous food is served in atmospheric, individual surroundings. The George Inn is one 17th-century coaching house that has met a slightly better fate. In the hands of the Whitbread company it's been thoughtfully preserved and kept relatively free of juke-box or space invader. The courtyard is usually clean and clear, the network of ground-floor bars (including a wine bar section) is a pleasant clutter of apt furniture, and the two upper dining rooms (the George and the Coaching Inn) feature beamed ceilings, leaded windows, scrubbed pine and tasteful hunting prints. For the most part, the food is in keeping with the surroundings. The George serves rather predictable set meals – soup, thin slices of meat, canned vegetables, bought-in trifles – while across the landing, the Coaching Inn is more up-market, better value and certainly a place parents would appreciate for its homely hospitality as well as its food. Touches of individuality are provided by the likes of excellent smoked salmon mousse, or a packed steak, kidney and mushroom pie, while safety is offered by steaks, Dover soles or escalopes. Drink reasonable house wine or tankards of beer.

About £10 a head.

## The Grange

39 King Street, WC2 (240 2929)
Covent Garden/Leicester Square tube
Open: 12.30–2.30pm and 7.30–11.30pm Monday–Friday; 7.30–11.30pm Saturday.

The very best of English cooking using prime ingredients where game predominates can be enjoyed at this initially austere restaurant. It's decorated in shades of dark brown with dark wood panelling, Victorian paintings and the tracery (lattice) of an oak confessional, with spotlights picking out stunning arrangements of vegetables. The place is formal and smart and is popular with après opera people dressed up to the hilt while at lunch it is most favoured by gents entertaining other gents. The menus are devised as set meals and start at £11.50 for two courses, £15.45 for three and £16.85 for four and include the choice of half a bottle of good wine.

The food is of a very high standard and shows English food, with regional specialities, at its best. Pâtés are served with their rather odd charcoal-charred bread, their crudités come in a large basket and their Gravad lax (marinated smoked salmon) is one of the most successful we've encountered. Main dishes tend to be plainly prepared, excellent roasts and poached fish but elaborate rabbit and duck dishes are rich and equal the best cuisine gourmande. The menu changes monthly.

From £15 a head.

## Hilaire

68 Old Brompton Road, SW7 (584 8993)
South Kensington tube
Open: noon–2.30pm (last orders) and 7–11.30pm Monday–Saturday.

The perfect place to discuss the inheritance. Everyone will be impressed with your sophisticated choice and no one will guess that this restaurant had a previous life as a burger joint (Brookes) and that it is part of the ubiquitous Kennedy Brookes chain. Strains of light classics waft on the air as you are ushered to your table by a bevy of formally-clad yet friendly waiters. You will all feel at ease with the stylish décor of creamy grey with white and the food will be memorable.

With the help of Anton (Dorchester) Mossiman's ex-sous chef, ex-Egon Ronay inspector Simon Hopkinson daily prepares a different lunch and dinner menu. His repertoire is eclectic though essentially French and of the nouvelle vague. Choices of blanquette of calves' brains, veal sweetbreads with wild mushrooms and goujons of sole with scallop mousse and sorrel sauce are typical of his dedication and have had us in ecstacies. The wine list is horribly serious with few half-bottles and house wine just under £6. If it's your treat, we'd advise a lunchtime visit when the set lunch is a mere £6.95 for two courses, à la carte is likely to be more than double.

From £10 a head.

## Hungry Horse

196 Fulham Road, SW10 (352 7757)
South Kensington tube
Open: 12.30–2.30pm and 6.30–midnight Monday–Saturday; 12.30–3pm and 7–11pm Sunday.

In the sixties, to sit at the bar and gorge yourself on a delicious home-made pie used to be quite 'the thing'. Sadly the Pie Shop is long gone, but you can still enjoy exactly the same combinations (steak and kidney with a delicious light crust is *the* one) in the surviving basement restaurant. The restaurant is tucked away down an alley behind the Fulham Road, and you reach it through a small courtyard which is laid with tables during the summer. Inside, the restaurant has a cramped feel; bare wooden tables are wedged into corners and rather beautiful life-size white ceramic horse head surveys the scene. All the food here is thoroughly British and it is apparently possible to eat Yorkshire pudding in every course. Soups come in tureens, pies are still the speciality and this is the place to find competently-prepared meat puddings, boiled beef with dumplings and fish cakes. Puddings are in the same vein and if you can make it, try spotted dick with lashings of Birds custard, or treacle tart.

From £12 a head.

## Julie's Wine Bar

137 Portland Road, W11 (727 7985)
Ladbroke Grove tube
Open: 11am–11pm Monday–Saturday; noon–10.30 Sunday; tea 3.30–6.30pm
Monday to Saturday.

If you can bag the best seat in the house – the comfy sofa at the back of the second room upstairs – you'll enjoy your tea, with Julie's home made cakes, flans, cheesecake or scones with clotted cream, all the more. Tea (choice of English breakfast, Earl Grey, Ceylon, Piccadilly, Lady Londonderry, China and Lapsang, or an equally long choice of herb teas) comes in a pot with extra hot water, portions of the delicious cakes are generous and Julie's is very nice when it's not full. Sit back and enjoy the splendour of the Victorian ecclesiastical furnishings, the touch of sixties bohemia and the (now) ageing beautiful people who favour the place. Julie's also serves wholesome home-made lunches and suppers.

Tea from £2.50; lunch and supper from £5 a head.

## Mustoe Bistro

73 Regent's Park Road, NW1 (586 0901)
Chalk Farm tube
Open: 1–3pm Saturday and Sunday; 6.30–11.15pm (10.45 Sunday) daily.

Discipline-minded parents might well appreciate the bluffness of this small restaurant's proprietor. A striking, Dickensian figure, his manner is part 'mine host' bonhomie and part scoutmaster, but his individualistic style happily spills over into the cooking as well. Dishes are frequently chalked up on the strength of morning market purchases and yet Mr Mustoe's obvious care and involvement doesn't find its outlet in exploitative prices. Starters are solid rather than spectacular – home-made soups, garlic mushrooms, tuna and beans – but there's flair in the main courses. The pork teriyaki or lamb with lemon and marjoram are worth a parental dip, but if it's safety first there's the likes of garlic or pepper steaks and beef and horse-radish casseroles. The cramped pine booths and bare wooden floors add to the no-frills but homely feel of the place. The Sunday lunch is particularly good value with roasts at a shade over two quid each.

About £16 for two.

## Pasta Connection

25–27 Elystan Street, SW3 (584 5248)
South Kensington tube
Open: 12.30–2.30pm and 7–11.30pm Monday–Saturday.

This elegant double-fronted restaurant offers a varied selection of very reasonably-priced fresh pasta and a limited choice of soundly-prepared Italian meat dishes. The restaurant is L-shaped and spartanly done out with bright white walls, the occasional plant and an incongruous selection of pictures. The staff are all Italian and the owner used to be one of the partners of the hugely popular King's Road Italian cafe, La Bersigliara. The menu is written up in Italian and only the popular dishes such as canelloni can be easily recognised so help from the waiters is essential; we wish you luck.

There's a short selection of non pasta starters, but a light pasta dish followed by a veal dish makes a perfectly balanced meal for around a fiver. Their zabaglione is very good indeed as are their sorbets. Increasingly popular with young Sloanes.

From £5 a head.

## The Perfumed Conservatory

182 Wandsworth Bridge Road, SW6 (731 0732)
Parsons Green tube
Open: 12.30–2.30pm Tuesday–Sunday; 6.30–11.30pm Monday–Saturday.

Trying to coax parents into eating anything other than plain grills or fish is usually a difficult business. If you want to stretch their horizons a little just tell them you're taking them to a thoroughly English restaurant called the Perfumed Conservatory, then let them see how adventurous it is when they get there. The distinctive plum-coloured awning will ease them into the small but prettily decorated (mirrors, paintings, wall-lights) premises, with a cramped, slightly chilly conservatory at the rear. The menu might seem familiar to them – English lamb, pork tenderloin, Aylesbury duck – but the cooking will surprise and delight them. The lamb is served in a crumbly pastry case, the pork is dressed in a sharp English grain mustard sauce, and the duck is nesting on leeks and green peppercorns. Other possibilities might include braised pigeon in elderberry wine, casserole of venison or kedgeree. Starters include delicious chicken livers with sherry, fresh asparagus in season, the lovely (in a visual sense too) quails' eggs on a smoked chicken and prawn salad, and the desserts are particularly attractive. The cloud pie – meringues embracing a purée of fresh fruit – and the chocolate thimbles are both smashing, and there are syllabubs and burnt creams as well if you've still got room. You could even try the fruity English wine Carr Taylor if the patriotism gets you.

About £30 for two.

## The Prospect of Whitby

57 Wapping Wall, E1
Wapping tube
Open: pub hours; restaurant, noon–2.30pm and 7–9.30pm daily.

The advantage of a parental trip here is that you can not only feed them pretty well, but give them a bit of history to boot. The Prospect of Whitby is one of London's oldest pubs (over 600 years apparently), and sitting as it does, in the heart of dockland (albeit derelict) it gives a great view of the Thames as a working river. It's reasonably well-preserved – stone-flagged floors, a jumble of barrels, polished wood and brass, and a striking pewter-topped bar. The clientele is usually an appealing mixture of East End low life and Gucci-clad tourists, so there's likely to be a bustle or a hustle going on. The upstairs restaurant, dedicated to Samuel Pepys, is atmospherically wood-panelled and littered with all manner of nautical knick-knacks. The menu is fairly safe, offering the value of a Berni Inn, but with slightly more choice. Seafood stuffed pancakes Prospect are generally reliable, but they can overdo the garlic in the scampi provençale. If escalope cordon bleu or fillet of pork in cider sauce don't appeal there's always steaks or Dover soles. Whitechapel artichokes or mushrooms Prospect (baked in cream) are pleasant starters. Afterwards retire to the comfortable upstairs bars for coffee, or if it's a pleasant evening, to the riverside terrace. Here you can nibble your After Eights on the very spot where Judge Jeffries had criminals staked out for the tide to claim.

About £15 a head.

## Rules

35 Maiden Lane, WC2 (836 5314)
Covent Garden tube
Open: 12.15–2.30pm and 6.15–11.15pm Monday–Friday, 6.15–10.45pm Saturday.

Steeped in literary history and virtually unchanged since it opened as an oyster bar in 1798, Rules serves traditional English food cooked to Edwardian recipes. It's in every foreign guide book to London and is much favoured by tourists who for the most part don't realize that the food is very variable and a lot of it downright stodge. Avoid the international side of the menu and opt for

172

smoked trout, jugged hare, steak and kidney or grouse with kidney pies, boiled beef and carrot with dumpling, braised oxtail or roast beef with Yorkshire pud.

The thoroughly English puddings are the highlight of the menu. House wine £5.40.

From £15 a head for food.

## San Carlo

3 Highgate High Street, N6 (340 5823)
Archway/Highgate tube
Open: 12.30–3pm and 7pm–midnight Tuesday–Saturday.

The speciality of this cool and elegant Italian restaurant is Italy's version of nouvelle cuisine – nuova cucina.

The restaurant is dominated by a truly impressive cold table and the menu is delightfully short. A selection of hors d'oeuvres (from £2.75) makes a good starter but chef Julian Biguzzi's light pasta dishes (from £1.75 starter, £3.75 main) shouldn't be missed. There are imaginative fish dishes – baby ink fish in a tomato and wine sauce and turbot with sweet red pepper – but also many classic Italian veal and kidney dishes and very plain meat dishes. The wine list is exclusively Italian and there is a good choice under £8 a bottle; the house wine is £4.75. There is a small garden for al fresco summer dining.

From £12 a head for three course meal.

## Simply Steaks

66 Heath Street, NW3 (794 6775)
Hampstead tube
Open: 7pm–midnight daily.

The name says it all really, and for any parents who want no-frills grills in no-frills surroundings – narrow room, bare wooden tables, orange upholstered chairs, dimpled windows – this is a useful venue. Starters are limited to tomato soup or sweetcorn chowder, but most people just head straight for the range of steaks (T-bone, 12oz rump, 9oz sirloin or 6oz fillet) served with a variety of sauces. These go from the simple sauce Béarnaise, via the steak stuffed with ham and mushrooms in a piquant sauce, to the fiery Mexican steak with a spicy chilli sauce. French fries, baked potatoes or salads accompany these. Puddings follow the same unpretentious lines with lemon syllabub, chocolate and orange mousse and fresh fruit salad providing welcome relief from the meat. Simply Steaks is

173

simply the sort of place you'd take your parents before packing them off on a train with no buffet.

About £12 a head.

---

## Tate Gallery Restaurant

---

Millbank, SW1 (834 6754)
Pimlico tube
Open: noon–3pm Monday–Saturday.

After you've shown mum and dad Boccioni's 'Still Life with Melon' they'll probably fancy a bite to eat, and fortunately the gallery's own splendidly attractive restaurant – wraparound Whistler rural mural, and peaceful views onto the lawns – is an ideal venue for a parental lunch. By killing two birds with one stone (giving them culture and a meal out) you will undoubtedly secure enough Brownie points to let you off going home for Christmas. There shouldn't be too many problems with the menu since it is thoroughly English, to the extent that it's partially based on rather odd historical recipes – omelette Arnold Bennett (with smoked haddock), Elizabeth veal kidneys Florentine (in puff pastry with a cream and spinach sauce), Hindle Wakes ('a medieval Lancashire chicken dish') and a Joan Cromwell salad (Oliver: 'What's for tea Joan, I'm starving!' Joan: 'Just a salad, you Puritan'). Some of the sauces on these dishes can go awry, so safest bets are usually the plainer dishes – steak, kidney and mushroom pie, poached salmon trout with mousseline sauce (hollandaise with whipped cream), game pie and alcoholic sherry trifle. To accompany these, there's a classy wine-list (which will be sent in advance on request so that wines can be ordered early enough to 'breathe'), reckoned to be reasonably-priced by London restaurant standards, which attracts serious plonkies from all over. There are some famous heavy-duty clarets (Château Latour), crisp, summer drinking white burgundies (Corton-Charlemagne) and a range of fruity Californians. There's also a thoughtful number of decent half-bottles – not something you come across too often. Another thoughtful touch is the provision of a no-smoking area (specify when you book), so if your mother's brought her pipe she may well get a table all to herself.

About £15 a head (more if you hit the serious wines!).

## Verrey's

233 Regent Street, W1 (734 4495)
Oxford Circus tube
Open: 12.30–3pm and 5.30–11pm Monday–Friday; 6pm–midnight Saturday.

For a restoring drink after a day pounding the pavements of Oxford and Regent Streets, or for a pre-theatre snack or meal, Verrey's is just the right place to take parents. Situated in a cosy basement below the excellent Lindy's Coffee Lounge and Pâtisserie, Verrey's looks and feels like an old-fashioned club. Oak-panelled walls, a cloakroom with counter, upholstered chairs, subdued but tasteful lighting and polite well-dressed staff set the tone for the place. There's even a padded piano bar to perch upon while the early-evening keyboard wizard tinkles through Dean Martin's greatest hits. The catering covers three angles – classic cocktails, what they term gourmet bar-snacks and a formal restaurant specialising in theatre meals, with a set-price menu at £10.50 a head. This offers standard items such as gammon with pineapple, hamburger steaks, Dover sole, sherry trifle and is unlikely to upset parental tastes. You're allowed to break for your show between courses, so you could come back from the nearby Palladium to have your dessert, coffee and mints. If it's just a quick snack you're after, try the short range offering steak sandwiches, chicken drumsticks, croque monsieur, tartelette aux crevettes and the like – they're pretty good value. At midnight on Saturdays, they even offer a traditional breakfast for hungry late-night revellers.

About £6 a head (bar); £10.50 set dinner, alc £15 a head (restaurant).

## Zen

Chelsea Cloisters, Sloane Avenue, SW3 (589 1781)
South Kensington tube
Open: noon–midnight daily.

Stylish, spacious and formally decorated with a red and gold colour scheme augmented by hand-painted Chinese horoscopes, a low, mirrored ceiling and curious rock pool complete with waterfall, Zen is a place to get dressed up for. The food is superb, great attention is given to its presentation and the speciality is unusual and lavish fish and shellfish dishes, vegetable dishes inspired by centuries-old Buddhist fare and meat and poultry specialities from the provinces of Kwong Tung, Hunan, Szechuan and Canton. The menu is more of a book than a list and there are no set meals to let you off the hook. We couldn't fault our choice of their special spring rolls served with curls of iceburg lettuce; pungent, dry, tangerine-peel flavoured beef slices; Szechuan sliced pork with garlic and chilli sauce; Cantonese crispy duck pancakes with all the trimmings, and sizzling Hunanese lamb slices with spring onions and ginger which arrived with Monks mixed vegetables and plain rice. To round off the meal, Zen offer a small list of unusual Chinese desserts like red bean paste pancake and honey melon tapioca pudding as well as the more familiar toffee apples. The restaurant seats 80 and there's a separate area for private parties of up to 30 when *the* thing to order would be the crispy Kwantung style roasted whole suckling pig.

From £10 a head.

*Also Good for Parents:*
L'Arlequin
Bates
Brinkley's
Capital Hotel Restaurant
Crystal Palace
Drake's
Feathers Hotel
Flanagan's
Haweli
Ho Ho
Joy King Lau
Jules Bar
Ken Lo's Memories of China
Masters
Mon Plaisir
Monsieur Thompson's
One Hampstead Lane
Paris House
Rowley's
Royal Academy Restaurant
Rudland & Stubbs
San Frediano
Sheekey's
Spaghetti Opera
Thé Dansant, Waldorf Hotel
Waterside Inn
Yesterday

## 13. When You're Out with Children

Meals out with small children can be delightful, but too often turn into a nightmare. They get bored easily, want to pee every five minutes and invariably whine if the food doesn't arrive instantly. There are places which make a feature of welcoming children by providing special infant-sized (and priced) portions, occasionally their own menu, high chairs and even chair bolsters. Some even go so far as to provide things for the little beasts to do and send them away with hats, sweets and balloons. Apart from the tailor-made places, we've also given details of large, ethnic restaurants which tolerate smalls, restaurants with large gardens in which they can tear about and those places with such novelty value that they'll be stunned into good behaviour – well at least for their first visit.

## British Home Stores Restaurant

99–105 Kensington High Street, W8
High Street Kensington tube
Open: 9.30am–5.30pm Monday–Wednesday; 9.30am–6.45pm Thursday;
9.30–5.45pm Friday and Saturday.

The wailing of children as they're dragged around department stores always triggers memories of the Beach Boys' 'Sloop John B' – the chorus is almost exactly the same, 'I wanna go home, let me go home'. Happily for ear-bashed parents trailing around BHS, relief is at hand. The first-floor restaurant, a spacious, well-appointed, modern self-service operation, has the sort of food to calm any distressed juvenile. A short under-12s menu offers choice gob-stoppers at just 80p a shot – junior burger in a bun with chips, two sausages with chips or beans, or junior fillet of plaice with chips. In addition, puds like jelly and cream, lemon meringue pie or custard tart should seal their jaws for the afternoon. High-chairs are provided for especially unruly characters and, on a more serious note, it's nice that a non-smoking area is operated so that kids don't get great lungfulls of smoke from shoppers seeking nicotine relief. Adults get a good deal too – one channel offers traditional fillers like roast beef and Yorkshire pudding, fried plaice and steak and kidney pie, while the 'Country Style' channel offers more contemporary items – macaroni cheese, fish crumble, chicken and mushroom pie, chocolate and hazelnut meringue – all of high quality. The provision of a wine and beers counter may result in your kipping down in the divan bed display at the restaurant's entrance. Breakfasts and afternoon teas are also served.

About £10 for a family of four.

## Canonbury Tavern

21 Canonbury Place, N1 (226 1881)
Highbury and Islington tube
Open: pub hours.

When London pubs advertise 'beer garden at rear', the reality is usually an old paved yard with a couple of bird tables and a recently-removed washing line. Here however, there is a large acreage of real, green grass, walled in so the kids can play in safety, and amply furnished with wrought-iron tables and chairs. They even provide swings for the little blighters and there are fairy lights on the trees so you can see where they've got to when it gets dark. The interior of the pub is spacious and well-kept, with a well above average buffet counter and cheerful efficient staff. You should find pineapple and tuna quiche, sweetcorn and tomato flan, prawn vol-au-vents, sausage savouries and splendid ham off the bone, as well as crisp, fresh salads. Hot dishes are restricted to high-quality cottage pie or steak and kidney puddings, unless you want to try your luck with their restaurant, where it's straightforward Dover soles and steaks. The beer is by Charringtons, and the swings are by Mothercare.

About £2.50 a head.

## Chuen Cheng Ku

17 Wardour Street, W1 (437 1398)
Piccadilly/Leicester Square tube
Open: 11am–11.45pm Monday–Saturday, 11am–11pm Sunday.

The first delight for children once they've got over the culture shock of Soho's Chinatown is the impressive dragon totem pole outside this bastion of Wardour Street. Inside, the restaurant is huge (seating for 400 in four rooms) and though the place has recently been revamped and cleaned up it's a functional sort of place, more of a canteen than a restaurant. Their menu is one of the largest known (which for a Chinese restaurant is no mean feat) and the more obscure and unlikely sounding dishes are likely to be the most successful; the curious mixture of crispy duck with lemon (curd?) is a perfect example. The highlight is the dim sum (Chinese snacks, most often stuffed and steamed or deep fried floury dumplings) which is wheeled round on heated trolleys during the day and (particularly) Sunday lunch. The idea is that you hail the trolley and take pot luck (few of the staff appear to speak English) but the tasty filled dumplings won't disappoint, whatever they've got inside them. Drink tea.

From £4 a head for food.

## Everglades Exchange

128 Hale Lane, Edgware, Middlesex
Edgware tube
Open: noon–11.30pm Monday–Friday; 11am–11.30pm Saturday and Sunday.

One of the great conundrums of English catering is whether or not you can take children into pubs or not. Generally speaking you can't, and you usually have to look for a garden, a children's room or a landlord with a blind eye if you want the family to stay together. Certain brewery chains have become aware of the disaffection these policies provoke however, which is part of the reason for the transformation of this pub from The Green Man to Everglades

Exchange. 'Theming' has taken place, which involves a great deal of tarting up – here on a swamp/deep South/good ol' Texas theme with murals, confederate flags, stuffed sharks and all manner of American bric-à-brac. More importantly, the former pub operation has been divided into a spacious, airy bar with cane furniture, and a colourful American-style restaurant. This therefore allows parents the chance to pile in for a solo drink while leaving the children in the restaurant, or indeed to dine and drink 'en famille'.

The menu is essentially Tex-mex favourites (chilli, enchiladas, burritos) together with a good range of burgers, club sandwiches and barbecue chicken dishes. A special junior menu offers burgers, hot dogs, chilli-dogs and ice-cream at about £2 cheaper than the adults' dishes. There's an appropriate range of sweets – apple pies, fruit sundaes, cheesecakes and, a child's delight this, a mocha mud pie, a concoction of fudge, mocha ice-cream and a cracker crust. Drinks are comprehensive, from French wines to American beers to Dr Pepper.

About £6 a head.

## Flags Restaurant and Coffee House

Commonwealth Institute, Kensington High Street, W8 (603 4535)
Kensington High Street tube, parking behind Institute.
Open: 10am–5pm Monday–Friday; 2–5pm Saturday and Sunday.

There's no admission charge to this cultural centre for 48 countries, where children will find much to enjoy. At the back of the Institute, close to the car park and overlooking the large lawn is a pleasant, comfortable restaurant. The tables are sensibly covered in brown and white plastic gingham and there's plenty of space for large parties. From 10am to noon they serve a traditional English breakfast of bacon, egg, toast and tea or coffee at £1.25, but the main feature of Flags is the international menu served between noon and 2.30pm Monday to Saturday. Prices are low so it's not too much of a disaster if little Johnny doesn't like his Sri Lankan chicken curry with rice (£2) or Indian omelette with diced curried chicken (£1.35). Traditionalists can stick to the ever popular fish or sausage and chips (under £1). The rest of the time Flags serves a rather indifferent selection of pre-wrapped sandwiches and stodgy Danish pastries.

A monthly What's On leaflet is available and Mum and Dad can regenerate over this with a bottle of the house wine at £3.75.

It would be difficult to spend more than £5 a head.

## Golders Hill Park Refreshment Bar

North End Way, NW11 (455 8010)
Golders Green tube
Open: 10.30am–8.30pm daily, March–October.

Over the past ten years Tony Pazienti has proved that food in parks doesn't have to be lousy. You'll find no pre-wrapped Mother's Pride sandwiches and stale Danish pastries here, just food you will be glad to eat as a snack or a nourishing full meal. There are daily specials, fresh crisp salads, fresh pasta dishes, decent home-made desserts with real cream, fresh Danish pastries and delicious gâteaux. The atmosphere is relaxed and pleasant and for those rare balmy days there are 30 tables outside for al fresco dining. The park is delightful, and children can explore the grassy slopes in search of the deer.

From £4 a head for a full meal.

## Hamley's

200 Regent Street, W1 (734 3161)
Oxford Circus tube
Open: 9.30am–4.30pm (7pm Thursday) Monday–Saturday.

What better place to take children than Hamley's, London's biggest toy shop? For parents and children with any money left to spend, Hamley's has a fourth-floor self-service restaurant and a basement soda fountain. The restaurant, operated by Grand Met catering, is a fairly functional cafeteria affair enlivened by the Edwardian theme – a large cut-out of an early-London omnibus, working puppets and table-clearers in straw boaters are just some of the touches of colour in a rather cramped array of white tables and folding chairs. The limited menu seems to make few major concessions to children, but the short range of hot pies with chips, soups and burgers, backed up by sandwiches, cakes and ice-creams, is the sort of all-purpose fodder to suit any age group. In theory the basement Soda Fountain with its list of ice-cream sundaes and milkshakes should be more attractive to children, but the brightly-lit, white-tiled counter is fitted with such high stools and besieged by so many throbbing video games, that it's a bit like eating on the flight-deck of the Starship Enterprise. On second thoughts, this sounds *exactly* what a child would want . . .

About £2.50 a head.

## Hard Rock Café

150 Old Park Lane, W1 (629 0382)
Hyde Park Corner tube
Open: noon–12.30am daily.

Reckoned to be the best hamburger restaurant in London, the Hard Rock is a good place to take kids over the age of nine or ten, but not much fun, I'd have thought, for anyone younger than that. The bustling atmosphere (there's nearly always a queue despite its warehouse dimensions), the loud, throbbing music, the wild range of wall decorations (anything from US College pennants to a Vitas Gerulaitis tennis racket) and the pin-ball machine by the bar, give it all the pazzaz the pre-pubescent child could desire – the post-pubescents will no doubt appreciate the regular parade of Lotharios and Lolitas at the bar. No price concessions are made for children, so be aware when choosing that most of the dishes are of huge proportions and should easily be enough for two kids. The essential ingredient of the menu of course is the hamburger – strapping hunks of char-grilled chopped beef served with large crisp salads, sesame seed buns and French fries. Sizes vary from ¼lb–½lb, with bacon, barbecue sauce and cheese being additional variations on the plain burger. Alternatives include bowls of chilli, and roast beef, club (chicken and bacon) or huge, toasted fillet steak sandwiches. Desserts are massive bowls of home-made apple pie, cheesecake or chocolate devil's foodcake, and while adults will enjoy the imported American beers (Michelob, Budweiser), thick milkshakes will probably get the vote from the young 'uns.

About £9 a head.

## Little Italy

175 New Kings Road, SW6 (731 6404)
Parsons Green tube
Open: noon–midnight daily.

No one could fail to feel relaxed at this comfortable and bustling restaurant which specializes in home-made pasta dishes. The menu features eight (all around £2) plus several burgers (£2.40–£3) and a long blackboard of specialities of the day. The owner has young children himself so Saturday and Sunday lunchtimes really are family occasions, and the half-price children's portions mean the visit doesn't break the bank. During the summer and early autumn, families can take advantage of the canopied hedged-off terrace which is set well back from the road. The children can drink shakes while mum and dad can do in a bottle of the very acceptable house wine (£4).

£8–£12 for a meal for a family of four.

## Luckys

1a Haven Green, Ealing, W5 (997 8859)
Ealing tube
Open: noon–midnight daily.

Located in a former 1840s coaching station, Luckys is a stylishly planned and executed cocktail bar cum restaurant. You can drink seriously at the bar – there is a list of nearly 50 cocktails averaging £2 each and a happy hour between 5.30 and 6.30pm Monday to Friday – or eat a snack or full three course meal.

The menu has a US bias and includes a Late Risers Brunch (£3.75) of egg, bacon, sausage with hash brown potatoes, muffin and orange juice; various elaborate sandwiches, charcoal grilled burgers from £2.95, salads, surf n turf (£5.25), steaks (from £5.25) and a short range of US desserts such as waffles, sundaes and cheesecake. The quality of the U.S. food is good and between noon and 7.30pm they serve a special 'kiddies menu at kiddies prices'.

Best of all though for parents is their Sunday lunch. Taking up Peppermint Park's smashing idea, they serve children a free burger, salad and chips (proper ones too) and grown ups can tuck into a traditional three course Sunday lunch for £5.95.

Between 1 and 2pm Smarty Arty (high-quality children's entertainer) takes the children off parents' hands and you can hear them whooping with laughter (and watch them from the bar).

Set Sunday lunch £5.95; à la carte from £8.

## Marine Ices

8 Haverstock Hill, NW3 (485 8898)
Chalk Farm tube
Open: 10am–10.45pm Monday–Saturday; 11am–9pm (6.45pm winter) Sunday.

Marine Ices have been based at the foot of Haverstock Hill since 1930, and were in the ice-cream business some 22 years before that. The history and pedigree of the Mansi family's operation is reflected in the quality of their product which is not only served in their bright, informal ice-cream parlour (gelateria), but which is also supplied to some 400 London restaurants. All their ice-creams contain non-milk fat, and all their sorbets are free of artificial flavouring or animal product – only fresh fruit or frozen pulp is used. None of this is likely to concern the hordes of youngsters who descend on the place throughout the year. They just enjoy the spectacular range of cassate (try the Siciliana with layers of vanilla, chocolate, strawberry and pistachio with a centre of nougat and candied fruit); bombes (the anacleto features coffee ice-cream with coffee syrup and hazelnut ice-cream); and their sundaes served with fresh cream (the Vesuvius is a mountain of vanilla, chocolate and marsala ice-cream with crushed meringues, cherries and marsala-soaked sponge). All these are served from a spanking new counter and refrigerated unit, custom-built in Italy.

At the rear of the parlour, they also operate a pizzeria (closed on Sundays) which boasts a short but well-cooked range of nine different pizzas, six pasta dishes, and three classic veal or chicken dishes. This section is fully licensed and is traditionally the spot where the divorced North London parent waits for his or her child to be handed over by the other divorced North London parent. The child, having been gorged on ice-cream already, then gets another tub of ice-cream to take home.

About £2.50 a head (gelateria) £6 a head (pizzeria).

## My Old Dutch

131 High Holborn, WC1
Holborn tube
Open: noon–midnight Sunday–Wednesday; noon–1am Thursday–Saturday.

Part of the trick of keeping kids happy in a restaurant is giving them food with some sort of novelty value – here, the interest is provided by a large variety (over 200) of sweet and savoury Dutch pancakes, served in, or rather across, huge china bowls the size of Desperate Dan's ash-tray. If they're stunned into thinking it's bath-time, you can try entertaining them with a picture game – as they eat the pancake, the scenic patterns on the bowls are revealed, showing familiar Dutch landscapes like windmills, ladies in clogs and canals. So, for example, the first child to uncover a windmill, can pick up the bill, have a cigar etc. Generally, the sweet pancakes (fruit, ice-cream, liqueurs) work better than the savoury (cheese, ham, garlic sausage) but they're all equally filling, one would be enough for two. To drink, there are assorted milkshakes. The functional pine tables and furniture would seem to be reasonably child-proof.

About £8 for two.

# No 1

Upper St Martins Lane, WC2 (240 3734)
Leicester Square/Covent Garden tube
Open: 11am–11pm Monday–Saturday.

Searching for something different for a birthday treat? No 1, a lavishly converted pub on the edge of theatreland, could offer the solution. Here, amid banks of greenery and to the strains of the latest sounds, try the speciality of the house-fondue. The do-it-yourself meal (either rump steak, lamb, chicken or cheese) arrives with a selection of dips, baked potato and sesame seed-coated bread. The rest of the menu at the Holsten-backed No 1 is international and includes their special platter of smoked meat and pickled cucumber, bratwurst, steak, calves' liver and crudités. Dessert is limited to apple flan, ice cream or fruit salad or the spectacular fondue dessert which is second best to being let loose in a sweet shop and includes home-baked marshmallows, macaroons, sponge fingers and fresh fruit for dunking in chocolate. All cocktails £2.50, Holsten beers and limited range of wines around £5 a bottle.

From £5 a head for food.

# Obelisk

294 Westbourne Grove, W11 (229 1877)
Notting Hill Gate tube
Open: noon–11pm Monday–Friday; 12.30pm–11pm Saturday and Sunday.

What could be better for kids than a crêperie dedicated to a comic-book hero? While Obelisk isn't essentially a child-orientated enterprise the informal atmosphere, the small patio at the rear, the interesting variety of crêpes and galettes and the provision of a couple of high-chairs are helpful considerations when dining en famille. The small, wooden-floored room is a pleasing jumble of tables, knick-knacks and ceiling fans, with enough bustle going on to keep kids occupied. The range of galettes (made from buckwheat flour) are threatened now by a more familiar café menu (Sicilian pasta, steak, kidney and mushroom casserole) but they're still tops for a snack. There's a wide variety of fillings, to be chosen in combination, from the humble cheese and tomato to the patrician smoked salmon and caviar. Mixtures of meat and vegetable (say ham and mushrooms) are generally most successful. The galettes arrive looking like Post Office parcels at Christmas but despite their appearance they are extremely filling. One should be enough for two junior tummies. Kids usually go straight for the fruit/ice-cream/

chocolate crêpes despite their teeth-rotting potential. Parents can relax with wine and the French papers.

About £4 a head.

---

## The Old Ship Pub

25 Upper Mall, W6 (748 2593)
Hammersmith tube
Open: pub hours.

On sunny days the length of the picturesque Hammersmith and Chiswick Mall presents a good pub crawl and healthy walk rolled into one. For those with children this large and comfortable pub is *the* place to head for and settle. The reason: they allow children inside the pub and they have a vast sloping terrace and patio set back from but overlooking the river where up to about 40 can be seated. The Watneys house daily prepares a cold spread and at lunchtime do a rotation of hot specials such as sausages, steak pie, pork chops and roast meats for around £2.50. It gets very busy and a long queue is normal. Children are quite safe as no cars are allowed on this part of the Mall and there's plenty for them to watch and loads of other children to play with.

From £2.50 for food.

---

## Peppermint Park

13 Upper St Martins Lane WC2 (836 5234)
Covent Garden tube
Open: noon–2am (last orders 1.30am) Monday–Saturday; noon–12.30pm (bar closes 11.30pm) Sunday.

The ultimate treat for pre-teen trendies would be to hold their birthday party at the pale pink and green Peppermint Park. The menu of all-American favourites such as burgers, steak, Reubens (hot pastrami with melted Swiss cheese, tomato and lettuce) and toasted ham and cheese sandwiches doesn't break the bank and they even do a kiddy burger with french fries for under £2. Their sundaes, splits and shakes are very impressive but a Belly Buster – serves from three to thirteen – will really guarantee a successful party.

Other things to note about Peppermint Park: there is dancing nightly from midnight and they are licensed until 2am; they offer a cheap egg-based lunch menu, vegetarians are catered for and on Sundays each child accompanied by an adult gets a free burger.

Cocktails served with all the trimmings are the speciality at PP, house wine £4.50.

From £6 a head.

## Pizza Hut

60 Hampstead High Street, NW3 (794 7090)
Open: noon–midnight Sunday–Friday; 11.30am–midnight Sunday.

Though they don't have a special children's menu at this or any other branch of Pizza Hut, here they at least take great pains to make a meal out with small children as easy on the parents as possible. They provide both high and bolster chairs, games, crayons, paper and balloons, and the waitresses have repeatedly been known to show great potential as childminders. The menu should also appeal to children – pizzas both 'Thin'n'Crispy' (these are best as they can be on the table within five minutes) and deep-sided Chicago-style. Either will feed two to three child-sized appetites, and with twelve toppings available there's plenty of choice. Another good wheeze is their 'one price, help yourself' salad bar where larger smalls can show off their balancing skills. There are no milkshakes but there are fizzy drinks and ice-cream, apple pie and cheesecake should be more than enough for pudding. A family of four could eat for a fiver; cheap house wine for fraught adults comes by the litre. Best to go during the week as it gets busy (and sticky!) on Saturday and Sunday.

## Sea-Shell Restaurant

35 Lisson Grove, NW1 (723 8703)
Marylebone tube
Open: noon–2pm and 5.30–10.30pm Tuesday–Saturday.

Not many children could resist a fish and chip lunch or supper, especially when they happen to be served at the best fish and chip shop in London. The Sea-Shell's reputation is founded on the freshness of its fish (bought daily), the high quality of its batter (secret recipe), its groundnut oil frying and the fact that everything's cooked to order.

Both the takeaway and sit-down sections generally have a queue outside, but the restaurant has a pretty quick turn-around time (it's pleasantly but functionally furnished and there's no licence) and now that VAT has appeared on takeaway prices you might just as well eat in as out.

It's hardly worth bothering with the starters – soup, prawn cocktail – so just get the off-spring stuck into delicious cod fillets, North

Sea plaice, Scotch haddock fillets or, if they've been very well-behaved, perhaps salmon cutlets or lemon sole. They can then finish off with cream gâteaux, apple pie or fruit cocktail. A good range of soft drinks is served as well as restoring cups of tea for parents.

About £6 a head.

## Texas Lone Star Saloon

154 Gloucester Road, SW7 (370 5625)
Gloucester Road tube
Open: noon–11.45pm Monday–Saturday; noon–11pm Sunday.
Also at 117 Queensway, W2
Open: noon–3pm and 5.30pm–1am Monday–Saturday.

You can't miss this large cowboy style tex-mex restaurant with the outsize Indian squaw guarding its door. Inside, the bare wooden floor boards, cowboy ephemera and music combine to give the place a real lived-in and authentic atmosphere. The tex-mex food is good and cheap and you'd be hard pushed to spend more than £5 a head. Their nachos (corn shells covered with cheese, onion and hot peppers) and hickory smoked ribs have devoted followers though the cowboy burger and french fries is popular with children. Cocktails are served in frosted half-pint mugs and there are US imported beers in frosted half-pint mugs and there are US imported beers and very reasonably-priced house wine. Children of all ages love the Lone Star because it's informal and exactly what you'd expect to find in the States. The place is particularly popular for weekday birthday parties and for Sunday lunch treats. Most evenings there's live music. Seating for 200 at Gloucester Road and 92 at Queensway.

Maximum £5 a head.

## Tootsies

120 Holland Park, W14 (229 8567)
Holland Park tube
Open noon to midnight daily
Also 117 New Kings Road, SW6 and 115 Notting Hill, W11

This small chain of pleasantly-decorated burger joints caters for children with their special mini burger, chips and baked beans or egg for under £2 – and they keep several special booster seats. All branches have a low-key and homely atmosphere with fresh flowers on the tables and cheerful waitresses. They serve wonderful thick milk shakes, ices, cheesecake and chocolate fudge cake. The Holland Park branch puts a few tables on the pavement during sunny weather and New Kings Road has a large deep al fresco space set well back from the road. The Fulham Road and Parsons Green restaurants will even organise a birthday party for you, complete with conjuror or Punch and Judy. (Minimum 15 children.)

From £3 a head for food.

*Also Good for Children:*
Bunga Raya
Bunny's
Café Pelican
Caffe Mamma
Chalk and Cheese
Fatso's Pasta Joint
Green and Pleasant
Henry J Bean's
Hung Toa
ICA Restaurant
Italian Connection
Joy King Lau
Kentucky Fried Chicken
Kowloon
Leeds Castle
Lord's Carver
Old Rangoon
One Hampstead Lane
Porter's
Pratt's Brasserie
Sidi Bou Said
Slinky's

## 14. When You Want a Bit of Fresh Air

Because we're not used to sun in this country we've never really developed a tradition of eating outside. This is especially true in London, where the limitations of space, not to mention carbon monoxide poisoning, make al fresco facilities few and far between. Certain restaurants, usually the continental ones, do always try, even if you have to suspend disbelief at a pavement turned 'sun terrace', and suspend terror at a table placed two feet from a bus-lane. While the Charlotte Street and Covent Garden areas are the most responsive to good weather, individual pockets of enterprise and flexible design do exist, and anywhere near or on the river (usually a pub) is a good bet for sea-breezes. If all else fails, there's always air-conditioning, so we've added a short list here of trustworthy places with this facility.

## Cap's

64 Pembridge Road, W11 (229 5177)
Notting Hill Gate tube
Open: 6–11.30pm Monday–Saturday; noon–3pm Sunday.

Comfortable, bric-à-brac furnished country-style restaurant with French inspired food by ex-Langan's chef. Popular gay haunt.

From £10 a head.

## The English Garden

10 Lincoln Street, SW3 (584 7272)
Sloane Square tube
Open: 12.30–2.30pm (2pm Sunday) and 7.30–11.30pm (10pm Sunday) daily.

Cool conservatory-style restaurant with rampant foliage. Companion restaurant to The English House but this has a lighter, more European menu.

From £15 a head.

## Gavvers

61 Lower Sloane Street, SW1 (730 5983)
Sloane Square tube
Open: 7–11pm Monday–Saturday.

The original Le Gavroche site, now the cheap relation where Roux trained chefs serve three course menus for a remarkable £16.75, including kir, half a bottle of wine and coffee.

## Gaylord

79 Mortimer Street, W1 (580 3615)
Oxford Circus tube
Open: noon–3pm and 6–11.30pm (11pm Sunday) daily.

Part of long-established, well-appointed up-market Indian restaurant chain. Kashmiri and mughlai specialities, together with traditional tandooris and curries.

From £10 a head.

# Kites

50 Woburn Place, WC1 (580 1188)
Russell Square tube
Open: noon–2.30pm and 6pm (6.30 Sunday)–11.30pm daily.

Elegant, subtly-lit, spacious raised ground-floor Chinese restaurant serving both Peking and Szechuan specialities. Good value set lunches.

From £8 a head.

# Ormond's

6 Ormond Yard, SW1 (930 2843)
Piccadilly Circus tube
Open: 12.30–3pm Monday–Friday; 6.30–11.30pm Monday–Saturday.

Spacious, arty, hi-tech ground-floor dining room hung with bamboo screens and modern prints. Modish menu of Franco–Italian dishes. Basement restaurant/members' club for late-night jazz.

From £10 a head.

# Overton's

5 St James's Street, SW1 (839 3774)
Green Park tube
Open: noon–3pm and 6–10.30pm Monday–Saturday.

Elegant, 18th-century style, long, narrow restaurant serving seafood in comfortable surroundings. Oysters are their speciality.

From £10 a head.

# Shezan

16 Cheval Place, SW7 (589 7918)
Knightsbridge tube
Open: noon–3pm and 7pm–midnight Monday–Saturday.

Northern Punjabi food served in elegant setting. Hidden in mews at rear of Harrods.

From £10 a head.

## Walton's

121 Walton Street, SW3 (584 0204)
South Kensington tube
Open: 12.30–2.30pm and 7.30–10.30pm Monday–Saturday; 12.30–2pm Sunday.

Lush, boudoir-style greenhouse of a place serving English regional food with touches of 'interpretation'.

From £10 a head.

## Woodlands

77 Marylebone Lane, W1 (486 3862)
Bond Street tube
Open: noon–2.45pm and 6–10.45pm daily.

Fashionably-appointed South Indian vegetarian restaurant with attractive lighting and booth-style seating. Excellent value set meals, 'thalis'. Companion branch in Wembley.

From £6 a head.

## Bar Crêperie

Unit 21, Covent Garden Market, WC2 (836 2137)
Covent Garden tube
Open: 10am–midnight daily.

Bang opposite the Portico of St Paul's Church, the outside tables at the Crêperie afford a perfect view of the acrobatics and buskings which go on all the time here. You can breakfast on hot croissant or one one of their delicious crêpes. During the day the crêpe menu (14 sweet filled and 24 savoury) is augmented by a couple of substantial mixed salads (£3.25) and steaks (£4.95) and the restaurant is a popular spot for an indulgent tea. Pig yourself on cream cheese and cherry filling or peaches with pernod (both £2.25). Inside there is a tiny trompe l'oeil room but the main restaurant is in the basement. It's a series of little pink-painted alcoves packed with tables for up to 80, and you have to queue. House wine £4.90.

From £5 a head.

## Brinkley's

47 Hollywood Road, SW10 (351 1683)
South Kensington/Earls Court tube, though neither is very close.
Open: 7.30–11.30pm Monday–Saturday.

This very pretty converted house, decorated with restrained style in
dark maroon with mahogany panelling, vast mirrors and numerous
tall trailing plants, has an equally attractive patio garden for al
fresco dining. Owner John Brinkley takes a firm hand in supervising
the short, essentially French menu which changes frequently
and shows a marked preference for game and fish. The following (all
tried from a summer menu) were tasty combinations, beautifully
presented and reasonably priced considering the quality of the
ingredients: duck ménage – parcels of filo pastry with a duck and
cucumber filling and barbecue sauce (£2.90); millefeuille of fresh
asparagus with sauce beurre blanc (£3.20); smoked salmon with
roulades filled with white crab meat (£4.20); a light puff pastry-
topped game pie (£5.50) and the nouvelle favourite, breast of duck
with a raspberry vinegar sauce (£6.50). Brinkley's keep good Stilton
and offer a selection of light home-made desserts such as sorbets
and chocolate bombe. The wine list is extensive and includes some
reasonably priced Château bottled and vintage wines. Their garden
really is one of the prettiest and most un-London-like that we know
of and during the summer they open for lunch.

From £12.50 a head.

## Café Des Amis Du Vin

12–13 Hanover Place, Covent Garden, WC2 (379 3444)
Covent Garden tube
Open: 8am–10.30am; noon–midnight Monday–Saturday (café); 11.30am–3pm
Tuesday–Friday and 7–11.30pm Tuesday–Saturday (salon).

When the weather is fine the passage in front of the ever-popular
café is filled with around 40 tables and still the 132 tables inside are
likely to be full. For the Café (with its wine bar downstairs and more
intimate Salon upstairs) is a brilliant concept and just scrapes into
being eligible for a Relais Routier listing – three courses for under
£7. The menu is short and features lots of snack-like meals. There is
no pressure to eat a three course meal, though most people do, and
you can be well satisfied with a couple of starters and a pudding.
Their frisée aux lardons (£1.25) with a plate of charcuterie (£2.45)
makes a perfect light meal but their boudin noir (£2.45) and
omelettes (£1.35) have devoted followers. Their bread is the real
thing (they were one of the first restaurants to import French dough

and bake their own baguettes) and their cheeses are superb. The wine list is appropriately well chosen (the company runs a popular club) and their house wines are some of the best in town (£4.30). Continental breakfasts are now also served from 8am in the café.

From £5 a head for food.

---

## Dan's

119 Sydney Street, SW3 (352 2718)
South Kensington tube
Open: 12.30–2.30pm and 7–11pm Monday–Friday.

Although Dan's patio isn't strictly speaking outside, it so resembles terrace eating that we have included it in this section. At the back of the restaurant (it is on two floors) there is an enclosed sunken patio, with seating for 20, which has so many plants and such cunning lighting that you feel you're in a garden. The rest of the restaurant is very pretty; pale green outside and beige and green inside giving a light, summery, airy quality even though the place is a small converted terraced house.

When Anthony Worrell-Thompson (now at Ménage à Trois) was chef Dan's achieved accolades from Michelin, but though the restaurant still offers above average nouvelle cuisine the current chef Tom Cheeseman is not in the same class as Warrell-Thompson. The menu changes frequently and we've enjoyed Dan's brioche of marrow, artichoke and wild mushrooms in a madeira sauce (£3.10) but the vegetable terrine with a tomato sauce (£2.95) would have been far better had it not come straight from the fridge. Rack of English lamb roasted with herbs (£7.95) was one of the few plain dishes on the menu and was spoilt by arriving luke warm.

From £15 a head.

---

## La Famiglia

7 Langton Street, SW10 (351 0761)
South Kensington tube
Open: noon–2.30pm and 7–11.45pm daily.

La Famiglia is a pleasant, popular, middle-of-the-road Italian restaurant which started off as a very fashionable haunt and is now resting on its laurels. It does have a very pretty garden which is honeysuckle lined and quarry tiled and can seat up to 40. Inside the restaurant is informal, with whitewashed walls hung with family photos and decorated with masses of greenery. Sister to La Nassa on the King's Road and ebulliently run by Alvaro, La Famiglia is good for instant bonhomie, flourish and suggestive grinding of the pepper mills but the food can be awful. The menu is long and we'd advise you choose the plainer dishes; avoid anything fried as it's invariably greasy.

Tuna fish with white beans (£1.95), Parma ham and melon (£2.45) or one of the home made pasta dishes make safe starters and breast of chicken with butter, parsley and garlic (£3.95) and grilled monkfish (£4.95) are wise main dishes. To follow zabaione (their spelling) is *the* pudding. The menu is very similar to La Nassa.

From £10 a head.

---

## Fontana Amorosa

---

1 Blenheim Terrace, NW8 (328 5014)
St John's Wood tube
Open: 12.30–2.30pm Tuesday–Saturday; 7–11.30pm Monday–Saturday.

This is a large Italian joint just off the busy Abbey Road boasting a spacious, raised pavement patio out front which comes into its own on sunny days. Inside, the restaurant's décor announces its slightly eccentric style – downstairs is a typical, bright Italian tiled-floor bar, while upstairs there's a parquet-floored, oak-beamed dining suite with upholstered chairs and the look of an English tea-room. The menu has its oddities, gushing prose descriptions of each dish included. If you're in an adventurous mood, start with uova alla granchio (eggs with crabmeat), salmone casanova (smoked salmon with sliced avocado), or the squid and prawn salad with a lemon and garlic dressing. Traditionalists can kick off with excellent pasta – fettucine aurora (cream, cheese, tomato sauce) or linguine with a seafood sauce. Main courses continue the off-beat themes, with fegato Marco Polo arriving Venetian style in a wine and onion sauce, while beef is filled with garlic and herbs in tomato sauce (vollatina alla guiseppina) and pancakes Blenheim Terrace are wrapped around a spinach, herb and cheese sauce filling. Scampi come in Pernod while chicken supreme comes in a champagne sauce. An apple mousse flavoured with vanilla (dolcezza di Adamo) and *French* house wine complete the eccentricities, making Fontana Amorosa an ideal value for those light-headed, frivolous summer lunches.

Set lunch £6.50 a head (excl wine); alc about £15 a head.

# Frederick's

Camden Passage, N1 (359 2888)
Angel tube
Open: 12.30–2.30pm and 7.30–11.30pm Monday–Saturday.

In the heart of antique-dealing Islington, Frederick's has established a firm local following, as well as getting regular support from the itinerant international set. The spacious, tastefully-furnished (rich brown colours) premises now extend to an outside patio (available for parties) and a quiet, pretty garden room at the rear, while the restaurant itself is air-conditioned should you fail to bag your seat in the sun. The solidly French menu changes fortnightly, but generally strikes an admirable balance between simplicity and invention, with thoughtful nods to the changing tastes of the public – both vegetarian and 'cuisine minceur' choices are also listed. Here you might find salmon trout baked in foil, with dill, lemon and coriander seeds, or a selection of deep-fried cheeses in light pastry, accompanied by a cucumber and yoghurt salad. A further indication of the restaurant's responsiveness is an excellent value, three-course Saturday lunch designed for starving shoppers – perhaps spaghetti vongole, blanquette de volaille en croûte, tartelette aux pommes. In truth, though, most people come here to fill their expensive boots on the likes of breast of pigeon fried in butter, carré d'agneau in rosemary butter or fresh sole in cream and herb sauce with strips of pancake. Dessert specialities include the smashing biscuit tulips filled with praline ice-cream, coated with caramelised zest and segments of orange – as you sit in the sun munching one of these, you can reflect how far you've come since Clacton sea-front and a '99' . . .

Saturday lunch £6.95 (excl wine); alc about £35 for two.

# The Garden Restaurant

616 Fulham Road, SW6 (736 6056)
Parsons Green tube
Open 12.30–2pm and 7.30–11pm Tuesday to Saturday.

Charles Brodie, who used to run La Poule au Pot and Maggie Jones has turned his hand to another very distinctive venture, called The Garden because it has one (small but 'real'). His intention is to provide an essentially vegetarian menu (free range eggs, poultry, wild game and meat 'not subjected to the horrors of the meat market' are permitted) in an up-market, comfortable setting. The menu changes frequently and is intended to delight vegetarians and prove to their carnivorous friends that a meal without meat can be an entirely painless experience.

Smoked salmon tartlets (cooked to order), spinach and cream cheese puffs, home-made soups and stuffed mushrooms are typical starters and mains are deliciously wholesome: chicken and artichoke pie, spinach loaf with tarragon sauce, nut stuffed canelloni and the dreaded nut rissole look-alike, croquettes of mixed nuts. Sorbets, apple snow, Greek yoghurt, honey and nuts follow. The wine list is short and sophisticated, ranging from a house French at £4, Elderflower £5 to Château-bottled and premier cru wines from £8.95 to £14.55.

Around £10 a head for three courses with wine.

## The Gardens

99 Kensington High Street, W8 (937 7994)
High Street Kensington tube
Open: 12.30–2.30pm daily.

This is probably the best place in London to eat on a summer day – a roof-top restaurant six floors up, stunningly finished in art deco style (flamingo murals, mirror tiles) and spilling out into its own exotic roof garden, complete with trees, lawns and strutting peacocks. The large parapet means you can't actually look down – a good thing in most cases – but the sense of airy freedom and quietness is astonishing. The menu tries to match the spirit of the place – colourful, fashionable and exciting. Start with deep-fried Camembert with gooseberry jam, smoked chicken salad, terrine of duck with green and red peppers, or their own fresh pasta with tomato and basil sauce. Main courses include the reliable calves' liver with onions and juniper berries, brochette of chicken or lamb with peppers and mushrooms, and a short list of choice fish dishes – Dover sole, poached salmon, fillets of lemon sole with ginger and coriander. There's good house wine to accompany these, and though the prices reflect the setting, and the cocktail bar is seductive, they *do* offer an extremely reasonable two course lunch at a fixed price of £5.50. Choosing à la carte, with the height and the air going to your head, well, the prices can go through the roof . . .

Set lunch £11 for two (excl wine); alc about £35 for two.

## Huffs

Chelsea Farmers Market Sydney Street, SW3 (352 5600)
Sloane Square tube
Open: 10am–5pm Monday–Friday; 10am–6pm Saturday; 11am–4pm Sunday.
Also at 28 Chalk Farm Road, NW1 (485 8296) but without al fresco facilities.

To the left of the entrance to the Farmers Market, a rather surprising venture to find in deepest Chelsea, is Huffs, the offspring of the popular Camden Lock wholefoods café. Like all the buildings which comprise this now two-years-old but deemed temporary venture, Huffs is a small wooden hut with seating for only 25. Outside though they have access to tables which can seat up to 100 and it's during the summer that the place comes into its own. Food is cheap, nourishing, home-made and caters equally for meat lovers and vegetarians. Hearty portions of lasagne, chilli and shepherd's pie, cauliflower cheese, salads, home made breads, puddings and pastries cost a maximum of £2 and though not licensed Huffs don't mind if you take your own. Incidentally the Market also features a live trout farm, tinned and bottled meals imported from France, a branch of the wholefoods bulk sales operation Neals Yard Food Co-op and excellent butcher, baker and greengrocer.

Food from £3 a head.

## Julie's Restaurant

135 Portland Road, W11 (229 8331)
Ladbroke Grove tube
Open: 12.30–2.30pm and 7.45–11.15pm Monday–Friday; 7.45–11.15pm Saturday; 12.45–2.15pm and 7.45–10.15pm Sunday.

After negotiating your way through the security door, down the narrow stairs, along a dark corridor with a low ceiling and back up some stairs, it's a relief finally to get through to the rear garden of Julie's Restaurant. With whitewashed walls, lots of potted plants and hanging baskets and an antique spiral staircase to the wine bar above, the courtyard is as quiet and as pretty a spot as you'll find in London on a summer day. Some of the rickety, wrought-iron chairs and tables can be less comforting, but it's still a pleasant venue for a light lunch. The largely English menu is broadly similar to the one in the companion wine bar, but with a few choices beyond the cold buffet. Chilled cream of cucumber soup, chicken with lemon and tarragon, fresh salmon with Hollandaise, grilled calves' liver with avocado, crème brûlée and chocolate mousse would give you a highly agreeable selection for an al fresco meal. There's a strong recommendation too for the house's French rosé wine, which can be a perfect accompaniment despite its unfashionableness. The dark network of alcove rooms that make up the interior are best enjoyed on cold winter nights, and it's worth mentioning that they have one large twenty-seater dining table that can be booked for private parties. It's also worth mentioning that Julie's, both inside and out, has a languidly romantic atmosphere.

About £12 a head.

## Meridiana

169 Fulham Road, SW3 (589 8815)
South Kensington tube
Open: noon–2.45pm and 7–11.45pm daily.

Meridiana has been one of the smartest of venues since it first opened back in the 'swinging sixties', and a goodly part of its attraction, apart from the fashionable Apicella ambiance, has been to do with its delightful first-floor roof terrace, decked with potted palms. Perched up there, you can keep an eye out for the ghosts of the Dave Clark Five in their white open-top E-type as they speed along the Fulham Road. Or you can just enjoy the sun. If you can't get a seat out here (and booking is essential almost all the time) the restaurant's cool interior – cream colours, ceiling fans, Venetian blinds, air-conditioning – is almost as worthwhile. Certainly there should be no problems with the food – a short but varied list of imaginative Italian dishes. The modish carpaccio (steak tartar) and poached sea-bream are there along with favourites like chicken sorpresa, Dover sole, scampi provinciale and calves' liver with bacon. For variety, try the excellent 'paglia e fieno', two different coloured pastas (green and white) laced with cream and Parma ham, or the garlicky linguine alle vongole (with seafood). Different starters include papaya with crab. Specials might include kidneys in white wine sauce. Smart waiters in white tunics strike just the right note between efficiency and informality.

About £20 a head.

## Old Rangoon

201 Castlenau, just over Hammersmith Bridge, SW13 (741 9656)
Hammersmith tube
Open: noon–midnight daily.

It took over a year to convert what was a huge pub into the colonial-style cocktail bar and restaurant it is now. The result is stunning and at night the candlelit restaurant which overlooks the floodlit garden is a lovely spot for a romantic evening. But the highlight of the Old Rangoon is the garden. Leading down from the colonnaded terrace, the large garden has a duck pond, a children's playground at the far end and a discreet video games shed. Benches, marble tables and chairs are arranged about the garden and in the summer tea can be taken (set tea for children £1.50, cream tea £3.50) and lunch hampers (from £3.50 per person), complete with blanket, are also available.

Inside, either drink at the bar (the place still has a full licence) or dine on vast portions of Americanized colonial food such as satay, various barbecued dishes, chicken tikka, burgers and steaks with sundaes, sorbets and ice cream puddings. Aside from cocktails try a jug of Sangria, bucks fizz, cider, Pimms or kir.

From £6 a head for food.

## One Hampstead Lane

Hampstead Lane, N6 (340 4444)
Highgate tube
Open: 12.30–3pm and 7.30–11.30pm Tuesday–Sunday; tea 3.30–5.30pm Sunday.

What was a motorbike showroom has been stupendously transformed (the £300,000 capital injection helped) into a huge restaurant that tries to cater to all types, moods and occasions. There are set meals, late set meals, children's menus, special Saturday and Sunday lunch menus and a live pianist but the speciality is dishes cooked 'au feu de bois' – on a wood fire covered with fresh herbs. This pungent smell, which occasionally wafts into the main dining-room, and the huge and impressive imitation log fire conjure up a rustic mood which takes the edge off the finery of the place. During the summer the upstairs south-facing roof patio is open for al fresco dining and here they operate a far more informal restaurant with help-yourself salads, cold meats, pâtés, cheeses and light desserts. This is the ideal place to recover from a look round pretty Highgate Village or restore the spirits after a peek at the famous cemetery.

Al fresco meals from £5 a head; restaurant proper from £10.

## Le Routier

Commercial Place, Chalk Farm Road, NW1 (485 0360)
Camden Town tube
Open: 12.30–2.30pm and 7–11.45pm daily.

Situated next to the Regents Canal in the heart of Camden Lock, Le Routier has a prize location to offer all Londoners thirsting for that wonderful summer day combination – fresh air and running water. The fact that the canal water often doesn't run but just lies there instead. and that Camden Lock is usually a teeming hell-hole of faded hippies and screaming kids, doesn't seem to deter the people who pack Le Routier and its canal-side patio. Le Routier is in a long, simple wooden building, basically furnished and decorated, but the food has ambitions beyond this. A seasonally-changing menu turns out chunky winter warmers – seafood lasagne, rack of lamb with rosemary, breast of duck with plum sauce – and correspondingly light summer dishes. Avocado, melon and mint or chilled tomato soup with basil, ham and croûtons are apt outdoor starters, while smoked salmon quiche and salad, calves' liver and tarragon butter or lemon sole fillets with cream and avocado have proved to be agreeable lunches. It's not really the sort of place where you can get away with just one course (which summer appetites generally demand) but by choosing simply you can still get a good deal. A half-price menu is offered for those children who haven't fallen in the canal.

About £30 for two.

## Royal Horseguards Hotel

Whitehall Court, SW1 (839 3400)
Embankment tube
Open: 12.30–2.30pm and 6–10.30pm daily.

The times given here are for Granby's, the hotel's formal restaurant, turned out in the style of a gentleman's club – leather furniture, bookshelves etc. It serves a table d'hôte menu of reasonable value (poached salmon, veal escalope) and one or two interesting à la carte specials. For instance, there's a short cuisine minceur section offering sole fillets with cider, and the lightweight salad Lisa, a pâté of avocado and cottage cheese, decorated with prawns, grapefruit and crabmeat on a nest of chicory leaves. The major attraction of Granby's however is the possibility of eating outside on the paved terrace, screened from the Embankment by a tall hedge. This is a pleasant spot, although a little too overshadowed by the undergrowth and the bulk of the hotel to be a true sun-trap. The terrace also extends along to the hotel's lounge, whence a useful, cheaper snack service is operated. During the summer months from 10.30am to dusk the Lounge's Garden Terrace is dotted with umbrella-tables where you can enjoy morning coffee, lunches in the style of club sandwiches, chicken or tuna fish salads or bespoke butties such as smoked salmon pâté or chicken breast. A traditional afternoon tea and cool ice-cream specialities are also served, and if tired Charing Cross-bound commuters nip in through the hedge entrance in Embankment Gardens, they can enjoy a peaceful g&t on the way home.

About £15 a head (restaurant); £6 a head (lounge).

## Salvador's El Bodegon

9 Park Walk, SW10 (352 1330)
Gloucester Road tube
Open: 12.30pm (1pm Sunday)–3pm and 7pm–midnight daily.

Chelsea's garden restaurants are, in the main, designed for sunseeking poseurs, but this modest, friendly little Spanish restaurant has a less sophisticated atmosphere. It's comfortably, even classily furnished – wood panelling, stone fireplace, tiled floor – but it's terrace at the rear is, thankfully, more Benidorm than Marbella. The tiled floor continues outside, and the walled patio, wafted by smells from the adjacent Indian restaurant, is packed with a dozen or so tables. Unless you get there early, the sun may have passed overhead – the garden is east-facing, you see.

Nevertheless, it's a pleasant enough spot in which to enjoy Salvador's rough and ready Spanish food. There's a spectacular array of cold hors d'oeuvres on a central table – crab cocktails, stuffed tomatoes or avocados, spiced mushrooms and sea-food salads – or you may choose the likes of stuffed squid, chilled gazpacho, tender, smoked Serrano ham or grilled sardines from the standing menu.

Main courses continue the solid 'peasant' theme, with a packed zarzuela (sea-food casserole), and heavily sauced (tomatoes, peppers, garlic, onions) dishes of chicken, beef and veal. The pechuga de pollo fundador (chicken breast with garlic and cognac) has been successful, and their paella Valenciana (for two or more) is also highly-rated. Sweets tend to revolve around fresh fruits and crème caramel. Sunday lunches can involve specials like the paella, roast lamb or even whole suckling pig. Generous coffee arrives in cafetières.

About £15 a head.

## South of the Border

8 Joan Street, SE1 (928 6374)
Waterloo tube
Open: noon–2.30pm and 6–11.30pm Monday–Friday; 6–11.30pm Saturday.

South of the Border is an oasis in a desolate maze of eerie streets, almost close enough to the railway line to feature 'Railway Cuttings' somewhere in its address. Inside the large and cleverly converted ex-bed factory you soon forget the dreary location and once you've found the place you are sure to return. Whitewashed walls hung with modern paintings, a farmhouse mood highlighted by bare wooden trimmings, a large bar and a two tier open-plan seating arrangement, tables laid with fresh flowers and the young friendly staff add up to a very pleasant set up.

Now that Paul Tutton has installed Australian John Downton in the kitchens the food has changed from the predictable to the adventurous and is truly international. The menu changes frequently and is augmented by several daily specials and always caters for the vegetarian. Satay (skewers of marinated meat served with a peanutty sauce), a vegetable soup and tempura prawns are typical starters and while everything isn't always perfectly executed, the menu is never boring. Chicken en croûte with a cheese stuffing and lemon sauce, pink roast lamb and Cumberland sausages are all reliably successful, should they be 'on'. Follow with crème brûlée or a pastry confection at which the chef excels. At the first sightings of a decent strong sun, the large, well-camouflaged terrace is laid with five tables and despite rumbles from the trains it's a very pleasant spot.

From £10 a head with wine.

## Spaghetti House

Avenue Chambers, Vernon Place, WC1 (405 5215)
Holborn tube
Open: noon–10.30pm Monday–Thursday; noon–11.20pm Friday and Saturday.

Better known as the Sicilian Avenue Spaghetti House, this member of the always reliable Italian chain takes full advantage of its 'pedestrianised' location during fine weather. The green awnings come down, the tables and chairs are dragged out, and the floral boxes are exhumed from hibernation to produce a little touch of

Rome comfort in darkest Holborn. With the traffic kept at a distance, it's actually possible to eat here without swallowing exhaust fumes, a fringe deficit of so many other al fresco venues in London. While the menu is essentially a reproduction of Spaghetti House standards, one or two items catch the eye – medallions of veal with oranges, sultanas, almonds and marsala, the polpettine (meatballs) with noodles in tomato sauce and the starter/main course spaghetti vongole (clam sauce). Also worthy of note are the tangerine flan and the delicious trifle, zuppa Inglese bamboo (with chocolate and bananas). Excellent capuccino and solid house carafes complete an open air picture that costs a lot less than it looks.

About £20 for two.

## Venus Kebab House

2 Charlotte Street, W1 (636 4324)
Goodge Street tube
Open: noon–3pm and 5.30pm–midnight Monday–Saturday.

The Greek restaurants in and around Charlotte Street are almost a barometer – pass one at 11 o'clock on a cloudy, grey morning, and if they're dragging tables and chairs out onto the pavement, you can guarantee the sun will break through within half an hour. While most of the kebab houses in the area are broadly similar, the Venus gets the vote because it occupies a sunny, open corner (tables curl round into Percy Street) and because its food is of a consistently reliable quality. Service too is always cheerful and efficient, no matter how big the crowds get. Best bets are their kleftiko, a piece of roast lamb the size of a house-brick but much more tender, the grilled red mullet, good kalamares in red wine and the minced lamb kebabs, sheftalia. Best of all though, are the chips – huge, golden and without a trace of oil. Make sure you order a side-plate of them to accompany your meal. Fine sticky pastries and coffee with Greek delight complete a smashing outdoor snack.

About £20 for two.

*Also Good for Open Air Eating:*
Anemos
Bagatelle
Bar du Musée
Bell, The
Bouzy Rouge
Café St Pierre
Chez Solange Wine Bar

Crêperie, The
Crusting Pipe
L'Estanquet
Golders Hill Park Refreshment Bar
House on the Bridge, The
Hungry Horse
Lemonia
Little Italy
Luba's
Obelisk
Old Drapery Stores Restaurant
Old Ship Pub, The
One Legged Goose, The
Picasso, The
Pomme d'Amour, La
Tickell Arms
Tootsies
Tuttons

# 15. When You Want To See and Be Seen

MICHAEL CAINE MASKS

There are many restaurants in fashionable parts of town that are packed out every night *despite* their food. That's not to say that the food is no good, at Langan's Brasserie much of it is downright brilliant, but people flock back time and time again because these places have established themselves as *the* haunt of certain coteries. These places are usually run by stylish maitre d's or have famous owners who often dine in their restaurant and whose friends do likewise. Mario, ex Mario and Franco, packs in the rich Sloanes at his new and pricey Chelsea restaurant Mario; Peter Langan (with partners Michael Caine and ex-Capital Hotel chef Richard Shepherd) turns away celebrities of stage, screen and media if they haven't booked at his Brasserie (*downstairs* is de rigeur) while young and trendy café society head for Zanzibar offspring 192 where chef Alisdair Little prepares stylish and modestly priced French-ish food and aspiring and real aristocrats might catch a glimpse of Patrick Lichfield and his famous pals who want a discreet night out at his basement Chinese restaurant, Tai Pan.

## Apicella 81

4 Mill Street, W1 (499 1308)
Oxford Circus tube
Open: noon–3pm Monday–Friday; 7pm–midnight Monday–Saturday.

As the name suggests, Apicella 81 is almost in danger of becoming out of date. Certainly, you're now less likely to see stars here than in the perennially fashionable Langan's Brasserie, and the evenings can be a lonely experience despite the excellent pianist. So settle instead for packed lunchtimes (booking essential) and glimpses of the powers behind the media thrones – agents, PR people and record producers, with the occasional journalist from nearby 'Vogue'. Sightings or not, you'll enjoy the white-walled, contemporary art-gallery décor and the imaginative Italian menu which changes with the seasons. The prosciutto (Parma or San Daniele) is reckoned the best in town, while grilled sea-bass or maecheroni Siciliana (with olives, capers, aubergines, tomatoes) have also scored highly. Service, already good, improves even further if you're carrying an Italian sports paper and know more about Enzo Bearzot than you do about Enzo Apicélla.

About £40 for two.

## Bombay Brasserie

Bailey's Hotel, Courtfield Close, SW7 (370 4040)
Open: 12.30–3pm and 7–11.30pm daily.

Great mystery and talk of astral planes surrounded the opening of this stunning and elegantly-done spacious, Raj-style restaurant but the place has been a huge success from the word go. The restaurant, at the back of the hotel, is beautifully designed; the tall windows are hung with louvred blinds, there are large photos and paintings of India and Indians and the room is most attractively lit with pretty oil lamps which give off a soft light. The delicious food is from the Bombay region, featuring many Parsee and Goan dishes. Fashionable in the evening, it is a very nice place to visit for lunch when they serve a hot buffet from a central table. Pig yourself at leisure; you can keep going back for a fresh load and new plate.

Set meal £7.50; alc £12–£15 a head with wine.

## Le Caprice

Arlington House, Arlington Street (just behind the Ritz), SW1 (629 2239)
Green Park/Piccadilly tube
Open: 12.30–2.30pm and 7pm–midnight Monday to Friday; 7pm–midnight
Saturday; noon–3pm Sunday.

Le Caprice is one of the few restaurants in this book to be reviewed twice. While it deserves special attention for its Sunday brunch it also ranks amongst London's most fashionable restaurants and this section would be incomplete without it. Nothing is too much trouble for the charming duo Christopher Corbin and Jeremy King who run this stylish haunt of anyone who's anyone in the worlds of media, stage and screen. It's starkly decorated in black and white with shiny chrome, deco light fittings and stunning black and white photos from Bailey's folio of sixties heroes, and the tables are sufficiently well spaced to preclude diplomatic seating plans. The short menu has been refined and now only includes the dishes which have proved popular with their faddy clientele. Hotly tipped by us are the Chavignol with walnut and frisee salad; ready prepared steak tartar which is served with a generous mound of perfect pommes allumettes or their steak. Follow with Marquise au chocolat, sorbets or Grand Marnier soufflé. Their house Italian is a modest £4.50 but their short wine list caters for all moods and pockets.

From £10 a head.

## Cecconis

5A Burlington Gardens, W1 (434 1500)
Green Park tube
Open: 12.15–2.30pm and 7.15–11pm Monday–Friday; 7.15–11pm Saturday.

Run by the ex-manager of one of Venice's most fashionable hotels (the Cipriani), Cecconis is a dignified, genteel sort of place which looks more like an Arab bank from the outside. Inside its gentility smacks of Money; bankers plan takeovers, businessmen talk money, famous American actors preen and ladies with all-the-year-round suntans show their girlfriends their latest find from Aspreys. Service is discretion personified, which is one of the reasons why the rich and famous favour the place.

The smartly presented menu is very expensive and the food, with a few exceptions, not worth it. The home-made pasta dishes are the choice and what most people who've been here before order. Tagglioline verdi gratinati – thin strips of green pasta with bacon, cream and cheese is one of the most popular. Desserts are yummy; delicious light crispy pastry stuffed with fruit and cream or potent zabaglione are highly recommended. There are a couple of wines under £5 but the short list of French and Italian wines is in the serious department.

From £25 a head; it is possible to dine for less but easier to do it for more.

## Eleven Park Walk

11 Park Walk, SW10 (352 3449/8249)
South Kensington tube
Open: 12.30–3pm and 7pm–midnight Monday–Saturday.

Behind a cream slab of wall, a natty little canopy and tall plants guarding the door is this elegant Italian restaurant that spawned Nova Park (recently re-opened as the Covent Garden Pasta Company) in Covent Garden. Drinks are taken upstairs while dining is done in the cream downstairs room made extra fashionable by David Litchfield and his team from Ritz, whose offices are just down the road. By Italian standards the menu is short and certain dishes are superbly executed; particularly the starters crepelle di quattro formaggi (£3.30), pancakes filled with four different cheeses; home-made fettuccine with smoked salmon and cream (£3.50); crudités with a bagna cauda dip (£2.80). Main dishes tend to be vastly over-priced and the best are carpaccio (£6.50) and king prawns with rice (£8). Desserts are worth keeping room for and like the starters are good value; meringues with Grand Marnier (£1.80), chestnuts and cream (£2) and stuffed crêpes (£1.80). House wine is Italian bottled and £5.

From £10 a head.

## L'Escargot

48 Greek Street, W1 (437 2679)
Leicester Square tube
Open: 12.15–2.30pm Monday–Friday; 6.30–11.15pm Monday–Saturday.

Re-opened a couple of years ago by a young team with their fingers on the pulse of London catering, L'Escargot quickly won support. Its combination of bar, brasserie and restaurant (and private rooms) all splendidly spacious and comfortable, offered a comprehensive service. Topping this off were two menus (the cheaper one for the brasserie) boasting a combination of familiar English dishes with inventive, modern French creations. The picture was completed by the signing of the charming Elena from Bianchi's to act as maîtresse d'hôtel. Before long, the literary and journalistic set followed her and have remained faithful since, despite minor ups and downs in the kitchens – over-flashy elements which frequently delivered less than they promised.

Eye-catching dishes remain – calves' liver with red onion marmalade, Dover sole with oranges and capers, veal fillets in madeira sauce, hazelnut pie with mango coulis – but they generally work rather than just look good on the plate. The seafood specials offered daily are also very successful – perhaps halibut with sorrel sauce in the restaurant, or trout with dill butter in the brasserie. Good salads (avocado, melon, cucumber), a strong selection of fruity Californian wines and a regular parade of faces from the dust-jackets of books are the other noticeable elements in a well-run operation.

About £25 for two (brasserie); £35 for two (restaurant).

## La Fontana

101 Pimlico Road, SW1 (730 6630)
Sloane Square tube
Open: noon–2.30pm and 7–11.30pm daily.

More than a few bob has been spent on this place in recent years as it's continued to move up-market. Fronted by miniature ferns and a lush window-box, La Fontana now has an interior to match – red upholstered benches, discreet lighting, paintings, neat white linen with contrasting blood-red napkins – and the dramatically stylish menu della settimana (weekly menu) has attracted top newspaper editors, arts moguls and, allegedly, a young female royal who's not supposed to eat very much.

If She has been here, She will have undoubtedly enjoyed such un-Italian items as terrine of venison, casserole of pheasant and delicious pot roasted lamb with flageolets. Even the more familiar Italian section boasts its own home-made tagliatelle (a sure sign of fashionableness), baked zucchini filled with spinach and cheese and tripe stewed in red wine with butter beans and herbs. La Fontana's ennoblement is confirmed by the offer of fresh truffles from Piedmont. Despite the rise in status, the staff remain both informal and cheerful. Puddings can range successfully across Europe from zabaglione to chocolate mousse via Mont Blanc. The only off note is provided by the slightly garish neon-sign that's been added to the restaurant's otherwise tasteful frontage – but then La Fontana is obviously determined to get noticed.

About £40 for two.

# Jamie's Wine Bar

Pelham Street, SW7 (584 4788)
South Kensington tube
Open: pub hours (upstairs); 12.30–2.30pm and 7.30–11.30pm downstairs
Monday–Friday.

Opened by Jamie Robertson, who used to co-own the once hugely-fashionable Chelsea-set haunt Monkeys (still going strong in Chelsea Green), this wine bar has quickly established itself as an in-spot for the area's Carolines and Henrys. It's actually a bit of a male stronghold and the small downstairs restaurant with its L-shaped gallery and refectory table has the atmosphere of noisy school dinners and an imminent bun fight. Upstairs looks more like a drinking club than a wine bar with its wood panelling, the day's qualities and comfy sofas. Bar sandwiches are available here but downstairs the food is prepared by a (probably) cordon blue gel and the food comes in substantial portions and though the menu changes frequently, it's based on good old English stalwarts such as kedgeree, vegetable soups, pies, hot pots, game in season and cold meats. The standard is very high and prices modest. For example soups average £1.50, potted shrimps £1.75 and main dishes £4.50. The ex-Mortons barman shakes a mean cocktail (the place has a full licence) and the wine list is wide-ranging.

From £5 a head for food.

# Joe Allen

13 Exeter Street, WC2 (836 0651)
Covent Garden tube
Open: noon–1am Monday–Saturday; noon–midnight Sunday.

'Prima donnas by the barrow load' is one regular's description of the clientele at the very theatrical basement replica of the famous New York branch. Waiters too are necessarily brusque to cope with their essentially famous (or would-be famous) clientele and aspiring trendies from the worlds of advertising and journalism. The formula is a long cocktail bar (where you can eat), dim lighting, red gingham clothed tables just far enough apart for privacy, bare brick walls covered with theatrical posters and a huge chalked-up menu. Booking is essential for both lunch and dinner and pre-theatre diners be warned; a two-hour limit is put on all meals before 9.45pm. Food is not the main attraction and regulars opt for the daily freshly-made soups, burgers (which aren't on the menu), liver and onion, chopped steak and similar plain dishes. Their salads are exceptional, vast and served in wooden bowls a foot in diameter.

Hot brownies, pecan pie and similar US stodge follow. All manner of cocktails, house wine just under a fiver and excellent rioja £5.80. There are no set meals but the occasional celebratory dinners such as Thanksgiving and Independence Day.

From £6 a head.

## Langan's Brasserie

Stratton Street, W1 (493 6437)
Piccadilly Circus/Green Park tube
Open: 12.30–2.30pm and 7–11.30pm Monday–Friday; 8pm–midnight Saturday.

Peter Langan, Michael Caine and chef Richard (ex-Capital Hotel) Shepherd have firmly established Langan's, now in its ninth year, as the hub of café society. Previously the Edwardian Le Coq d'Or, the large and elegant premises is the haunt of media fashionables and the stylish place (be sure to book a table *downstairs*; upstairs is ideal for intimate or private occasions) is a delightful and comfortable place to dine. Drink in the plush bar first and take in the scene; mirrors, photos and contemporary art cover just about every inch of space on the wall, ceiling fans whirl, adept waiters rush about and the constant buzz of conversation belies the need for background music although there is a live turn late most evenings.

The menu is dauntingly long (written over a Hockney pencil colouring of the dynamic threesome) but the place is run as a brasserie and it's not necessary (though tempting) to get into an arm and a leg situation. The light dishes such as Shepherd's famous spinach soufflé with anchovy sauce and frisée au lardons – an endive salad with crispy bacon, croûtons, thin mayonnaise dressing and coddled egg, and poached egg with smoked haddock are reliably excellent, so too are the plain fish dishes and the puddings almost without exception (the rice pudding is one) are superb. Try the crème brûlée, profiteroles with chocolate sauce or fresh fruit salad. The house white is very fair and better than several more expensive whites on the list; £5. There are plans to re-do the back bar and open up for after-theatre snacks and drinks from 11pm.

Food from £10 a head.

## L'Olivier

116 Finborough Road, SW10 (370 4199)
South Kensington/Earls Court tube
Open: 8–11.30pm Tuesday–Sunday.

After the fashionable success of his French fish restaurant chain (La Croisette, Le Suquet and Le Quai St Pierre) Pierre Martin has given his special treatment to a meat restaurant. As at the fish restaurants, the formula is simple. There is a small bar/reception area at street level, but the restaurant is an L-shaped basement prettily decorated in navy blue and white with stylish Provençal print table-cloths and carpet and wood-panelled walls decorated with attractive flowery prints.

The main highlight of the menu is the roast meats, served as a joint and carved with panache at a central carving table. The set meal costs £16 and is a gargantuan feast which starts with a large platter of mixed hors d'oeuvres, followed by a plate of saucisson, a succession of vegetables farcis, a spicy soup and then your choice from les rôtis. *The* dish is gigot d'agneau, cooked to order and served with a side plate of vegetables. A huge salad and then cheese (from an outstanding board of French cheeses all in tip top condition), a dessert and coffee are also included. The alc features some of their wonderful fish dishes including the notable fish soup and bouillabaisse as a main dish. The set meal at £16 is only really worth it if you have a large appetite; a starter, rôti, salad, cheese and dessert is more manageable and will average £12 a head. Wines from £6 or try their pichet (enough for two glasses) at £2. Booking is essential.

Set meal from £16; à la carte from £12 a head.

## Mario's

260–262A Brompton Road, SW3 (584 1724)
South Kensington tube
Open: noon–3pm and 7pm–midnight (last orders 11.30pm).

Mario, of Mario and Franco fame, has forsaken his retirement and proved (despite everything) that he can still pull the fashionable crowd just like he did in his heyday. The large, dimly lit dining room is stylishly done with smoked windows (which slide open on hot days) and black venetian blinds, with brilliant white walls hung with an assortment of very colourful and peculiar modern art, and the tables are prettily dressed in cream with blue napkins. Unfortunately the service and the food don't match the beautiful room but that doesn't seem to stop the rich and fashionable crowd filling the place nightly. The menu is short but we are hard pushed to recommend anything. Cream of mussel soup with saffron and the unruinable bresaola with an oil and lemon dressing are better bets than the home-made pasta dishes. The dessert trolley is a disgrace and amazingly for an Italian restaurant there's no zabaglione. The cheeseboard too is an afterthought and cheeses are presented wrapped in sweating cling film. What one has to put up with to be fashionable.

From £15 a head; house wine £5.50.

## Maxim's de Paris

32 Panton Street, SW1 (839 4809)
Leicester Square tube
Open: 12.30–3pm Monday–Friday; 6.30–11.45pm (last orders) Monday–Saturday, but remains open far later.

Last June Pierre Cardin and the Kennedy Brookes chain brought the famous Parisian Maxim's to London. Modelled on its 1893-opened parent, the new Maxim's is a lavish replica intended to become the hub of London's high society. Dressing for the occasion is de rigeur; at lunch collar and tie, at dinner dress clothes. Door-men greet you and whisk away your coat (a service they'll extend to your car with prior notice – the restaurant has its own garage and can even lay on a Rolls) and you are then ushered into an enormous reception room which leads off the main dining room where up to 200 can dine without feeling squashed. A discreet string quartet sets the scene for romantic dancing, and service is suitably accomplished. Upstairs there are a series of sumptuously decorated rooms for private parties and a champagne bar. A select few are being invited to join Maxim's Club and will have access to the champagne bar and substantially cheaper set meals. The food is of course French and de haute qualité. 25 chefs led by Christian-Paul Moury prepare a nouvelle-influenced menu with plat du jour, seasonal specials like oysters and international favourites Russian caviar and finest smoked salmon. Naturally a night out here is piggy bank time; managing director Laurence Isaacson quotes a figure of £70 for two just over a year ago.

## Melange

59 Endell Street, WC2 (240 8077)
Covent Garden tube
Open: noon–2.30pm and 5.30–11.30pm Monday–Friday; Saturday dinner only.

Fashionable with art students and young trendies who come to Endell Street to visit the next door PX and nearby Detail, Melange is an ambitious venture undertaken with zeal and energy by its young owners. Done out modishly (but on the cheap) with a fifties-inspired look, the odd obligatory half pillar, dragged walls and fabric and rope false ceilings, the room is a surprisingly relaxed place, and is intended to be a venue for snacks downstairs and more formal meals upstairs. The food is interesting and imaginative and while not always successful obviously comes from an inspired young (only 22) chef. And it's cheap.

There are perfect light lunch dishes such as home-made noodles with bacon and leeks in a cream sauce (£1.20), feuilleté of brocolli with a hollandaise sauce (£1.20) and bangers and mash (£2.80) which is a little too nouvelle (ie mean) on the mash, though more is available on request. Main dishes are both plain (grilled steak and french fries) and imaginative, such as noisettes of lamb with slivers of crab and slices of chicken in a mint and honey sauce with mango. Equally adventurous puddings include pears cooked in a paper parcel with raspberry liqueur. Wines come by the carafe at £2.50 or by the bottle at £4.

## Ménage à Trois

15 Beauchamp Place, SW3 (584 9350)
South Kensington tube
Open: 11.30am–2.30pm and 5.30pm–12.15am daily.

As soon as it opened, Ménage à Trois quickly became the haunt of what one might call London's 'jeunesse hoorée' – alternatively known as Sloane Rangers, Nigels or upper class twits. The particular reason for its fashionableness – apart from a Beauchamp Place location – was the style of menu offered by chef-patron Anthony Worrall-Thompson, described in the words of their own publicity as 'just starters and puddings, no intercourse'. The weight-conscious Carolines and Vanessas of SW3 (not to mention Diana of SW1), flocked here to nibble these delicately-proportioned morsels derived from 'nouvelle cuisine' but now rechristened 'cuisine éclectique'. While there's no denying the prettiness of the food – nor indeed the prettiness of the cramped basement rooms (an indoor garden effect with tiled floor, white brick-work, stripped pine, mirrors and potted plants), eating here can be less impressive than the publicity suggests. The three hot, cheesy pastry parcels, for example, will tickle the tastebuds with their imaginative flavours – Camembert and cranberry, Roquefort and leek, boursin and spinach – but you'll finish the plate asking for another bread roll. Similarly the fillet of Welsh lamb, suggesting strapping hunks of meat, in fact comprises four 50p piece sized slices fanned around a scallop mousse and a purée of leeks – five tiny mangetouts accompany this, but no roast potatoes.

If you can adapt to this fiddly style, and don't mind paying for artistry rather than quantity, you should enjoy the likes of chicken breast stuffed with asparagus, with a chive butter sauce and lemon-scented florets of broccoli, cream soup of mussels, saffron and baby vegetables, baked pig's trotter en croûte, assorted French salads (pigeon breast and wild mushrooms) and puddings such as fromage

216

blanc with kiwi fruit and raspberry sauce. Whether you'll like the people or not is another matter – in truth, there generally seems to be an older, straighter crowd now, but still, from the darker alcoves and corners, you'll hear the hoots and brays of the Ménagerie du Ménage à Trois.

About £18 a head.

## Odette's

130 Regent's Park Road, NW1 (586 8766)
Chalk Farm tube
Open: 12.30–2.15pm Monday–Friday; 7.30–10.15pm Monday–Saturday.

Tucked away in a desirable enclave off Primrose Hill, Odette's is still sufficiently close to town and to Hampstead to draw a media crowd, albeit more self-effacing than the one at Langan's. The customers here might be described as lower-profile stars – radio broadcasters, painters and photographers (whose work adorns the walls) and writers – but there's still a sly, intensive array of mirrors so nobody can pass unnoticed, at least not in the gloomy main dining-room. The white-walled, sky-lit room at the rear is actually more pleasant to be in, but until they lay on periscopes, you won't get *seen* there. Odette's menu is knowingly fashionable but generally delivers the flavours promised by its avant-garde combinations. Braised duck with turnips and port, game pâté with madeira jelly, freshwater shrimps with Indian spices and the delicious banana brûlée have all featured regularly. And just to remind the rich and the famous of the times when they weren't, there's always the likes of carrot soup, vegetarian moussaka and rice pudding to be had. A cosy basement wine bar also deals in this less exalted fodder, and has a furtively sexy atmosphere.

About £30 for two (restaurant); £18 for two (wine bar).

##  192

192 Kensington Park Road, W11 (229 0482)
Ladbroke Grove tube
Open: 12.30–2.30pm and 7.30–11.30pm (booked last orders).

Offspring of the fashionable Covent Garden membership-only watering hole the Zanzibar, this place was originally conceived purely as a wine bar. However when the downstairs room fell vacant and chef Alisdair Little (ex-L'Escargot and of his own Simpsons) became free at the same moment, owner Tony Macintosh threw in his chips and opened the tiny basement as a restaurant (or as Alisdair prefers, café).

217

Modishly designed by architect Michael Chassey, the bar is presided over by partner Ben Wordsworth and is a fashionable drop-in spot for young trendies and café society. Downstairs Alisdair runs his tiny kitchen as if he were continually cooking for a private dinner party; which he almost is, there are only eight tables. He changes his menu twice a day, is choosy about his ingredients (meat comes from the Roux Lamartine in Ebury Street, the fish from the back of an ice-packed van which imports daily from France and the veg is fresh daily). Alisdair is a very talented and dedicated chef and his food is always imaginative, delicious and, though influenced by nouvelle cuisine, remains distinctive. The place is run on a no-extras basis – no cover, no automatic tip, vegetables included, no VAT – and this coupled with a very reasonable drinks list results in a very keenly-priced meal for which you'd happily pay double. You can snack or eat one course upstairs; a three course meal for two with wine will see change from £25. Chef Little will be well worth following if he goes ahead with plans to open his own restaurant in Soho.

From £8 a head.

## San Lorenzo

22 Beauchamp Place SW3 (584 1074)
Knightsbridge tube
Open: 12.30–3pm and 8–11.30pm Monday–Saturday.

The entrance is deceptive to this, one of London's most consistently fashionable restaurants which opened in the swinging sixties. Maybe it's been superseded by Langan's Brasserie and Le Caprice, but you can still reckon on meeting the eyes or catching a glimpse of the glitterati. Joan Collins apparently loves it. The decoration is quite bizarre and most unexpected. It's very dark and comprises a series of rooms stunningly decorated with wicker screens, tall frondy plants, bamboo furniture, candle light and an eclectic mix of modern graphics and huge Balinese paintings, all of which add up to a sort of sub-tropical bohemia. Waiters are handsome and bored-looking and aren't overly friendly unless you have stardust in your hair. The menu is short, is essentially Italian with Anglicised touches and is expensive. There are unexpectedly naff touches like individually wrapped butter and stale rolls but their crudités with a very warm bagna cauda and fresh pasta (fettuccine al pesto in particular) are reliably good. The wine list is exclusively Italian and, unless you're familiar with your Barolos and Frascatis, leaves you at the mercy of the waiters.

From £10 a head for food; £15 is more realistic.

## Signor Baffi

195 Shenley Road, Borehamwood (953 8404)
Elstree BR–St Pancras
Open: noon–3pm and 7–11pm Monday–Friday; 7–11.30pm Saturday.

Question: Why should an ordinary-looking Italian restaurant in a suburban London shopping parade be a place in which to see and be seen? Answer: Because Signor Baffi's just happens to lie between EMI's Elstree Film Studios and the BBC's new production base (formerly Central TV). The line-up of autographed photos on Signor Baffi's walls reflects the different faces of the entertainment world who've dined there – Sophia Loren and John Wayne rub shoulders with Cilla Black and Jimmy Tarbuck. It's a place then that feeds stars, writers and film moguls, as well as middle-management from the local trading estate. The familiar Italian menu is therefore geared to accommodate these exotic beings with Châteaubriand, fresh lobster, Scotch salmon, pheasant and even asparagus flown in specially from sunny California. For the less well-heeled, there's the usual range of escalopes, pastas and chicken dishes, all excellently cooked, as well as a bespoke blackboard list of daily fish specials which might include fried halibut or a Mediterranean sea-food salad. Other notables include roast crown of spring lamb (for two persons, or one Orson Welles) and a delicious filleto all Quercia (cooked between oak boards and flared with brandy). The premises are tastefully, but not extravagantly, furnished and there are one or two tables in corners for shy superstars to hide in.

About £30 for two.

## Tai Pan

8 Egerton Garden Mews, SW3 (589 8287)
Knightsbridge tube
Open: noon–2.30pm and 7–11.30pm daily.

Stylish basement restaurant part-owned by aristocratic Patrick Lichfield, tastefully decorated colonial-style with ceiling fans and huge and stunning photos of latterday China. It attracts reclusive stars of the George Harrison/Catherine Deneuve type. Service is formal and efficient but most of the waiters are young and friendly so it's in no way intimidating. The food is a mixture of the spicy and hot Szechuan and Hunan (noted for its peppery, dry sautéd, Ganshow and seaspice dishes) and the menu is clear and explicit. There's generally a lunch special for under £5 a head but choosing à la carte reckon on spending from £15 a head. Best value and ideal for first timers is their six-course (plus rice and dessert) feast at

£12.50 a head, but à la carte choices should include bang-bang chicken with cucumber in hot sesame sauce, Tigers' whiskers and whole Ganshow steamed fish which are all particularly good. Drink sake, big, full-blooded cocktails or house wine at £5.25.

From £15 a head for food.

*Also Good for Seeing and Being Seen:*
Barca, La
Blake's Hotel
Camden Brasserie
Gardens, The
Keats
Leonardo's
Meridiana
Nineteen
Pier 31
Soho Brasserie

## 16. When You Want To Get Healthy

Hungover? Overweight? Ready for a purge? We offer a selection of restaurants that take the nut rissole and limp lettuce out of healthy eating. Find out that vegetables can be cooked imaginatively, presented attractively and taste good at proven vegetarian restaurants Manna and Food For Thought or notice that you haven't noticed there's no meat in the delicious spicy Indian food at The Sharuna and Diwana Bhel Poori House. Eat healthy fish informally at Grimes in trendy Covent Garden, get dressed up for it at stylish Le Suquet in South Kensington or try it more interestingly raw, deep fried (tempura) or spiced at Japanese Ajimura. If you really want to pamper yourself, try a cuisine minceur (French gourmet slimmers food) at Capability Brown in West Hampstead or Frederick's at the Angel.

# Ajimura

51 Shelton Street, WC2 (240 0178)
Covent Garden tube
Open: noon–3pm and 6–1pm Monday–Saturday.

Behind a profusion of plants which totally obscure the window, the lively and informal Ajimura has more the ambiance of a left bank café than the austerity usually associated with Japanese restaurants. The tables and seats are refectory-like, lighting is from faded paper lanterns and a rather rude animal frieze runs round the room. The staff, both Japanese and English, are young, and the place attracts an essentially young bohemian clientele. The menu is long but well explained and there is no pressure to eat a full meal. Take a snack at the tempura/sushi bar or try either dish in the main part of the restaurant. Aside from the traditional tempura (fish and vegetables coated in a very light batter and deep fried for a couple of minutes) and sashimi (an arresting display of finely sliced raw fish served with pungent and very hot green mustard) there are several set meals and dishes of the day. This is one of the few Japanese restaurants in town where you won't come out hungry and with a light wallet or a second mortgage. A nice detail is that you will be offered a selection of sake cups and you choose the one that appeals the most.

Set meal £5; à la carte from £8 a head; dishes of the day £3.

# Aykoku-Kaku

9 Walbrook, EC4 (236 9020)
Bank tube
Open: noon–2.30pm and 6–9.30pm Monday–Friday.

City gents blanching at the prospect of another three-hour assault course on sauté potatoes, steak pudding and sherry trifle might do well to emulate their Japanese banking colleagues and head here for lunch. Situated in a large, brightly-lit, pine-furnished basement beneath Bucklersbury House, the Aykoku-Kaku is almost an office canteen for the Nipponese banking fraternity – the prompt, regimented departure of one shift of workers to be replaced by the next one moments later is a wonder to behold. Further cultural shocks for Brits are in store, with the offer of a light nutritious and well-balanced Japanese lunch – no falling asleep at the desk for them. Complete set meals are served on wooden, airline-style trays, with a traditional main course accompanied by appetiser, soup, rice, green vegetables, tea and fresh fruit. Main dishes might include fish, both raw (sashimi) and deep-fried (sakana kara-age), yakitori (chicken and vegetable pieces with sauce) sukiyaki (lean beef fillet strips) or the exquisite tempura prawns in lightweight batter. If you can't restrict yourself to this refreshingly frugal fare, you can always head for the likes of kushikatsu (deep-fried, bread-crumbed pork with onions on a skewer), the potent tokkurai (flasks) of sake or the cans of imported Suntory beer.

Set meals £8–£12; alc about £15 a head.

## Capability Brown

351 West End Lane, NW6 (794 3234)
West Hampstead tube
Open: noon–2pm and 7–11.30pm Monday–Saturday.

If you're on a diet or just on the culinary wagon for a day or so, it's still difficult to resist the temptation of a full meal. The pretty, plant-festooned Capability Brown solves this problem by offering beautifully-cooked, adventurous food which is nevertheless lightly sauced and sensibly proportioned. Inspired by a combination of 'cuisine minceur' (literally cooking for slimness) and 'nouvelle cuisine' (emphasis on presentation and invention), the menu offers dishes of striking combinations, decoratively served and which will leave you feeling well-fed as opposed to well-stuffed. Thus, while carré d'agneau en croûte might be unthinkable to a slimmer dining elsewhere, here it's served in the most delicate of pastry cases, surrounded by a thin but delicious sage sauce. Among the starters, the mousse of duck liver with green peppercorns is so light you can hardly feel it on your tongue, and while the artichoke pastorale, incorporating a cheese soufflé, might not be to everybody's taste, there's no denying its subtlety. Some of the combinations do sound a bit over the top – venison with bananas, duck with lychees and ginger – but the invention generally seems to keep pace with the kitchen's ability. The only minor snags are the occasionally over-long waits between courses and the fact that, unless you're on their excellent three-course prix fixe menu (£7.95 lunch, £8.95 dinner) you'll leave with your wallet feeling as light as your stomach.

About £50 for two.

## La Corée

56 St Giles High Street, WC2 (836 7235)
Tottenham Court Road tube
Open: noon–3pm and 6–11pm Monday–Saturday.

For those who find Japanese food light and nourishing, a dip into Korean cuisine may prove equally rewarding. Most of their dishes are broiled or grilled and accompanied by light but spicy sauces, all of which leaves you feeling well-fed but not over-blown. Indeed the spicing may make it more attractive to Western palates than the plainer Japanese food. La Corée is a good place to have a try anyway – friendly, helpful staff, pleasant surroundings and a range of set meals to act as an introduction. Korean appetisers are particularly agreeable with the koo-jeul pan, offering nine varieties, a meal in itself. Try delicious dumplings (goone man-doo), pa jeon (beef and oyster with spring onion) or gaesal jeon (crab and vegetable fishcakes). The simple-sounding main courses (eg bulgogi jungshik-fried beef) arrive with so many dishes of accompanying savouries, soups and vegetables, you'll feel you're having a feast. So if you order Chinese-style, you may wind up breaking the table. For drink, try delicious warm sake, or the highly potent rice wine so-joo.

Set meals £8–£12 per person; alc about £20 for two.

## Diwana Bhel Poori House

121 Drummond Street, NW1 (387 5556)
Euston tube
Open: noon–11pm Tuesday–Sunday.
Also at 50 Westbourne Grove, W2 (221 0721)
Bayswater tube
Open: noon–3pm and 6–11pm Tuesday–Sunday.

The spicy South Indian food served at these small, functional and brightly lit bistro-style restaurants is so tasty that we doubt you'll notice it includes no meat. In India the Bhel Poori House is the place for a snack and that is exactly what you'll find here – a series of tasty snack meals. The panni poori – hollow round whole wheat wafers which you crack and add chick peas and spicy sauce – is the most spectacular dish while the dosas – a thin buckwheat pancake stuffed with curried potatoes and onions and samosas (triangular pastries) served with a tomato sauce are the most popular. Everything is very cheap but best value is had from the Thali – a set meal served on a stainless steel tray and likely to include dal, rice, vegetables, a savoury dish and chapati or pooris. The Diwana is not licensed but they don't mind you taking your own. Some people though go purely for their yoghurt-based drink, lassi.

From £3.

## East West Restaurant

188 Old Street, EC1 (251 4076)
Old Street tube
Open: 9am–9.30pm Monday–Friday; 9am–3.30pm Saturday.

Run by the Community Health Foundation, who operate various

worthy and healthy (for mind and body) courses, East West specializes in macrobiotic and wholefood meals and snacks in a peaceful
and friendly atmosphere. There is a definite Japanese influence to
the food here and stir-fried vegetables, tempura, miso-based soups
and wholesome stews are light and tasty. Everything is made on the
premises and tea, coffee, fruit juices and sugar and dairy-free
desserts are available all day. The food and the atmosphere are the
ultimate in mind and body cleansing despite the fact that you will be
offered alcohol; they are licensed to sell wine and beers. The dining
room is a pleasant space which has a twinge of the school room
about it. At lunch they serve an amazing value set meal for under
£2.50.

From £3 for a full meal.

## Food For Thought

31 Neal Street, WC2 (836 0239)
Covent Garden tube
Open: noon–8pm Monday–Friday.

Most restaurants posing as health food places are as guilty as
anywhere of using lashings of sugar and refined flour, and serving
food so overcooked that texture, flavour and goodness are gone.
This place is an exception and manages to make healthy food not
only palatable but tasty. The small restaurant, despite its very
cramped seating for 50, is *the* place for take-away and rare is the day
that there is no queue outside between noon and 1.45pm. Now in its
tenth year, Food For Thought has a definite policy for its food. They
bake all their own bread and pastries, use fresh ingredients and aim
to serve food that's appealing to the eye and palate and makes no
great hole in the pocket. Everything is prepared by hand and the
daily-changing menu always includes four hot savoury dishes, usually their famous stir-fried vegetables (cooked fresh every 20 minutes)
extremely innovative salads, fruit salads, proper puddings like
crumble and a range of rich but healthy cakes. Takeaways are
packed in heat-retaining pots, portions are extremely generous and
average £1. Not licensed. Tea and home-made cakes are served
each afternoon.

## Govinda's Vegetarian Restaurant

9–10 Soho Street, W1 (437 1835)
Tottenham Court Road tube
Open: 9am–9pm Monday–Saturday.

Bouts of excess frequently bring on spiritual as well as physical
self-examination, so it's as well to know that this brightly-furnished,

self-service vegetarian restaurant is operated by members of the Radha Krishna Temple. You're not exactly lectured on your previous debauchery, but there are well-meaning booklets hanging around and a general air of 'we're here if you need us, sinner'. Still, when they're not wandering up and down Oxford Street knocking seven ages of man out of their tambourines, the Temple members provide a nifty line in nourishment. Apart from a good range of salads, pastries and non-alcoholic drinks, there's a short list of hot dishes to warm the stomach as well as the soul. These may include a wholemeal pizza, spinach pie, stuffed peppers, soup jardinière or the appetising bean-pot, and if you don't find these filling enough, there are always jacket potatoes. Finish off with fresh fruit, flans or carrot cake and a relaxing cup of herbal tea. The functional pine furniture unfortunately, makes it no place to linger – perhaps that's why they're always on the move?

About £8 for two.

## Green and Pleasant

Covent Garden General Store, Long Acre, WC2 (240 7781)
Covent Garden tube
Open: 10am–midnight daily.

In part of the vast basement of the gift shop, Green and Pleasant is both those things; it claims to bring back fresh fruit and veg to the market and is a pleasant enough place to be. Queue to serve yourself from the impressive salad bar and wide choice of bits (bacon, cheese) or be less health conscious and opt for one of the microwaved hot dishes – pasta, chilli, quiche, pitta sandwich, crêpe or soup. Finish with fresh fruit, American apple pie, fudge cake or frozen yoghurt. Seating is in rather upright banquettes and the colour scheme is green and white. House wine £3.95 carafe.

From £5 for food.

## Grimes

6 Garrick Street, WC2 (836 7008)
Covent Garden tube
Open noon–3pm and 5.30–11.30pm Tuesday–Saturday.

Grimes is a stylish place to eat healthily. Their idea is to serve sparklingly fresh produce and as it's slightly off-putting subtitle 'The Cold Fish Café' suggests, the produce on offer is mainly from the sea and mostly cold. Oysters, shrimps, potted prawns, smoked salmon and gravad lax (marinated raw salmon), crab salad with home-made mayonnaise, cold poached fish platter and hot dishes like sea bass

226

with beurre blanc and monkfish with tomato concassée are typical. There are a few meat dishes and the healthiest (and cheapest) is the fashionable steak tartar. The wine list favours white wines, with the house blanc de blanc at a reasonable £4.75 and house champagne £10. The place is pleasantly decorated in white with pretty silvered chairs and its brasserie air is accentuated by the French waiters. Upstairs is nicer than down, which is stark and characterless.

From £5 a head.

## Juicy Lucy

23 Conduit Street, W1 (629 9426)
Bond Street tube
Open: 8am–6.30pm Monday–Friday; 9am–4pm Saturday.

With ten years' catering experience and over 100 branches in Africa, America and Australia, the first London Juicy Lucy has got its formula right. The idea is to provide cheap, filling, wholesome and healthy food either to eat in or take out in a pleasant bright comfortable and fully air-conditioned restaurant. Food ranges from freshly-squeezed fruit (from 59p to 99p) breakfasts of cereal and croissant, kidneys and bacon, tomato, onion and bacon and scrambled eggs; salads all sorts (self-service bar; 99p for a full plate), various daily baked quiches (£1.25), wholewheat rolls (from 69p) and a range of chicken, fish, vegetable or pasta hot pots (£1.30 without meat, £1.70 with). During the afternoon they serve tea. Not licensed.

From £2 for a good feed.

## Kalamaras

66 and 76–78 Inverness Mews, W2 (727 9122)
Bayswater tube
Open: 7–11.30pm Monday–Saturday.

Stelios Platonos has two Greek restaurants in this narrow mews behind Queensway, both famed for the high quality of their food and for the 'healthiness' of its presentation – minimal oil, and no great plates of chips or rice. The larger premises ('Mega' at 76–78) are highly atmospheric, with dim lighting, live bouzouki music and a close-packed jumble of tables. The smaller taverna ('Micro' at 66 – 727 5082 after 6.30pm) is much more spartan (dark red walls, no music) with a shorter, cheaper menu and, for the purposes of this section, a healthier potential because it's unlicensed. There's no corkage if you bring your own wine, but the food is so fresh and clean-tasting, a bottle of Perrier often seems the best accompaniment. There's a vast array of starters (up to 24) including simple items like Greek salad with fetta cheese, plates of olives or taramasalata, together with more unusual dishes. These can be combined to produce a cheap meal in itself – try the spanokotyropites (spinach and cheese in light, parchment thin pastry) or the lightly-fried marides (whitebait) and make a point of asking for the spiced lamb in pastry which doesn't appear on the menu. Combine these with a salad, excellent dolmades, octopus or squid and you have a healthy, well-balanced meal. Avoid though, the melitzanes scordalia – an overpoweringly strong garlic and aubergine dip – which may well be good for the blood, but will haunt your mouth for days. If you've room for a main course, the suckling gouronopoulo (pork) is served deliciously lean and savoury, with simple salad accompaniment. Good Souvlakia and grilled red mullet are other possibilities. Keep healthy to the end by ignoring the sticky sweets in favour of fresh fruit and a Greek coffee without sugar – ena skehto parakalo.

About £12 for two (Micro); £25 for two (Mega).

## Mandeer

21 Hanway Place, W1 (323 0660)
Tottenham Court Road tube
Open: noon–3pm and 6–10.30pm Monday–Saturday.

This place would probably be better termed 'Mandeer Enterprises' since the network of basement rooms houses an Indian art gallery, food shop, meeting hall, as well as two restaurants. Despite the diversification, attention is obviously still paid to the vegetarian cooking offered, self-service style, in the Ravi Shankar hall at lunchtimes only, and in the more formal restaurant next to it. In truth, the self-service deal can be a bit over-functional – drab queue, limited choice, harassed service from a waiter handling samosas one moment, dirty fivers the next, and, above all, a really bare, dull room with plastic chairs and cutlery to match. Choices are restricted to a couple of savouries – samosas or aluvada (fried, spiced potato balls), mixed vegetable or excellent butter bean curry, with brown rice, bowl of dal and paratha to complete the jigsaw on your little steel tray. It is ridiculously cheap to eat there, though, and unquestionably better for you than a jumbo sausage with french bread (isn't everything?). More stylish eating can be enjoyed in the restaurant – tiled floor, low-slung lamps, artwork on the walls – and a more extensive menu, with the set meals particularly good value. Chef's specials include deliciously moist vegetable dopiaza or butter masala, and there are familiar vegetarian dishes like mateer panir (yoghurt, cottage cheese and peas), chana chat (boiled chick peas with tamarind chutney) and of course, masala dosa.

About £2.50 a head (self-service); £7 a head (restaurant).

## Manna

4 Erskine Road, NW3 (722 8028)
Chalk Farm tube
Open: 6.30pm–midnight Tuesday to Sunday

Manna was regarded as a hang-out for the cranky lovers of nut roast and dandelion leaves when it opened 15-odd years ago. By providing a consistently high standard of vegetarian and macrobiotic food over the years in a very pleasant country kitchen-style room, Manna has firmly established itself and now has devoted carnivorous regulars as well as confirmed vegetarians.

Sit at the massive pine tables and choose from the daily-changing chalked-up menu; they have no pretensions in describing the food and you invariably end up with a far more delicious looking and tasting dish than you'd expected. Everything is made on the premises including bread and yoghurt and regularly features a soup, various casseroles, unusual salads, bakes and delicious fruit puddings. Manna has and continues to prove that food without meat can be delicious. Drink organic cider (natch) or wine under £5 a bottle.

From £5 a head for food.

## Neals Yard Tea Rooms

Upstairs at The Dairy, 6 Neals Yard, WC2 (836 5199)
Open: 10.30am–8pm Monday–Friday, 3.30pm Wednesday and 4.30pm Saturday.

## Neals Yard Soup and Salad Bar

2 Neals Yard, WC2 (836 3233)
Open: 11am–5pm Monday–Friday; 11am–4pm Saturday.
Covent Garden tube

Neals Yard is firmly established as the centre for the health-conscious who only want to eat organically grown vegetables (The Farm Shop); buy grains, pulses, dried fruits and other healthy stables in no-nonsense packs, usually in bulk (The Co-Op); stock up on naturally-cultured dairy produce (The Dairy); stoneground flour and who take their own bottles to be filled with wine (Seven Dials Wine Co); purchase herbal remedies (from the Apothecary) and even seek alternative medical help from the Therapy Rooms. Upstairs at the Bakery are the Tea Rooms. Here there is a comfortable space to munch on the salad-stuffed pitta sandwich; a doorstep made with one of their tasty breads; a slice of brown pastry quiche or on one of the strange-looking array of cakes made with unusual mixtures of fruit, banana or carob. To wash it down there is a choice of teas – herbal, Chinese, Indian, obscure and familiar. Diagonally opposite the Tea Rooms is the Soup and Salad Bar. It's a large quarry tiled room which opens directly onto the Yard, has some bar stool seating but like the Bakery is most geared to providing a takeaway service. Aside from thick and nourishing daily-made soups, there are wholesome snacks such as vegetables in peanut sauce, cheese bake, baked potato, fruit crumble and numerous and changing salads.

From £2 a head for a snack meal.

## Raw Deal

65 York Street, W1 (262 4841)
Baker Street tube
Open: 10am–10pm Monday–Friday; 10am–midnight Saturday.

Periods of gastronomic and alcoholic excess can be shaken off here by an appetising range of hot vegetarian dishes. These might include chickpea savoury bake, a delicious nut roast or stuffed vegetables. Home-made soups and fruit crumbles, together with an imaginative display of salads, complete a robust, unapologetic menu. Drinks are restricted to fruit juices, though you may bring alcohol if you wish. The cramped jumble of tables and the common-room atmosphere make it easy to strike up conversations. If this is not your wish, take a book to hide behind.

About £7 for two.

## Sabras

263 High Road, Willesden Green, NW10 (459 0340)
Dollis Hill tube
Open: 12.30–8.30pm Tuesday–Sunday (winter); 12.30–9.15pm Tuesday–Sunday (summer).

The traditional response to a bout of excess eating and drinking is to go on the wagon and adopt a healthier diet. You can achieve both at this small, unlicensed, brightly-lit but pleasantly-appointed Indian vegetarian restaurant, which also operates as a shop. The refrigerated display features all manner of pastries and sweetmeats, while giant jars contain exotic beans, pulses, spices and rice. It's a comprehensive and well-run enterprise, which is reflected by the long, helpfully-annotated menu which explains every dish in detail – a consideration many Indian vegetarian restaurants ignore. The descriptions will make your mouth water and it's very easy to go berserk and over-order. But be warned that the portions are generally meant to serve two and are uncommonly large. Among the farshan (hot spicy savouries) which serve as 'starters' are the usual samosas and bhajiyas as well as less familiar items – patra, slices of dark, dense Indian yam leaves mixed with tamarind, garlic and sesame seeds, or moong dal vada, a lentil, spring-onion and yoghurt cake. The cold Bombay specials are smashing too – puris (puffed wheat bread) filled with potatoes, yoghurt, chutneys, coconut, coriander leaves and the like. Among the larger dishes, the masala dosa (rolled, crisp pancakes stuffed with spiced potatoes) are superb and there's an inventive range of vegetable curries of varying degrees of 'dryness', like the juicy char-ratna with peas, cauliflower and tomatoes. Traditional sweets – shrikand, shiro (semolina and wheat flour with saffron, almonds and cardamoms), keri no rus (mango pulp), are delicious too. Healthy fruit or yoghurt drinks should accompany these, although there's no corkage charge for boozers with their own wine. The early closing times are presumably an attempt to avoid the 'ten pints and a curry brigade'.

About £10 for two.

## Sharuna

107 Great Russell Street, WC1 (636 5922)
Tottenham Court Road tube
Open: noon–10pm Monday–Saturday; 1pm–9pm Sunday.

Most of the time, eating 'health' food means enduring spartan surroundings and earnest atmospheres. Here however, beautifully-cooked regional Indian vegetarian food can be enjoyed in considerable comfort, and with music and drink to deflate any seriousness or introspection. Situated beneath the hotel and wholefood shop of the same name, the Sharuna's basement dining-room is fitted out with red upholstery, smoked glass mirrors, comfortable chairs and a thick, tweed-like wall-covering. The classy, cosy atmosphere means that you can actually make an occasion of a vegetarian meal. There's a small list of starters offering such as sambhar, a hot lentil curry, or the Gujerati dish kadhi, a spiced yoghurt creation. Best main course is the de luxe thali, a complete meal on a tray, with individual bowls of vegetables and dal, pilau rice, raita, a couple of puris (wheat pancakes), poppadoms and a choice of sweets. Serious health freaks can try the tabiat wala, a dish of mixed salad topped with nuts, almonds, raisins and cheese. If you're choosing a selection of individual dishes, try the kashmiri rice, steamed basmati rice with saffron, nuts, almonds, etc. Drink beer or wine, or if you're still serious about your health, the sweet yoghurt concoction, lassi. Skip the port and cigars.

About £8 a head.

## Slinkys

49–51 Whitehall, SW1 (930 9877)
Charing Cross or Embankment tube
Open: 10am–8pm Monday–Friday; 10am–6pm Saturday and Sunday.

If you really want to diet seriously then Slinkys is the restaurant for you. A specially designed weight watchers menu is based on calorie intake and at Slinkys the tills not only tot up your bill but also give a calorie count total on each part of the meal. The restaurant is a fast order operation and the daily-prepared and frequently-changing menu caters for all types of dieters. One of the regular hot dishes is home-made steak pie and chips, which is billed as a high energy meal, but quiches of all sorts, vegetable casseroles and salads are most popular. All the hot dishes are served with either brown rice, jacket potato or salad and are remarkably good value at between £1.70 and £2.95. Salads are a far cry from the limp lettuce and soggy tomato brigade and combinations such as orange and carrot, garlicky provençale vegetables and Chinese greens are typical. Salads cost 80p a small portion and £1.70 as a main. The aim of the operation is to re-educate us into eating healthily and economically. Needless to say, Slinkys isn't licensed.

From £2.50 for a full meal.

## Le Suquet

104 Draycott Avenue, SW3 (581 1785)
South Kensington tube
Open: 12.30–2.30pm Wednesday–Sunday; 7.30–11.30pm Tuesday–Sunday.

Part of the Pierre Martin group of French fish restaurants, this one is reckoned by many to be the best. The food is certainly superb; sea bass, bream and oysters from Boulogne, lobster, langoustine and salmon from Scotland and whatever's good in English waters from Billingsgate. Here the menu is strictly à la carte and although they do have an oyster bar it's not bookable and the chances of finding an empty space for their spectacular ice-packed tray of Fines Claires, Belons or Colchesters is unlikely. Their stunning plateau de fruits de mer (which includes all three types of oyster) is a meal in itself and so healthy – that you'll wonder why you don't eat here more often. The fish is soundly prepared, the only drawbacks about the place are its surly French waiting staff and the noisy Sloane Ranger clientele. That is, apart from the price.

From £15 a head.

*Also Good for When You Want to Get Healthy:*
192
Busabong
Garden Restaurant, The
Golden Duck
Joe Allen
Joy King Lau
Jun
Linda's
Masako
South of the Border
Woodlands

# 17. When You're Out Late

London, unlike New York, is not a late-night city but it is peppered with places that will serve a snack or a full meal after 11.30pm, and this has been our dividing line for inclusion in this section. There are very few places open after 1am and even fewer open all night. To get alcohol with a late meal, the restaurant must have an entertainment license, and this is why you can dance after midnight at Peppermint Park in Covent Garden or watch a magician at midnight at Fatso's in Soho. Soho is the most reliable place for late meals and is where – at The Diamond in particular – many of London's chefs are to be found between 1 and 4am taking a busman's holiday. White nighters, club folk and punters have their own regular haunts such as Harry's in Soho and the aptly-named Sunrise (open until 6am) in Covent Garden. London's Lebanese community dines till 5am at Maroush in Edgware Road, 3am at Fakhraldine in Piccadilly and very late at the most relaxed of them all, the Phoenicia in Abingdon Road.

# Agra

135–137 Whitfield Street, W1 (387 4828)
Warren Street tube
Open: noon–3pm and 6pm–midnight Monday–Friday; noon–midnight Saturday and Sunday.

Now getting a well-deserved lick of paint, the Agra is a long-standing tandoori and curry house spreading across two capacious rooms which are well used to late-night frolics from UCH medical students. The plain walls and neat white tablecloths are indicative of a simple, no-nonsense style. There's a short range of tandoori specials, of which the king prawn, the fish and the mixed grill (chicken, sheek kebab and mutton) are well worth trying. Beyond that it's good quality curries all the way, from the patrician lobster at the top of the range (£3.60), via chicken vindaloo and mutton Madras (light up the night with your tongue afterwards), down to the humble egg curry at £1.40, which has saved many a penniless student from starvation. It doesn't always escape attention from those recently ejected from licensed premises, but the late Sunday hours are a boon when you don't want your weekend to finish.

About £6 a head.

# Café Pacifico

5 Langley Street, off Long Acre, WC2 (379 7728)
Covent Garden tube
Open: 11.30am–3pm and 5.30–midnight Monday–Saturday.

This is one of the many converted warehouses in Covent Garden, and the owners have done a good job, creating an airy and informal restaurant, with constant music, which seats 100 (25 at the bar). Ceiling fans and two huge windows keep the large, busy space cool even at the height of summer. Food is Southern Californian/Mexican and while it's not the most authentic food of its type, it is cheap and filling. Most things are either chilli-laced or avocado-based and the following are our favourite dishes; nachos sonora – crispy tortilla spread with beans, avocado and sour cream (£2.95) and LA Burrito (£3.75) a flour tortilla stuffed with mince and avocado, which are both more than enough for two average appetites. If you like it hot, pile on the piquant chilli sauce which should be on the table. We'd advise sharing a dish of guacomole to start.

The Café serves good strong cocktails, tequila of course, Mexican beers and rather watery Sangria by the jug. Ideal for late night munchies.

From £5 a head.

## Chez Solange

35 Cranbourn Street, WC2 (836 0542)
Leicester Square tube
Open: noon–3.15pm and 5.30–12.15am Monday–Saturday.

One of the longest-established theatre-land restaurants in London, Chez Solange commendably tries to convince itself and its customers that London is suddenly Paris and that all-day and late night opening are quite the norm. A two-tiered affair, with sedate Edwardian décor downstairs and racier, alpine-lodge interior upstairs (with live piano music some nights), it has an intimate, slightly furtive atmosphere ideal for late-night dining. The menu offers an extensive range of 'cuisine bourgeoise' dishes, strapping plates of decently-cooked food with only a few nods here and there to modern fashions. Such standards as coq au vin, scampi provençale, côte de porc and ris de veau are always available and there's an additional, mimeographed sheet detailing a 'menu de la semaine'. Choosing from this may prove better value because there's slightly more adventure displayed here – saddle of lamb stuffed with meat, mushrooms and herbs; salade gourmande cuisine nouvelle (fresh artichoke heart and avocado on a salad bed with almonds and a red wine vinegar and double cream sauce); sweetbreads in white wine with wild mushrooms. No matter how late it is, don't miss their summer coupe de la saison, a strawberry and raspberry creation laced with cassis. Other classics are the mont blanc (chestnut purée with whipped cream), rum baba and the jam omelette with Grand Marnier and ice-cream. There is also a set pre-theatre dinner and an adjoining wine bar.

Set meal £10 a head (excl wine); alc about £17 a head.

## Chez Zorba

11 Charlotte Street, W1 (580 5948)
Goodge Street tube
Open: noon–3pm and 5.30pm–3am daily.

Chez Zorba is no peasant hut, but a smart, red-velvet chaired premises on two floors, with live bouzouki music and dancing in the basement most nights (no charge). If it's just a quiet late night snack and drink you want it's best to stay upstairs – don't be tempted by the siren sounds of smashing plates, because the menu tells you that

all breakages **must be** paid for. Charcoal-grilled kebabs and 'inter-national' steaks (Diane, Châteaubriand) probably aren't the most digestible of bedtime meals, but you have to weigh their freshness against the likelihood that the arni kokkinisto (lamb casserole) has been around all day. French onion soup and lamb cutlets are probably the safest route to an undisturbed night, though the entrada (traditional broth with lamb pieces) and a couple of veal escalopes might be worthy alternatives. If you're planning to work through the night, the comprehensive meze will keep you fuelled up and the sheer excitement of being able to drink until 3am may make the 'mouzouki' worthwhile. Altogether now, 'It's quarter-to-three
. . .'

About £12 a head.

## The Diamond

23 Lisle Street, WC2 (437 2517)
Leicester Square tube
Open: noon–4am.

Many of London's leading chefs are regularly to be found tucking into a late night supper at this Cantonese café in the heart of Chinatown. Everyone who is a regular claims that the best dishes aren't on the menu but unless you happen to be or speak Chinese, finding out 'what's on today' can be heavy going. Scallops on the half shell; prawns fried in garlic; squid in breadcrumbs with prawn and Emperor chicken steamed with a salty sauce are some of those dishes. Choosing from the menu we'd recommend the traditional Cantonese favourite of crab with ginger and spring onions and very garlicky Hoi Hoi prawns. They are licensed, but avoid their wicked cocktails.

From £5 a head for food.

## Fakhraldine

85 Piccadilly, W1 (493 3424)
Green Park tube
Open: noon–3am daily.

This huge and elaborately decorated L-shaped restaurant with its fountain, lavish plants and extensive use of mirrors is run by two Lebanese brothers. Named after the sixteenth-century founder of modern Lebanon, Fakhr El-Din, they make great claims in their publicity that 'only the best will do'. In our experience the best does do for the many Lebanese diners but Europeans, even if they show a good grasp of the cuisine, don't get such good food or service. Avoid anything sounding vaguely international and make up a meze meal. If the uncut and undressed salad (this should arrive automatically with a dish of olives) is limp send it back. There is a vast choice of meze (snacks) and it is the perfect late night pick-me-up which can be extended into a feast or be simply a light meal. There are 45 different hors d'oeuvres to choose from; hummus, moutaboul (very tasty aubergine puree with sesame, lemon and olive oil), lambs' liver, stuffed vine leaves, kibbey (raw fresh meat pounded with crushed wheat, onions and spices) give you an idea. The food is treated as dips to be shared, eaten with the salad and pitta bread. They come round with a trolley of honey-drenched pastries; they are deceptively easy to eat and very pricey. Drink aniseedy Arak.

From £8 a head, £15 is more likely.

## Frère Jacques

37 Long Acre, WC2 (836 7639)
Covent Garden tube
Open: noon–1am daily.

Bang next door to the tube, this must be the prime site in Covent Garden. Sensibly the owners (Kennedy Brookes, who also run the Wheeler's chain) run this fish restaurant as a brasserie so you can snack or go the whole hog any time, although the menu is reduced between 3 and 6pm.

The table piled high with shellfish at the door is a good omen and most crustacea from the humble shrimp (£1.75) to tiny French Fines de Claires oysters (six, £3.75) are available both au naturel and cooked. There's a choice of seven main fish dishes and three meat plus light dishes and a few desserts. Not everything on the menu is as successful as it should be though their plateau de fruits de mer and uncooked shellfish have been brilliant.

The restaurant is large and very pretty, decorated in white and green with a striped awning, lots of greenery and mirrors.

From £5 a head; house wine £4.25. £12–£15 for a three-course meal.

## Harry's

6 Kingly Street, W1 (734 8708)
Oxford Circus or Piccadilly Circus tube
Open: 8.30am–6.30pm and 10.30am–6am.

By day Harry's feeds the locality's office workers with large portions of English fare such as breakfasts of egg, bacon, sausage and chips; cauliflower cheese; liver and bacon; roast beef and two veg and home-made puddings, and nothing costs more than £2.

By night they catch the night club punters and staff (they are bang opposite the Valbonne) and serve just tea or coffee, breakfast any way you want it, grills, scampi and slightly more sophisticated international dishes. It's a friendly, family-owned café which is known to its regulars for generous portions of good quality plain English food at very reasonable prices. They are not licensed.

From £2.50 a head.

## The Italian Connection

Strand Palace Hotel, Exeter Street, WC2
Covent Garden tube
Open: noon–2.30pm and 6pm–midnight Monday–Saturday.

At the rear of the Strand Palace Hotel (entrance in Exeter Street, or, more stylishly, through the main hotel foyer) is an operation variously described as La Premieta Pizzeria or The Italian Connection. Whichever you decide to call it, the modern, brightly-lit but rustically-furnished room is a useful place for that ideal late-night snack, the pizza. The ones served here seem genuine enough, despite being dressed up with silly names like La Cosa Nostra. Most are basically garnished with tomatoes, mozzarella and other cheeses, with additional toppings offered in the form of salami, sausage, ham or mushroom. Best bet if you're in a small party is to carve up La Gigante, a 21-inch-wide number. If you're starving, La Rustica, a deep-dish pizza-pie or one of the non-pizza specialities (gnocchi in beef sauce) are real fillers. Good ice-cream sundae-style desserts (coppa padrino with brandy, cream and pistachio nuts), serviceable wines and excellent cappuccino are The Italian Connection's other notable points. The prices aren't too bad either.

About £6 a head.

## Lanes

The Inn on the Park, Hamilton Place, Park Lane, W1 (499 0888)
Hyde Park Corner tube
Open: 12.30–2.30pm and 6pm–midnight daily.

Adjacent to the Four Seasons Restaurant Lanes is a smartly-fitted, brightly-lit modern restaurant taking orders until midnight. This allows late-nighters the prospect of a high-class full meal (and drinks!) without the usual 'chairs going up on tables, waiters brushing the floor' pressure of so many other places. At the centre of the room is Lanes' buffet display, incorporating a stunning 'harvest festival' array of appetisers, hors d'oeuvres and salads. You are invited to select from this after choosing a main dish whose price (between £10–£14) includes either soup or an appetiser. Soup might be chicken broth, while the appetiser might include dressed Cornish crab, giant prawns, melon or marinated salmon. Main dishes embrace mainly grills – seafood, salmon steak, lamb cutlets, fillet of beef, sirloin steak – although there's poached Dover sole in rosemary butter for those wanting something lighter. Desserts, at £2.25 extra, include sherbets, exotic ice-cream and a selection of fruit tarts. At lunchtime, Lanes offers an enticing range of set three-course meals from around £11–£14, which include wine, service and coffee. These are very popular and should be booked in advance, though the late suppers are more readily available.

About £15 a head.

## Luba's

6 Yeoman's Row, SW3 (589 2950)
Knightsbridge/South Kensington tube
Open: noon to 3pm and 6–11.45pm Monday–Saturday.

For years Luba's has been a popular spot for impoverished South West Londoners who enjoy the light hearted bistro atmosphere and save a bob or two by taking their own wine (Luba's is not licensed). The food is Russian peasant-style with Italian and French overtones and the restaurant is renowned for its large portions. Popular dishes include the bortsch, piroshki (deep fried mincemeat pancakes), galubtzy (minced beef in cabbage leaves with rice and wine sauce) and pojarsky (veal with mushroom sauce). It's not a place for faint-hearted eaters; particularly not the puddings – cernic (a pancake stuffed with cream cheese and smothered in cream) is typical. In summer a few tables are placed outside on the quiet Row.

From £5 a head.

## Maharani

117 Clapham High Street, SW4 (622 2530)
Clapham Common tube
Open: noon–3pm and 6pm–midnight Monday–Friday; noon–midnight weekends.

This long-established (over 20 years) Indian restaurant has a devout following which is not just confined to 'Clarm' Commoners. A long, bustling room, lit by coloured panels, has seating (some in the form of pleasant wooden alcoves), ranging along both walls. Service is both informal and efficient, even into the late hours. The menu is dominated by well-prepared tandoori specialities, from lobster, prawn and mutton to the deliciously moist butter chicken. Particularly worth trying is the murgimusallam, a combination plate of tandoori chicken, minced meat, egg and tomato, served with pilau rice. Among the curries, the fruity chicken Kashmir (with lychees and pineapple) and rogongost (their spelling, mutton with tomato and onion) deserve attention. If you're feeling adventurous, you might ask the manager Mr Khan in advance if he has any of his fish speciality, cooked delicately in yoghurt. Drink lager, or light German wines.

About £8 a head.

## Mayflower

68–70 Shaftesbury Avenue, W1 (734 9207)
Piccadilly tube
Open: noon–4am daily.

This popular haunt of night owls is a lot more lavish and comfortable than other nearby all-night Chinese cafés. Lavish rose-coloured velveteen covers the walls, there are numerous pictures, the starched linen is not characteristic of Chinese restaurants in this part of town and the food is good too.

Its main-drag location and tackily lavish decor give the Mayflower a two-pronged role. By day and some of the night, tourists fill the place but by night it is most frequented by Chinese who have their own menu. Not surprisingly there is a dual standard of service, size of portions and availability of dishes but, despite that, the Mayflower has many non-oriental regulars. It is a Cantonese restaurant and while much is stir-fried (like their famous crab) and steamed (their scallops with garlic are superb) they are known for their baked dishes. The menu is long and varied and there is plenty of opportunity for experimenting (Hung Sau fish head and yam stuffed fried spiced duck give you an idea) but safe and sound dishes too are on offer. Lemon chicken, Cantonese roast chicken with cinnamon salt are popular dishes here and reliably good. Eat either a one course meal for under £5 with a drink or try one of the set meals from £6 a head; à la carte from £8. They are licensed, and can seat up to 130.

## M'sieur Frog

31a Essex Road, N1 (226 3495)
Angel tube
Open: 7–11.30pm Monday–Saturday.

For a neighbourhood restaurant such as M'sieur Frog to have last orders at 11.30pm is commendable – but then this place is so popular it has to stay open late just to accommodate all those wishing to eat there. Enter through a side door into a converted terraced house, cocooned from the noisy Essex Road by thick half-curtains and pine-panelled walls. Further atmosphere is created by the low-slung (mind your head) basket-shaded lamps and the red-check oil-cloths on the closely-packed tables. While the name may be questionably naff, the menu is eclectic and robustly French, and it takes time to digest the possibilities. Start with massive slabs of slushy garlic bread, or tender frogs' legs (they had to have them) in a creamy fennel sauce. Good 'peasant' soups, plates of country ham and fish mousses are frequent alternatives. The main courses might include calves' sweetbreads and kidneys, a chunky veal casserole with pine kernels and oranges, coquilles St Jacques or a great skillet of Alsacienne cooked meats and sausages. Fish specials should appear on the blackboard list. Puddings (and cheeses) are usually tremendous – ice-cream with hot chocolate and orange sauce, crème brûlée, crêpes au Grand Marnier. Such riches might not be too wise too late at night, but if you're on your way home from town, or Sadler's Wells, this must be worth a visit. Beware only of service which sometimes imitates the restaurant's evident hero – Marcel Marceau.

About £15 a head.

## Pucci Pizza Vino

205 King's Road, SW3 (352 2134)
Sloane Square tube
Open: 11am–12.30am Monday–Saturday.

The owner of this pizzeria is a frequenter of fashionable haunts himself and his interests, connections and friends, plus his habit of whisking whoever's left at closing time off to clubland have made this a fashionable haunt itself. Regularly full of trendy young things in search of the high life, Pucci's has a lot to offer apart from being in or watching its clique. In a busy atmosphere and to the latest sounds, good and cheap basic Italian food is served on sturdy marble-topped tables. Pizzas average £1.50 and steak meals under £5. Wash it down with above average house wine at £4.50.

Well under £5 a head.

## Semiramis

4 Hereford Road, W2 (727 4272)
Notting Hill Gate tube
Open: noon–3pm Monday–Friday; 7pm–midnight daily.

A tiny, seven-tabled Greek restaurant off Westbourne Grove,

Semiramis has to keep long hours or it would presumably go out of business. Cork-tiled walls and low-slung basket lampshades give it the feel of an architect's studio rather than a goatherd's hut, but the food is pure, well-cooked peasant fodder – pastourma (spicy Armenian sausage), halloumi (grilled goat's cheese), kleftico and the pork stew afelia are the card's strong points, especially with their roast potatoes filling in for rice. Charcoal grills and the reasonable meze (selection of dishes) complete a small Greek presence, with the limited covers pushing the prices higher than you might expect, but quality gaining accordingly. At lunchtimes, the kitchen assumes an additional, bizarre persona, with English, European, Asian (Thai chicken) and even Japanese food (ocean stix fish in lemon) appearing on the menu. No road test, as yet, on this, but avocado metarama (avocado stuffed with prawns and taramasalata) sounds a little dangerous compared to the hot Sussex smokies (pots of smoked haddock in cheese sauce) or the beef and spinach bake.

About £26 for two.

## Soho Brasserie

23–25 Old Compton Street, W1 (439 3758)
Piccadilly Circus tube
Open 10am–11.30pm Monday–Saturday.

Almost immediately Westminster Council introduced its 'clean up Soho' campaign a new clutch of restaurants opened on the essentially Italian side of Soho. Quite the best, and very fashionable (particularly with the film and media worlds), is the Soho Brasserie. Beautifully converted by a large brewery, the place is very much its Paris counterpart with a large bar (French-style, *without* stools), a few tables in front of the bar and a mirrored banquette-seated restaurant at the rear. Despite ceiling fans, the temperature rises dramatically as the place fills and as it's one of the few places (apart from pubs) in Soho to drink without having to eat, it gets very full. The menu caters for breakfasts, offers tasty and well-executed snacks such as warm duck livers with spinach salad (£2.75); fish soup with croûtons, rouille and Gruyère (£1.75), mixed saucissons and salamis with gerkins and olives (£2.65) and meat dishes such as the classic grilled steak (£7.50) and calves' liver and bacon (£3.65). There are daily specials which generally include a couple of fish dishes; recently on offer was delicious turbot with beurre blanc and fillet of brill on a bed of sliced chicory in a cream sauce. Crême brulée here is excellent but fromage blanc with fruit purée or French cheeses are slightly easier on the cholesterol intake. Drink and any of the food is available until 11.30pm (they actually close at 12.30am) and the snack menu is available throughout the afternoon. The wine list is well thought out and caters particularly to London's increasingly discerning and sophisticated wine drinkers; Fleurie (£7.95)/Brouilly (£8.90)/Muscadet de Sèvre et Maine (£6.85) are typical; for those just wanting drink, house wine is £4.85.

From £2 for one course; £10 for three.

## Sunrise

3 Long Acre, WC2 (836 2816)
Covent Garden tube
Open: noon–3pm and 6pm–2am, breakfast 2–6am.

The menu at this newish late-nighterie on the edge of Covent Garden and round the corner from Stringfellows caters to most moods. The food is wide ranging from 'lite bites' such as ambitious salads (melon, pear, grape and cream cheese dressed with honey, ginger and lemon juice, £4.75 or parma ham, sweetcorn and pineapple, £5.25) and meats on toast (chicken Maryland, £3.15 and veal à la crème, £3.50) to international dishes such as surf and turf (£7.25), kebab (£5.50) and veal stroganoff (£5.75) with brownies, sundaes, crêpes, cheesecake or Stilton to follow. From 2am they serve breakfast; BLT £3.75, omelettes £3.95 and traditional English breakfasts £4.50. Around 20 can be seated on the ground floor but downstairs, where up to 90 can foot tap to jazz-inspired music, is cosier. Décor is dark pink with co-ordinated Gatsby style pictures, bentwood chairs and lots of greenery, fake and real. It's not a place to cross town for but is a useful late-night stop and they're licensed until 1.30am; cocktails all £2.75, house wine £5.50. As yet there is no dancing but it's on the cards.

From £10 a head.

## Swiss Centre

2 New Coventry Street, W1 (734 1291)
Leicester Square tube
Open: noon–midnight daily.

The Swiss Centre is almost a last resort as a late-night venue. The baffling complex of restaurants and cafés makes it forbidding to all but the most desperate night owls. Still, if you can't face the prospect of a Chinese in nearby Lisle Street, the Centre at least offers a European alternative. The Swiss Imbiss (the what?) offers breakfast and snacks, The Chesa is the formal, up-market restaurant serving 'international' food, The Locanda reflects the Italian element in Swiss cuisine (pastas, escalopes), while the Taverne offers more of what you might expect from your 'William Tell' watching days. Cheese fondue and raclette (melted cheese with boiled potatoes, pickled gherkins and onions, belch) are the main items along with grilled veal, lamb brochette and steaks. There's also a short list of regional specialities, ranging from basler bebbi topf (fried pork mignons with sautéed pimentos and potatoes au gratin, belch again), and suprême de volaille aux prunes (belch) to steak de porc Jurassienne (grilled pork steak with mushroom, glazed with tomato sauce and Swiss cheese, belch, expire). If you can handle all this, and the maze of alpine décor with twinkling lights at close to midnight, you probably qualify for a Duke of Edinburgh Award. But then it *is* open late and you can get a drink.

From £5 a head to £15 a head.

## Toscanini

330 King's Road, SW3 (351 3634)
Sloane Square tube
Open: 12.30–3pm and 7pm–midnight Tuesday–Sunday.

Related to La Bersagliera, the Italian café down the road, Toscanini is a comfortable, functional place run by a friendly Italian family. Brightly lit and unspectacular in its fittings and decoration, its walls are painted with quaint and very elaborate harps and musically inspired paintings. Background music is generally Toscanini. The long menu features all your favourite Italian dishes and they specialize in home made pasta with a blackboard of daily-changing dishes. Most of the food is cooked to order and portions are stunningly large. Gnocchi, when it's on, is a cheap and filling choice and their offal dishes are particularly good.

Toscanini deserves to be far more popular than it is.

From £8 a head.

*Also Good For Late-Night Eating:*
192
Ajanta
Apicella '81
Astrix
Au Bois St Jean
Bamboo Kuning
Bar Creperie
Bates
Brasserie, La
Brasserie St Quentin
Bunga Raya
Café des Amis

Café Pelican
Café St Pierre
Caffe Mamma
Camden Brasserie
Caprice, Le
Caravan Serai
Carlo's Place
Chelsea Pot, The
Chez Victor
Chicago Pizza Pie Factory
Chicago Rib Shack
Chuen Cheng Ku
Covent Garden Pasta Bar
Creperie, The
Crystal Palace
Don Pepe
Eleven Park Walk
L'Estanquet
Fatso's Pasta Joint
Flavio
Gallery Restaurant, Camden Palace
Geno Washington's
Golden Duck
Grange, The
Green and Pleasant
Grimes
Hard Rock Cafe
Haweli
Ho Ho
Hungry Horse
Jake's Restaurant
Joe Allen
Joy King Lau
Jun
Kowloon
Langan's Brasserie
Leoni's Quo Vadis
Little Italy
L. S. Grunt's
Lucky's
Manzil's
Manzi's
Mario's
Maroush
Masters

Ménage a Trois
Mrs Beeton's
My Old Dutch
Nassa, La
Nineteen
Old Rangoon
One Hampstead Lane
Oval Tandoori
Palookaville
Parsons
Peppermint Park
Petit Prince, Le
Phoenicia
Pier 31
Pizza Express
Pollyanna's
Pratt's
Rowley's
Salvador's El Bodegon
San Carlo
Serendipity
Sheppard's
Shireen
Sidi Bou Said
Suquet, Le
Tai Pan
Texas Lone Star Saloon
Tuttons
Zen

## 18. When You Want Breakfast

Nutritionists reckon that breakfast is the most important meal of the day because it bridges what is usually a fourteen-hour gap between last night's dinner and today's lunch. Too often, however, that bridge consists only of a hurried slice of toast, a cup of lukewarm tea and a Silk Cut. Yet if you have the time, a breakfast out can be a stylish and relaxing way to start your working day – you can check the stock market reports and the racing tips, while soothing your stomach acids with a bowl of porridge. And business people are becoming increasingly aware of the possibilities of holding hotel breakfast meetings – there are attractive surroundings, it's cheaper than lunch, there are no phones ringing at your table and there's a good chance that your business rival will still be half-asleep.

# Bar Italia

22 Frith Street, W1 (437 4520)
Tottenham Court Road tube
Open: 8am–7pm Monday–Saturday; 9am–7pm Sunday.

Not so much a bar, more a community centre for Soho's Italian waiters and restaurant workers, the Italia is a narrow, functional room, lined with formica counters, fruit machines and wobbly stools. Nevertheless, it's as vibrantly atmospheric and macho as a Scorsese film. A pictorial tribute to Rocky Marciano hangs behind the bar while further up, some 20th-century Michaelangelo has depicted Dino Zoff brandishing the 1982 World Cup. You don't really go for the food here, but what there is, is excellent. Terrific espresso and cappuccino, slabs of home-made cake, rolls filled with salami, mozzarella and tomato, while for breakfast, there are additional items like fruit juice, Italian brioche or croissants. Most customers just stand at the counter dunking in their cappuccino and jabbering in Italian over a Gazzetta dello Sport, while the younger blades comb their hair in the mirror which runs the length of the room. More legitimate entertainment is provided by the regular, large-screen videos of Italian league soccer matches.

About £2.50 for two.

# Blue Sky Restaurant

106 Westbourne Grove, W2 (229 0777)
Notting Hill Gate tube
Open: 7.30am–10pm Monday–Saturday.

In keeping with its tropical name, the Blue Sky is such a busy breakfast haunt that the windows invariably steam up and the customers wind up with a sauna as well as their sausages. The large, brightly coloured Italian restaurant (spot the Chianti bottles, Rimini posters and World Cup team photos) is packed with five ranges of formica booths, two of which are joined to allow early morning discussion of the papers ('Cor, look at 'er!') to spread noisily. The large menu is standard caff stuff in the main – grills, steamed puddings, pizzas – but its comprehensiveness allows a good breakfast choice. There are the usual good quality fry-ups, backed up by the likes of mushrooms on toast, the 'farmhouse egg' range offering such favourites as ham, egg and chips, the grills offering steaks, liver or lamb chops and even a pancake section with plain, jam or fruit-filled numbers. With thick toast and hot, creamy coffee to support these, you can enjoy a stomach-bulging breakfast and still come out of the heat with a weight-loss.

About £2 a head.

## Brasserie St Quentin

243 Brompton Road, SW3 (589 8005)
South Kensington tube
Open: 10–11.15am Saturday and Sunday, for breakfast; otherwise, noon–3pm and 7pm–midnight (11.30pm Sunday) daily.

At the weekend, the Brasserie St Quentin tries to live up to the first part of its name by opening at 10am for 'café complet' – continental breakfast to you and me. While this may not sound such a big deal, it should be pointed out that the atmosphere and stylish trappings of the room – mirrored walls, chandeliers, brass-topped bar, gilt chairs and white table-linen – make breakfast here a real occasion. Regular customers park their Mercedes gull-wings Parisian-style on the pavement outside and pose moodily by the window for two hours (last orders for breakfast are roughly 11.15 am as lunch starts promptly at noon). The provision of papers and service by black-tied, waistcoated waiters complete the French illusion.

The breakfast, though limited, is extremely good – strong, flavoursome coffee with a jug of warm milk, and a basket of lightly sugar-coated croissants and crisp, fresh bread with tiny jars of Tiptree preserves. At £2.50 a head, you shouldn't have to ask for another cup of coffee but it's usually necessary. Otherwise, as the French say, formidable. You may be tempted to stay on for one of their good three-course lunches at £8.50 – fish soup, foie de veau aux herbes, feuilleté aux fruits. Then at 3pm (on weekends again only) it's afternoon pâtisserie, and then dinner starts at 7pm . . . in fact, just take a toothbrush and spend the whole day there.

Breakfast £2.50 a head; set lunch £8.50 (excl wine); alc about £18 a head.

## Carriages

Euston Station, NW1 (387 9400)
Euston tube
Open: 7am–10pm Monday–Friday; noon–7pm Saturday.

What was once The Lancastrian Grill, British Rail's 'Travellers Fare' restaurant in the Euston station complex, has now been transformed by them into Carriages. New alcove seating, smart carpets and attractive globe lighting give it a more welcoming air, and the breakfast there is still one of the most enjoyable in London.

This is partly to do with the view – the first floor room gives a marvellous panorama of the station concourse, with commuters flocking in, and Scottish football supporters flocking home. The traditional British breakfast (£3.60) matches the quality and size of the one available on Inter-City trains – and that's meant as a compliment. The deal offers various starters – fruit juices, corn flakes, grapefruit, muesli and, full marks, porridge. The ensuing grill is a cleanly-presented plate of sausage, egg and bacon and tomato with kippers as a lighter alternative. Toast and preserves are plentiful, and the individual pots of coffee and tea have enough in them to allow you a linger over your newspaper. The continental breakfast is about a pound cheaper but not nearly as much value. From 11am hot meals, grills and teas are served.

About £4 a head.

## Cathay Restaurant

417 King's Road, SW10 (352 2135)
Sloane Square tube and bus to Worlds End
Open 7am–5pm Monday–Saturday.

This large and functional café/restaurant serves large portions of cheap international fillers such as spaghetti bolognaise for around £1 but is best known for its fry up and breakfasts all-sorts served throughout the day. Egg, bacon and chips cost £1.15 but best value are their specials such as egg, bacon, sausage, tomato, fried bread and tea at £1.30. Hidden on the 'wrong' side of increasingly fashionable Worlds End, this place is used most by local tradesmen and knowing trendies and is a useful place to refuel cheaply if you've 'done' one side of King's Road and intend walking back to Sloane Square to do the other. They are licensed and offer a cheap (£3.50) house wine on the bearable side of evil.

About £1.50 a head.

## The Coffee House, Hotel Inter-Continental

1 Hamilton Place, Park Lane, W1 (409 3131)
Hyde Park Corner tube
Open: 7am–noon daily.

Anyone who's ever been to New York can't have failed to have been impressed by the range of breakfast bars scattered all over the city. An early-morning meal there seems much more of an institution than in this country, with the result that breakfasts have both nutritional appeal and variety. Trying to track down these qualities in London isn't easy, but the Inter-Continental Hotel's breakfast-room, The Coffee House, must be about the best there is. Their morning menu (served until noon) boasts such substantial plates of Americana as corned beef hash with fried egg, waffles or pancakes with maple syrup, fillet minute steak on toast with egg, bacon and tomato and a variety of omelettes. Supported by such British standards as porridge, kedgeree and kippers or haddock in butter, and the familiar continental pastries, cheeses and cold meats, The Coffee House's menu is as comprehensive as any in London. The self-service buffet (open till 10.30am) is restricted to the cold elements, freshly squeezed orange juice, and cereals, allowing pleasant, efficient service to take care of orders for hot meals and the endless provision of coffee and tea. The food is high quality and the furnishings, starkly modern despite the Coffee House theme, are comfortable on the seat if not on the eye. Three fixed-price menus are offered as well as the à la carte selection, but even choosing extensively from there shouldn't amount to more than £8 a head for a smashing morning meal.

Set menus £4.40 (continental); £6.80; alc about £8 a head.

## The Coffee Shop, YWCA

16 Great Russell Street, WC1 (636 7512)
Tottenham Court Road tube
Open: 8am–8pm Monday–Friday; 8am–2pm Saturday; 8.30am–2.30pm Sunday.

With most of London's cheaper breakfast venues giving off a strident macho air – all fry-ups and 'Star birds' – a pleasantly feminine alternative is offered by the YWCA's Coffee Shop. It's open to both sexes of course, but the surroundings – large, quiet, airy refectory-style room decked with floral posters – and the lightweight menu, obviously have women in mind.

The self-service counter offers a decent display of packet cereals and muesli, assorted fruit juices, prunes or grapefruit segments, croissants, wholemeal bread rolls and pastries, and boiled eggs. There's also a hot-plate decked with rashers of bacon, sausages and creamy porridge should you feel tempted to stray from your diet. The Cona machine is kept well-stocked with freshly-brewed coffee and the place has a pleasantly unhectic atmosphere. Savouries, soups and sandwiches are served throughout the rest of the day.

About £1.30 a head.

## The Connaught

1 Carlos Place, W1 (499 7070)
Bond Street tube
Open: 7.30am–10.00am daily.

The Connaught provides the most civilised setting in London for breakfast – a quiet, mahogany-panelled room, lined with red velvet chairs and banquettes and pink linen covered tables, all topped off with crystal chandeliers. A clutch of tail-coated waiters in starched shirts completes the elegant picture, so it's no surprise that a) high standards of dress are required (no velour jogging suits or Gucci sweatshirts, but jacket and tie, please), or that b) you can pay more for breakfast here than for dinner in many other restaurants.

Of course if you can afford to eat at The Connaught, cost is not a consideration really, so just sit back and wallow in the comfort and enjoy their splendid and extensive breakfast menu. It covers a complete range of options, from a simple continental breakfast to à la carte selections such as kedgeree, finnan haddock, bacon and eggs, frankfurters, omelettes and even Dover soles, steaks or grilled calves' liver. There's a wide range of cereals (porridge, Swiss muesli, grape nuts) and fruits or juices to get you started, and huge croissants and copious toast to finish. Coffee and tea are served in individual pots and are both of the highest quality. The only disruptive note is struck by the rather obtrusive console where the dishes are co-ordinated. But then it's rather touching to hear the stuffed shirt waiters, as at any breakfast gaff, arguing over whether it's sausages or haddock at table three . . .

Continental breakfast £4.50; alc about £10 a head.

## The Fox and Anchor

115 Charterhouse Street, EC1 (253 4838)
Barbican tube
Open: 6am–2.30pm Monday–Friday.

Smithfield's nocturnal working routine gives breakfasts a greater importance than it might have for day workers. The need to fill up and beat off the cold and starvation plays a large part in dictating the kind of food Smithfield's population goes for – so at the Fox and Anchor, a large, well-preserved old pub in a northern corner of Smithfield, you won't find muesli or Special K on the menu. No, it's fuel food all the way, and in huge quantities to boot. There's no set breakfast, you simply reel off a list of your favourite items and wait for them to appear, piled high on the Pyrex plate. A typical selection might include sausages, bacon, liver, tomatoes, mushrooms and fried eggs for about £2.50. Steaks, kippers and poached eggs are variations, and there are chips and beans if you want to fill every corner of your stomach. The home-made spicy sausages are especially worthy trying, but everything is both freshly, and well, cooked. If you've only just got up, you might be pushed to face a pint at 7am, but a brandy 'heart-starter' with excellent coffee should certainly set the pulse racing. There's a snug dining area at the rear of the pub – place-mats, napkins, formica booths – but most regulars eat at the bare pub tables or at the bar itself. Lunchtimes see massive steaks and mixed grills served to the meat barons in their suits, but by then, the lads in the blood-stained white coats are tucked up in bed . . .

About £6 for two (breakfast); £14 for two (lunch).

## Hampstead Pâtisserie and Tea Rooms

9 South End Road, NW3 (435 9563)
Hampstead BR
Open: 9am–5pm Monday–Friday and 9am–noon Saturday and Sunday.

At the back of this pâtisserie is a small, cramped and functional breakfast and tea room. Before you set off to discover the Heath, fill up on poached or scrambled eggs on toast for under £1; ham and cheese with poached egg on toast for just over £1 or breakfast continental style on warm croissant and butter and one of their delicious pastries which are 50p a piece. Tea comes by the pot, coffee by the cup.

## The King's Head

132 Edgware Road, W2 (723 6433)
Edgware Road tube
Open: 9am–3pm daily; 5.30–10.30pm Monday–Saturday; 7–10pm Sunday.

The idea of having breakfast in a pub might seem a little stomach-churning if you've only reeled out of one a few hours previously, but if you can stand the faint whiff of stale beer, the Kings Head is a useful venue for breakfasts. They're served in the first-floor dining-room, which is sufficiently well-appointed – half-panelled walls, tartan wallpaper, Grenadier Guard posters and prints – and comfortable to play host to informal business meetings. It's particularly cosy on winter mornings when the old-fashioned radiators generate a thoroughly warming climate. The simple breakfasts are offered on a two tier basis, continental (£2) and English (£3), with ten-per-cent service added. The lightweight breakfast is fruit juice or cereal with plentiful toast, or rolls, and preserves, and generous supplies of tea or coffee. English breakfasts offer well-cooked scrambled eggs, omelettes (plain or with a variety of fillings at a small extra charge) and sausages or bacon with eggs (fried, poached or boiled). Preceded by cereals (Cornflakes, Weetabix) and followed by a big basket of toast with individual sachets of marmalade and jam, it's a pretty reasonable deal in hospitable surroundings. Breakfasts are generally served right up to noon, when the restaurant's unpretentious lunch menu (home-made steak and kidney pie, roast chicken, roast beef and Yorkshire pudding) takes over.

£2–£3 a head.

## Messrs C

10 New Row, WC2 (836 0563)
Leicester Square tube
Open: 7.30am–7.30pm Monday–Saturday.

For years the rather dull Dairy, this corner site has been given a lick of maroon paint, smartened up and re-opened by an energetic young team who serve good English grub. They do almost any variation on the English breakfast and a Full House of egg, bacon, sausage and chips with a slice, tea or a strong cappuccino will see change from £2. The rest of the day they do a takeaway service for rolls, pizza and sandwiches and you can sit down to a hearty plate of steak and kidney pudding, fish and chips or pasta dishes of the day. They aren't licensed but don't mind you bringing your own. Very handy for nearby Covent Garden without the Garden's inflated prices. During the summer they have some seating outside in the Row.

From £2.50 a head.

## Le Metro

28 Basil Street, SW3 (589 6286)
Knightsbridge tube
Open: 7.30am–10am daily (breakfast); 11am–3pm and 5.30–11.30pm Monday–Saturday.

This is the latest venture from Margaret and David Levin, owners of the Greenhouse and the adjacent Capital Hotel. It doubles as a wine bar and continental breakfast room for inmates of their L'Hotel, 28 Basil Street, and for the general public. Freshly-squeezed orange juice precedes warm croissants which are served with good strong cafetiere coffee, and the meal costs £2.50 a head.

Aside from its breakfast operation, the Metro, which is a basement annexe to the Capital Hotel, is an L-shaped wine bar, functionally decorated with a fair sized bar and short menu. The food is cheap, sophisticatedly simple (supervised by the capital's chef Brian Turner) and served on nice china; coffee comes in smart green and gold rim apilco cups. The light dishes include a good smoked goose breast with a salad frisée (£2), a plate of cheese (£1.35) and main dishes (from £4–£5) include fried chicken with garlic croûtons, skate with capers and blanquette de veau with little vegetables. Another highlight of Metro is its cruover machine, a French invention which enables opened wines to be stored without deterioration, and this means the bar can serve ten fine wines by the glass. The more modest wines in the long, well-chosen list start at £5.25; cruover wines from £5 *a glass*.

From £2.50 for breakfast. A la carte meals from £5.

---

## Pâtisserie Française, Maison Pechon

127 Queensway, W2 (229 0746)
Bayswater tube
Open: 8.30am–5pm Monday–Saturday; 10am–5pm Sunday.

Breakfast continental-style at this large, functional dining room behind the pâtisserie. The chef finishes baking the day's croissants by dawn and when the place opens at 8.30am they are still nicely warm. Indulge yourself on one of the tempting array of pâtisserie on sale in the shop, which are all made to the current owner's grandfather's (who started the shop) recipes. They also bake a very good baguette.

Throughout the day a variety of inexpensive and filling French dishes such as chicken vol au vent are available.

£1.50 for breakfast; £3 for a light meal. Licensed.

---

## The Pavilion

Grosvenor House Hotel, Park Lane, W1 (499 6363)
Marble Arch tube
Open: 7am–11pm Monday–Saturday; 7.30am–11pm Sunday.

By their very nature hotels are obliged to serve breakfast, but only a few of the bigger ones put sufficient energy into it to attract customers from outside. The Grosvenor House's recently-opened Pavilion, however, is a thoroughly out-going enterprise. With its large, colourful awning and huge windows looking out onto the Park it certainly gets noticed. Inside, the modern décor is just as striking – green perspex pillars, flashing lights, brightly coloured floors and walls – definitely making it a place that shouts 'yes' to breakfast. The well run operation offers set morning meals of a traditional and nutritional nature. The waitresses will seat you at one of the spacious tables and provide you with tea or coffee, thereafter you simply help yourself to as much as you like from two well-stocked counters. One offers cereals, fruit juices, cheese, cold meats, pastries and fresh fruit, while the other boasts a packed range of sausage, bacon, tomatoes, mushrooms, eggs and so on. For those with lesser appetites a third counter offers just croissants and coffee. It's a well-organised restaurant, and from 11am it goes on to serve set-price lunches, afternoon teas, early evening cocktails and light suppers.

Set breakfast £4.75 a head.

## The Picasso

127 King's Road, SW3 (352 4921)
Sloane Square tube
Open: 8.30am–11pm daily.

Largely because of its location on the 'arty' end of the King's Road, and also because they allow visitors to brood over a cappuccino for hours and because it has tables outside on the pavement, The Picasso has been an 'in' place for years. Run by Dino's, the Italian cheap and cheerful café chain, the food is basic Italian-ish café fare, is most popular for breakfasts and cheap one-courses (lasagne, cannelloni, egg florentine, omelettes, and liver and bacon). Inside, it's very functional with formica-topped tables and wooden bench seats. In its way it's a very fashionable place.

From £2 for food.

## Quality Chop House

94 Farringdon Road, EC1 (837 5093)
Farringdon tube
Open: 6.30am–4pm Monday–Friday.

Mount Pleasant Post Office sorters regularly start their day, or finish their night, in this glorious throw-back to the Pre-Muesli Era. The polished wooden tables, tiled walls, Victorian prints and banquette seats give a clue to the style and it's no surprise, but a real pleasure, to find porridge and bubble and squeak on the breakfast menu. Sausage and bacon fry-ups, boiled bacon, hot toast, strong tea and even buttered rock cakes will send you out onto the street sporting one of those eerie glows last seen in the 'Ready Brek' adverts. Come back at lunchtime for liver and onions, home-made pies or fish and chips.

About £5 for two.

## Raoul's

13 Clifton Road, W9 (289 7313)
Warwick Avenue tube
Open: 9am–6pm Monday–Saturday; 10am–6pm Sunday.

This small but pleasantly-appointed coffee shop and pâtisserie does a good trade throughout the day, drawing custom from local shoppers and passing tourists. There's an exotic array of continental cakes and pastries always available, several of which make ideal breakfast snacks – croissants both plain and filled with ham, delicious chocolate or almond bread, cheese-flavoured pastries and the hot, filling Strasbourg (frankfurter in pastry). Allied to excellent cappuccino and superb Viennese coffee (with fresh cream and flaked chocolate), these can provide a good, if sweet, start to the day – but you need something to boost the old blood sugar first thing don't you? For less adventurous palates, there's always scrambled eggs on toast, and if it's more of a brunch you're after, their filled vol-au-vents, quiches and pancakes will bridge any midmorning gap. The padded, wrought iron chairs are a bit of a tight fit for lounging round with the papers, so these, and the constant time-checks from the piped Radio One, should still get you to work on time.

About £1.50 a head.

## The Seven Steps

3 Highbury Place, N5 (no phone)
Highbury & Islington tube
Open: 8am–5.30pm Monday–Saturday.

No problem getting breakfasts here, since – salads, omelettes and sandwiches apart – that's all they serve throughout the day. Nestling at the foot of Highbury Fields and just far enough back from Holloway Road to be quiet, The Seven Steps is a bright and cheery venue for a morning meal. The wallpaper is almost as loud as the fruit machine, but neither should detract from a decent range of seven set breakfasts, from the basic bacon and egg to the de luxe two sausages, fried bread and egg, with beans, In between, mushrooms (with egg and bacon), ham (with two eggs and mushrooms) and tomatoes (with bacon and egg) come into the equation, though I'm not entirely sure if you're allowed to mix up the elements beyond the fixed combinations offered – shades of the diner scene in 'Five Easy Pieces'. Anyone wanting a break from the fry-up parade might try their decent buck rarebit – Welsh rarebit with a poached egg. With thick, hot toast and good tea inside you as well, you can go off to fight the throng on the Victoria line.

About £1.70 a head.

## The Tudor Grill, Hilton International Hotel

179–199 Holland Park Avenue, W11 (603 3355)
Holland Park tube
Open: 7–11am daily.

Handy for the M40 and on a direct express bus route to Heathrow Airport, the Kensington Hilton is ideally-placed for that breakfast meeting with incoming American businessmen or outgoing Swedish air-hostesses. As you might guess from the name, the Grill's done out in a mock-Tudor style with beams (probably not original), heraldic pennants and minstrels' gallery above the serving console. This gives it a rather dark, gloomy atmosphere, best suited to winter mornings – as indeed is the food. The operation is essentially self-service once you've been led to your table and fixed up with coffee or tea. A quick walk round the central counter reveals racks of croissants and Danish pastries, a shelf filled with fruit juices and cereals, a grill bar offering traditional English sausages, bacon, mushrooms, eggs (scrambled or fried), and a final choice of cold meats. The disadvantage of self-service is that it rather tends to 'functionalise' what could, indeed should, be a stylish occasion. The big advantage of course, is that you can pig yourself to your heart's (stomach's?) content. The food is of a reasonably good quality (excellent scrambled egg) but if you catch the tail end of a batch of bangers, they can look rather tired. Expect queues too at their infernal toast machine – you slip your slice of bread into a ferris-wheel contraption and wait until it reappears browned to your choice, but then is it your slice or the person's behind/in front of you? People should not have to think this hard so early in the morning.

English breakfast £4.75; continental £3.50.

*Also Good For Breakfast:*
Bar Crêperie
Bolton's
Brasserie, La
Buttery Grill
Café Des Amis DuVin

Café Pelican
Café St Pierre
Diana's Diner
Dome
Filling Station
Fortnum & Mason's Fountain
Juicy Lucy
Perdoni's
Peter's
Pratt's
Restaurant, The
Soho Brasserie
Sunrise
Tire Bouchon, Le
Widow Applebaum's

## 19. When You Want Something Different

Cosmopolitan London offers the chance to sample the cuisines of the world. Chinese and Indian food have been upgraded here over the past ten years and it's now possible to enjoy many regional specialities and less of the ubiquitous curry and chop suey. It's common knowledge that if you know where to look you'll find better Greek food in London than is available to most English tourists in Greece and London now boasts two Vietnamese restaurants. These ethnic restaurants not only offer the opportunity to try their countries' food in atmospheric surroundings without having to board a plane, but can also be remarkably cheap. Our selection includes the cuisines of Russia, Thailand, Burma, Korea, Afghanistan, Lebanon, Indonesia, Tunisia, the Caribbean and Sri Lanka.

## Ali Baba

32 Ivor Place, NW1 (723 7474)
Baker Street tube
Open: 11am–midnight daily.

You should guess from the name that this place has Arab connections – in fact it's predominantly a Moroccan venture with southern Mediterranean and European overtones. Tucked away in a narrow street off Gloucester Place, the small premises have a takeaway counter in the front to dish out kebabs, and a simple but smartly-furnished dining area at the rear. There's a list of Euro-grills to contend with, but obviously you'll ignore these in favour of authentic Moroccan couscous, the Ali Baba special (lamb stuffed with rice, raisins and nuts), the Saudi Arabian stew capsi and the tangy saiadia (fish in spicy tomato sauce, with rice). Best starters are the savoury kubbeh (fried meat-balls with crushed wheat), or the falafel (fried balls of ground beans and spices), though the dips-hummous, mutabel (aubergine and sesame seed) and foul (brown beans with lemon and garlic) – are all worth trying. To offset the slightly dry texture of most main courses, the desserts are refreshingly sweet – mohalabieh (cold milk pudding) or om ali (bread pudding with raisins). If you can't face the prospect of the house's Moroccan red, you can always bring your own wine.

About £10 a head.

## Bahn Thai

35 Marloes Road, W8 (937 9960)
Kensington High Street tube
Open: noon–2.30pm and 6–11.15pm (last orders) Monday to Saturday.

Stunningly decorated in black with clusters of small Thai parasols covering the light fittings and adding the only splash of colour, this small basement restaurant is candlelit for lunch and dinner. The place is run with dedication by an Englishman who lived for years in Thailand and his Thai wife, and the food is some of the best of its kind in London. The long menu is daunting but explicit and there is help on hand for those unfamiliar with the hot and fiery food. Don't miss their mini spring rolls served with a sweet sauce dip; the grilled garlic and peppered spatchcock prawns served with a hot, spicy chilli sauce or the steamed silver pomfret (Thai flat fish) served with julienne vegetables and a light soy sauce. Soothe the palate with mangoes or oranges in syrup served on a bed of ice. Drink chrysanthemum or jasmine tea or take your own wine (there is an off license open until 8pm in the same block) or try their excellent house wine at £3.75. Pigging it you'd have difficulty spending more than £10 a head on food but the average is £7.50.

## Calabash

The Africa Centre, 38 King Street, WC2 (836 1976)
Covent Garden tube
Open: noon–3pm and 6–11pm Monday to Friday; 6–11pm Saturday.

This large and sparsely decorated dining room in the bowels of the Africa Centre is one of Covent Garden's least pressurized and delightfully untrendy restaurants. The walls are hung with African tie-dyed fabrics and the only other decoration is a huge display of the fruit and vegetables used in the cooking. The staff are so laid back and the music so rhythmic it's impossible not to feel relaxed here. The food represents most African countries – Kenya, Nigeria, North Africa, Ghana – on a rotation basis so it takes quite a few visits to sample the entire menu. However, you can always be assured of a hearty meal, usually a stew-type dish, and some interesting flavours. The Calabash is very good value with main dishes around £3 and their carafe wine £2.70. Fried plantains with a spicy tomato sauce makes a perfect shared starter and Zanzibar, a wing of chicken in a tasty coconut milk sauce and Nigerian Egusi, a musky dish of huge chunks of steak stewed in palm oil with spinach and melon seeds are regular favourites. We go regularly for their fried sweet potatoes. End with fresh African fruit or OD on the batter-fried pineapple flambéed with rum.

From £5 a head for food.

## Caravan Serai

50 Paddington Street, W1 (935 1208)
Baker Street tube
Open: noon–3pm and 6–11pm Monday–Saturday; 6–11pm Sunday.

## Also **Afghan Tandoori**

Chelverton Road, SW15 (788 0599)
Putney tube
Open: noon–3pm and 6–11.30pm Monday–Saturday; 6–11pm Sunday.

Offspring of the Putney Afghan Tandoori, which for years was London's only authentic Afghan restaurant, Caravan Serai offers a delightful slice of Afghani culture as well as food and has the added advantage of a very central location. Spotlessly clean, the white walls are hung with evil-looking scabbards, colourful rugs and tasseled pouches which, together with fabric-decorated doorways, the rug-strewn floor and indigenous waiters the places fits its name like a glove. The food is rich, spicy and tasty with some interesting and contrasting flavours and textures. Tandoori is popular and there are endless variations on the kebab but the explicit menu will tempt you towards the more adventurous dishes.

Murgh beryon – marinated barbequed chicken served sizzling in a frying pan with tomatoes and onions, ashak – pasta filled with leek, minced meat and yoghurt; and the curious Borani badejan – a tasty aubergine dish – are all especially recommended starters. Main dishes tend to be heavily spiced and some are very hot. Their gigantic mixed grill would probably satisfy Big Daddy while those who prefer subtlety might try one of their delicious Basmati rice dishes with Subzi Goshed, a dish of diced lamb with spinach, or a rich prawn dish such as Mahi Kuner. Put the fire out with a Firni – a tasty rose water and ground rice dish peppered with pistachios and almonds.

At lunch (Monday to Friday) they serve an excellent value three course meal for £4.95; à la carte expect to pay £10–£15 a head with their strong house wine.

---

## Caribbean Sunkissed Restaurant

49 Chippenham Road, W9 (286 3741)
Maida Vale tube
Open: noon–3pm and 6–11pm Monday–Saturday.

If you're lusting for a taste of sunshine and an evocation of that long-ago (or still to come) Caribbean holiday, this is the place to go. The sunshine begins even before you get inside – there's a huge burst of orange rays painted across the window, and while the décor of the two floors is an odd combination of garish carpet and tasteful paintwork and table-linen, the atmosphere is friendly and professional. The food covers a wide and attractive range of Caribbean cuisine from the straightforward crab and avocado cocktail or callaloo (spinach soup), to the exotic roast pork Calypso (with rum, garlic, ginger and lime juice) and the threatening Caribbean deep-water shark (that's a slice not a whole fish). Other winners include the beef and vegetable stew (peas, yams, chilli and coconut cream), tuna á la Sunkiss (fried tuna with peppers, onion and garlic sauce) and marinated fried chicken (with rum, soya and pepper sauce). The liberal splashings of alcohol certainly help the sauces, so it's worth having the plain mixed vegetables (plantain, sweet potatoes) to soak up the juices. Don't miss the banana surprise as your pudding, because, not surprisingly, there's yet more rum involved.

Pleasant French house wine, pre-meal rum punches and lilting reggae will add to the holiday spirit.

About £24 for two.

## Cuisine Sri Lanka

57 Cleveland Street, W1 (636 9098)
Goodge Street tube
Open: noon–3pm Monday–Friday; 6–11pm Monday–Saturday.

'Didn't know they had one, squire' might well be a typical response to the notion of a Sri Lankan national cuisine. Even this gloomy, simply-furnished (white plaster walls, Air Lanka posters) little restaurant isn't quite sure, hedging its bets with an 'international menu' of soups, starters and grilled meats. What remains though, gives an intriguing hint of strong but subtle flavours, a confident way with fish and a pleasant line in desserts. Essentially, Sri Lankan food is an extension of the South Indian style – highly-spiced, potentially very hot vegetable curries – boosted by greater use of sea-food and defused, where necessary, with coconut milk. The small, fertile island also has a huge range of herbs and spices, and some of these find their way into the dishes here, albeit anonymously under the description 'Sri Lankan ingredients'. Fish ambul thiyal, for example, is Indian ocean fish (rather like mackerel) sourly but deliciously spiced with a little number called gambage, as well as more familiar elements such as cinnamon and garlic. The combination works very well, as does the mixture of ginger, garlic, cloves, cardamom, Sri Lankan curry powder and coconut milk in the tender mutton curry. To accompany these, there's delicate, short-grain yellow rice or devilled potatoes, steamed then fried in coconut oil with onions, chilli powder, curry leaves, maldivefish and cinnamon. Other curries include beef, lentil and okra, and there are further appealing fish dishes, including fried rings of cuttle-fish. Start with the traditional egg hopper, a bowl-shaped corn pancake containing a fried egg, spiced ad lib with delicious seni sambol, a pickle of tamarind, lemon grass, cardamom, cloves and coconut milk. Finish off soothingly with a fine passion fruit sorbet, the fruity, liquid wood-apple cream or Sri Lankan crème caramel, watlappan. Drink lager, cheap house wine or full-bodied Ceylon tea.

About £9 a head.

# Don Pepe

99 Frampton Street, NW8 (262 3834)
Edgware Road tube
Open: noon–2.30pm and 7pm–12.30am Monday–Saturday; noon–2pm and 7–11pm Sunday.

Anyone wishing to recapture the flavour of their Spanish holidays could do a lot worse than dropping in at the Garcia brothers' authentic Galician restaurant. The pleasant display of shrubbery outside and the cool, white-tiled, white plaster interior will waft you gently away from the Edgware Road. To add to the atmosphere there's a smart, stainless steel-topped bar draped with friendly local Spaniards drinking beer, talking football and playing the fruit machine, and there's occasionally a guitarist in the evenings. The short card is strong on seafood with three or four scampi dishes, all laced with garlic, and a couple featuring Mediterranean prawns. Rape al aillo (monkfish with garlic) also lurks among the starters, though for non-garlic fans, recommendations can be given for the tender pincho moruno (basically a pork kebab) and wonderfully tender, unoily calamares fritos. Alternatives to King Prawn's régime in the main courses include the large and succulent fillete de ternera (grilled veal chop in a thick tomato sauce), a fillet of sole (lenguado) with a cream and mushroom sauce and a chicken breast cooked in a Rioja and mushroom sauce. One of the well-reported house specials is lomo de cerdo (pork fillet in cayenne sauce). Crêpes and zabaglione are offered on the dessert list but are not always available, leaving you to make do with a cream caramel. Pleasant, helpful service and the freshness of the food (they have their own delicatessen adjacent) distinguish Don Pepe as a valuable 'holiday' haunt. Among the fine Spanish wine list there's the excellent Marquès de Cacères Rioja (both white and red).

Set meal £6.90 (excl wine); alc £15 a head.

# L'Estanquet Bistrot

158 Old Brompton Road, SW5 (373 9918)
Gloucester Road tube
Open: noon–3pm and 7.30pm–2am Monday–Saturday.

Fed up with familiar French food whether it's nouvelle cuisine or coq au vin? Then why not try L'Estanquet where they deal in the regional specialities of Gascony, the south-west corner of France that merges into Basque country. The décor reflects the Spanish influence – a small, highly atmospheric ground-floor café style restaurant, with white brick walls, a tall wooden counter, red tiled floors and red patterned curtains covering the 'slit' windows. The colourful oilcloths on the tables, and the rugby union posters on the wall (Gascon towns like Bayonne and Dax are the heartland of French rugby) restore the French flavour, while the menu comfortably straddles both countries.

There's a long, appetising list of starters (which include 'petits plats' for solo eating at the bar), most of which can be taken in combination to form a complete meal. There's traditional mountain-dried saucisson sec (salami), fried scallops, potage garbure (ham and vegetable soup), cold smoked breast of duck with mushrooms, stuffed Spanish mussels, arachon fish soup and simple jambon de Bayonne. The piperade Béarnaise (scrambled eggs with Bayonne ham and peppers) is a meal in itself, while the stuffed snails, crusted with garlic breadcrumbs, are scarcely less so. If you can manage a main course the chipîrons farcis (squid stuffed with sausagemeat) can look rather charmless, but is delicious nevertheless, while the magret de canard is sliced tenderly. Other main dishes include poulet Basquaise (with peppers), daube de boeuf au vin de Cahors or tourte de poisson (fish in puff pastry). Essential desserts are the crêpes azarra (soaked in local liqueur). Fragrant house wine (Menjucq) is served in large litre carafes, perhaps to help you forget the delays between courses. The gloomy downstairs restaurant (open evenings only) offers a similar but larger and more expensive menu, and live 'ethnic' music to contend with. Tables outside in the summer complete a multi-faceted operation.

About £10 a head.

## Great Nepalese Restaurant

48 Eversholt Street, NW1 (388 6737)
Euston tube
Open: noon–3pm and 6–11.45pm daily.

On the flanks of Euston Station, the Great Nepalese belies its rather drab, net-curtained exterior with a bright, comfortable interior (flock wallpaper, yes, but classy flock) and a warm welcome. The name, the crossed kukri emblems and the gurkha prints on the walls give evidence of an independent Nepalese national identity, which shines out from a largely Indian menu. While most of the food simply extends the north Indian régime of tandooris and mild meat curries, individuality is asserted by the appearance of several unusual dishes. Among the starters there are kalezo ra chyyan (chicken liver with mushrooms), haku choyala (diced mutton with hot spices, barbecued on skewers), mascobara (black lentil bread with curry sauce) and delicious meat-filled mamocha (pastry dumplings) in a tomato and garlic sauce. Main dishes embrace tandoori, curry and vegetable dishes, though probably the best deal first time out is either the Nepalese set meal or the Nepalese tandoori mixed grill. The set meal, based around chicken, mutton or, unusually, pork curries with rice and chapati, also includes copious dishes of black dal, aloo bodi tama (black eye beans, potatoes and bamboo shoots), achar (potato and cinnamon seed chutney) and sag (spiced spinach). The tandoori mixture grill is a colourful, moist mound of tender chicken, mutton, prawns and minced lamb with onions, cucumbers, tomatoes and hot spices. Cleanse the palate with chunky mango kulfi or Nepalese rice pudding laced with raisins and flavoursome cashew nuts in their shells. Don't miss the Nepalese rum as a digestif – imported by the boss's friend at the Royal Nepalese Embassy, it's a light, brown ethereal rum that's nowhere near as fearsome as the bottle – a glass Gurkha dagger – might suggest.

About £9 a head.

## Han Kuk Ko Kwan

2 Lowndes Court, Carnaby Street, W1 (437 3313)
Leicester Square tube
Open: noon–3pm and 6–11pm Monday–Saturday.

In an alley off the now extremely depressing and very un-swinging Carnaby Street is this cheap, pleasant and authentic Korean restaurant. Aside from an astounding display of enormous ginseng roots, and the delightful friendly native staff, the two floor restaurant (a hidden upstairs room seats 50) has very little to suggest that it serves some of the best Korean food in town. The place is run by the diminutive Mrs Park, and her husband does the cooking. The menu is long but describes each dish fully and for those who'd rather not attempt a selection there are set meals varying from £4.20 per person up to £17.50 for two and which include the cuisine's most popular dishes. Koreans seem to go in for appetisers in a big way and if ordering à la carte these average 80p each (most Koreans would order several). Flavours are spicy, musty and tangy and include some unlikely-sounding combinations; squid in brine, bracken shoots, pickled radish with red pepper and pickled Chinese cabbage. Main dishes are reminiscent of Chinese food; much is steamed or crispy deep-fried with either chilli or variations on sweet and sour flavours, served with rice or chop-suey-style with noodles, which make a substantial and cheap one course meal.

Traditionally the appetisers are eaten as an accompaniment to a main dish and if you're lucky, your waitress will show you how to 'assemble' the food correctly. For example, Bulgogi, which is one of the most popular dishes and resembles the Japanese Sukiyaki (slices of raw marinated beef and vegetables cooked on a burner at the table), is cooked and then rolled with a little of each relish in a lettuce leaf and eaten like a sandwich. Puddings don't really feature; tea will appear automatically and is on the house and their house wine is £4.50 a bottle.

Set meals from £4.50; à la carte from £6 a head.

## Linda's

4 Fernhead Road, W9 (969 9387)
Maida Vale tube
Open: noon–3pm and 6–11pm Monday–Saturday.

London's best Vietnamese restaurant – others are the Mekong in Victoria and Bistro Vietnam off Oxford Circus – is a small and modest affair. Black and gold flock cover the walls, Chinese lanterns and Christmas lights provide the colour. It's run by the Blaney family; Linda, a Vietnamese, is a powerful maîtresse d, her mother and sister cook in the tiny adjoining kitchen and her handsome son serves. The menu offers snacks, single courses, à la carte or various set meals and the food is similar to Thai cuisine but uses lots of fresh coriander and ginger. Dishes tend to arrive simultaneously so if you opt for one of the set meals you'd better brush up on your chopstick skills first. Their mini spring rolls (beef and bean sprout filling), which come sliced and decorated with cucumber and leaf coriander, are a delicious nibble and will leave you wanting more. The spare ribs don't come covered in gunge but are chopped small and are deliciously spicy. Chicken in a gingered brown sauce, sliced quarters of tortilla-like omelette and any of the vegetable dishes are highly recommended as main courses. Everything is so cheap (though portions are small) that it doesn't cost much, or take long, to try the whole menu. Their Muscadet (£4.75) is a perfect accompaniment.

From £5 for food.

## Mandalay

100 Greenwich South Street, SE10 (691 0443)
Greenwich BR–Charing Cross
Open: 7.30–10.30pm Thursday–Saturday.

At the Deptford end of Greenwich South Street, in a small, unprepossessing terrace of shops, is the Mandalay, which makes the not unreasonable claim to be the only Burmese restaurant in the country. It's run by a pleasant young couple, Gerald and Suzy Andrews, with Gerald employing his Burmese background to good effect in the kitchen while Suzy chats to and chivvies the customers who fill this place on each of its three opening nights. In their informative menu they describe Burmese cuisine as a cross between Indian and Chinese – the curry (sebaur) is a standard dish, but there's also much use made of noodles, spices, ginger and garlic in other recipes. Some of the starters are 'tasters' for larger main courses such as the brilliantly light and savoury punta kow suar, a dish of noodles with spiced fried chicken, egg fry and spring onion. Other starters are the tempura-style budhi jow (deep-fried slices of marrow with chilli and garlic dip) and the tremendous pet-to, minced pork balls, deep-fried in wun-tun with chilli and soy sauces. Apart from the sebaurs (freshwater 'green' king prawns, fish, pork, beef), main dishes include Burmese fish-ball curry (slightly too dry and watch for the garlic) and another big scorer, the nun nun bin curry – beef or chicken pieces with coriander leaf, tomatoes, onions and spices. Stir-fried vegetables (foogar) and a traditional soup, hincho (either tomato, potato or marrow), should accompany these, with either plain or coconut rice. The soup comes in handy as a tongue-balm if you over-indulge in the relish tray – cauliflower pickle, crisped prawns, burnt chilli and fish gravy and the lethal green chillies all add heat to otherwise mild and subtle tastes. Desserts include tasty mango ice-cream, kyauk-kyew (a sort of clear sea-weed jelly with coconut topping) and the delicious semolina cake with fruit and almonds. The premises – padded, floral benches and bamboo canes in reception upstairs, open white-coloured dining-room with private alcoves downstairs – are slightly primitive but pleasant nonetheless.

About £22 for two.

## Masako

6–8 St Christopher's Place, W1 (935 1579)
Bond Street tube
Open: noon–2pm and 6–10pm Monday–Saturday.

The increasing popularity of Japanese food owes something to its ceremonial style of service as well as to its health-enhancing qualities. At Masako, a long-established restaurant that's part of the Ninjin food importing group (hence authentic ingredients), you can enjoy both these aspects of Japanese cuisine without fear of embarrassment or blunder. The traditionally-dressed waitresses are gracious and courteous, and well used to explaining dishes to puzzled Europeans. The restaurant offers two styles of service – conventional seating on the ground floor, albeit in a beautiful, bamboo-screened, red velvet upholstered room, and traditional, low-table, stockinged-feet, cushion seating in the complex of basement dining rooms. This facility is not always readily available, so it's worth checking in advance if you require it. Even so, it's probably best enjoyed in the company of a Japanese friend to show you the ceremonial ropes. The best access to the lightly-cooked, highly-nutritious food is via Masako's excellent, reasonably-priced set lunches, which are based around a standard Japanese main dish, with appetisers, soup, pickles and rice to accompany it. The most familiar dishes are sukiyaki (slices of fillet broiled at your table with assorted vegetables and soy gravy) and the delicious tempura seafood with vegetables (huge prawns in a delicate batter, dipped into a sharp tempura sauce). Other dishes to be safely enjoyed are the yakitori (lean chicken pieces on a skewer in savoury sauce), yosenabe (a seafood, chicken, bean-curd and noodle casserole), sashimi moirawase (salmon and scallops) and the delicious appet-iser oshitashi (chilled spring greens with dried bonito flakes). You should enjoy the light, clean taste of it all and unless you're really cack-handed, the wooden chopsticks should be used at all times, except when dealing with the soup, which is drunk straight from the bowl as an accompaniment to the main dish. Drinks available include expensive imported Japanese beer, expensive but seditious flasks of saké rice wine, and cheap green tea. Fresh fruits or sorbets are the usual climaxes to a light and nutritious meal with a difference.

About £15 a head.

## Le Mignon

2 Queensway, W2 (229 0093)
Queenway tube
Open: noon–3pm and 6–midnight Tuesday–Sunday.

While the choicest, most imaginative Hungarian food in London is undoubtedly served at the Gay Hussar (see page 71), Le Mignon is a reasonable alternative, spreading more toward Austria it must be said, but boasting a rich, continental ambiance. The location – right on the corner of Queensway and Bayswater Road – gives it a splendidly busy aspect, and the 50s interior (net curtains, panelling, long ranks of tables crisply covered in white) make it an ideal venue for those days when you see life as a European art movie. The cosmopolitan, multi-lingual staff in their white jackets add a further touch of foreign mystique. Hungarian food is no friend to slimmers, dominated as it is by rich, creamy sauces, noodles and escalopes, but to robust constitutions, it offers strongly-flavoured winter fuel. The familiar, drab Eastern European starters (marinated herrings are typical) are best ignored in favour of the delicious, highly-seasoned fish soup hongroise. Plats du jour will usually include meatballs, goulash (naturally), paprika schnitzel, fried spring chicken and the tangy beef lecsó – tender beef in a relatively mild tomato and pepper sauce. Finish off with dobos, a traditional Hungarian cake topped with caramel. Good European beers are worth trying as alternatives to wine. Beware of live, ethnic (violins and cimbalon) music in the evenings.

About £24 for two.

## Nikita's

65 Ifield Road, SW10 (352 6326)
Earls Court tube
Open 7.30–11.30pm Monday–Saturday.

To date this is London's most authentic Russian restaurant (The Bortsch and Cheers and the homely Luba's in Knightsbridge are nowhere near as pure) but the food is 'interpreted' by a French chef. Upstairs is a small bar where you can knock back the speciality of the house; small ice-packed carafes of spiced vodka – these set you up for anything. A steep staircase leads down into the candle-lit restaurant with its many alcoves and corners. The décor is simple and stunning; the bold striped wallpaper (designed by Tony Little) still looks as impressive as it did when the place opened seventeen years ago. The food is delicious and from the long, well-explained menu the following is a foolproof choice. Start with borscht and prawn chowder (solyanka) which is served with hot and tasty little pancakes (piroshki) stuffed with different savoury fillings. Follow with the lean fillet of lamb (shashlik karski) which arrives dramatically on a flaming sword and is eaten with a mint and yoghurt sauce. Good alternatives include a lavish steak tartare spiced with vodka and caviare. Finish with their superb pancakes filled with cream cheese and coated with syrup. If you've kept to vodka throughout the meal you are likely to add to their long list of guests who fall *up* the stairs.

About £10 a head.

## Ognisko Polskie

55 Princes Gate, SW7 (589 4670)
South Kensington tube
Open: 12.30–2.30pm (3.30pm Sunday) and 6.30–10.15pm daily.

Part of the purpose of this section is to guide you to places not only with different styles of food, but with different atmospheres as well. This certainly applies to the restaurant of the Ognisko Polskie (Polish Hearth Club), set in a large terrace opposite Imperial College. The Club offers its members concert rooms, libraries, a bar and even a theatre, but the friendly restaurant is open to the general public and it's not necessary to speak Polish or to be accompanied by a member to enjoy its marvellously robust, Eastern European food. The quiet, elegant, pale yellow dining-room with its pillars, oil-paintings, mirrors and a view onto the gardens is an excellent venue for a stylish meal with a difference. The menu, printed in Polish and English, changes daily but invariably offers such standards as chlodnik (cold beetroot soup), pierogi z miesem (tender meat dumplings), excellent boiled beef with horse-radish sauce and cold beetroot salad, kabanos (sausages), veal cutlet with mushrooms, and pork chop with sauerkraut. Variations might include leniwe (cheese dumplings), smoked pork loins with onion sauce and sauerkraut salad, chicken Kiev or wild mushrooms in cream (usually a Sunday lunch starter). Desserts might offer pancakes with apple or cheese, prunes with custard or a choice from the luscious array of cakes on display in the adjacent bar. Speaking of which, while Polish pils lager is a sensible accompaniment to a meal here, it's criminal not to have a go at their range of native vodkas, ranging from the straight, through the rowanberry (jarzebiak) via bison herb to the cherry flavoured. After going through the card on these try not to be disrespectful to the serious-looking gentlemen on the top table – they are in fact senior members of the Polish Government in Exile.

About £8 a head.

## Phoenicia

11/13A Abingdon Road, W8 (937 0120)
Kensington High Street tube
Open: noon–midnight daily.

Hani Khalife and his wife live above the Lebanese restaurant they run with dedication, following traditional recipes ('the same way my mother cooks for her guests in the village back in Lebanon'), and the authenticity of the food is borne out by the many regular Lebanese diners. The spacious restaurant is the sort of place where you'll feel comfortable dressed up or down. The odd hookah pipe, constant Arab music and attentive Arab waiters are the only real indication that you are in a Lebanese restaurant – that is, until the food starts arriving. A bowl of plump olives and hot chilli peppers and a huge dish of chilled and undressed salad will appear automatically and if you order Arak, the traditional aniseed drink, this will be dispensed with ceremony and a clean glass for each slug.

The best way to sample as many of the rich, tasty and spicy dishes as possible is to order a meze meal of several small shared dishes which are eaten with the salad and hot pitta bread. There is a set meze meal at £7.40 per person, with a choice of a meat or vegetarian meal. Garlicky chicken wings and lemon marinated livers, creamy and surprisingly pungent aubergine moutabal, hot hummus with shawarma (smoked beef) and the traditional taboulleh (chopped salad) give you an idea of the treats in store. They make their own pastries, both light pancakes stuffed with a cream cheese topped with chopped pistachios and the honey-drenched variations on shredded wheat. A separate jug of honey will be served. Arak costs from £6.45 (for four glasses' worth) and they keep a very silky Lebanese wine at £9.20 (French house wine £4.90). Almost everything on the menu is available to take away and they will cook a whole lamb (either to take away or for a party in the restaurant) which feeds up to 30 and costs £90/£100 respectively.

Set meal £7.40, alc £12.

## Pomegranates

94 Grosvenor Road, SW1 (828 6560)
Pimlico tube
Open: 12.30–2pm and 7.30–11.15pm Monday–Friday; 7.30–11.15pm Saturday.

Pomegranates boasts one of London's most varied and truly international menus with dishes chosen as a result of owner Patrick Gwynn-Jones' world-wide travels. Cantonese roast duck, glazed poussin with Muscat de Beaumes de Venise and chicken satay rub along with crab bisque with oysters and Cognac, Burek with Sudanese pepper sauce and poached pigs' kidneys with spicy sesame sauce. The comfortable, dimly lit and clubby-style basement is liked as much for chef Pang's astounding menu as for its relaxed style and good wines (Gwynn-Jones is also in the wine business and keeps a very fairly priced and well-chosen list). While not everything on the menu is as authentic as you'd find in a specialist ethnic restaurant, we doubt you'll be disappointed, and the tranquil opulence of the place with its Tiffany lamps, carefully-chosen paintings and private party rooms makes up for any failings in the food.

From £8 a head for food.

## Sidi Bou Said

9 Seymour Place, Marble Arch, W1 (402 9930)
Marble Arch tube
Open: noon–3pm and 6pm–midnight Monday–Saturday.

With the help of a chef, Faouzi Amroussi manages single-handed at his pretty two-year-old Tunisian restaurant named after the delightful town near Tunis. The one-room restaurant is decorated in

274

powder blue and white, the lower part of the walls lagged with raffia, and a clutch of those ubiquitous white wire birdcages that everyone brings back from their first visit to Tunisia complete the total Tunisian look. Food is served on the characteristic blue and white china and traditional music plays on relentlessly. The menu is confined to the country's most popular dishes; salads mechouia (chopped grilled peppers, tomatoes, onions, garlic and tuna fish) and Tunisienne (raw chopped vegetables with mint and vinaigrette dressing); the wonderful brik à l'oeuf – a filo pastry triangle enclosing an egg, chopped parsley, capers and onion which is deep fried, served propped on a wedge of lemon and eaten like a sandwich without spilling the soft yolk; couscous (cracked wheat, chick peas, vegetables and meat, chicken or fish) and various Tajine (a filling souffle-like oven baked dish of lamb, grated cheese, eggs and vegetables). To follow there are tasty little Tunisian pastries, the traditional mint tea or Greek-style coffee served with orange water. Faouzi has temporarily lost his license so you can't try Tunisian wine but the nearby off license offers plenty of alternatives. The Lebanese Chateau Musar is a brilliant accompaniment.

Set three course lunch £4; alc £8 a head.

## Solopasta

26 Liverpool Road, N1 (359 7648)
Angel tube
Open: noon–3pm and 6–10pm Tuesday–Saturday; noon–3pm Sunday. Shop: 11am–10pm.

This small and friendly shop makes its own pasta continually, and cooks up a range of authentic Italian sauces to go with it. Adjoining the shop is a bistro which serves all the food sold for take-away, plus those dishes such as zabaglione which need to be cooked to order. The food is cheap and delicious – try their light and creamy cannelloni farciti (stuffed with spinach, bacon and walnuts) with a crisp mixed salad and garlic bread, followed by peach and chocolate mousse. The style of the place is more café than bistro with its woodgrain formica tables, but it does offer astounding value. A two course meal for two with half a litre of wine will see change from £10.

*Also Good When You Want Something Different:*
Ajimura (Japanese)
Aykoku-Kaku (Japanese)
Bamboo Kuning (Far East)
Beewees (West Indian)
Bloom's (Jewish)

Bunga Raya (Malaysian)
Busabong (Thai)
Cafe Pacifico (Mexican)
Chaopraya (Thai)
Corée, La (Korean)
Efes (Turkish)
Fakhraldine (Lebanese)
Gay Hussar (Hungarian)
Jorgen's Weinstube (German)
Jun (Japanese)
Kalamaras (Real Greek)
Luba's (Russian)
Maroush (Lebanese)
Petit Prince, Le (Algerian)
Rasa Sayang (Malaysian/Singaporean)
Salvador's El Bodegon(Spanish)
Siam (Thai)
Sukothai (Thai/Far East)
Suntory (Japanese)
White Tower (Greek/Balkan)
(For Indian and Chinese Restaurants, see separate index at back
of book)

## 20. When You Want to Get Out of London

It may seem perverse of a London restaurant guide to recommend places outside London, but there's no doubt that we all feel the urge to get out of the city at some time. A summer evening dinner or a weekend lunch in the country can offer much needed changes of pace and scene to minds and palates dulled by the familiarity of London restaurants. Of course, country retreats can often be rude awakenings if Ye Olde Mansion House's chef buys all his food from a freezer centre, or if the locals still think Londoners have the plague. Generally speaking though, a meal in the country should give you a genuine taste of the field and the farmyard. The places we've listed here cover all points of the compass and are roughly an hour to 90 minutes' drive from central London. British Rail stations are given where the restaurant is also accessible by train. And as the cross-channel day-trips have increased in popularity, we've included reports on venues in Calais and Boulogne.

# The Bell Inn

Aston Clinton, Buckinghamshire (0296 630252)
A41
Open: 12.30–1.45pm; 7.30–9.45pm Tuesday–Saturday; lunch Sunday.

It's a relatively painless hour's drive up the fast-moving A41 to Aston Clinton. As the road nears Aylesbury and passes through more rural scenery the roadside hotels, inns and pubs get more lavish-looking and the charming cottage-style country house Bell Inn, set in a pretty garden, is altogether classier. The Bell is a member of the Relais et Chateaux (there are only 15 in Great Britain and 300-odd world wide), was originally a coaching inn and retains an old brewery, stables and malthouses which surround a cobbled courtyard. The current owners' father took over the Bell in 1939 and he established the Inn's fine wine list (the Gerard Harris Wine Shop opposite is owned by the family) and the current chef, Jack Dick, produces French food of a complementary sophisticated style. The dining-room is large and comfortable, with discreet wall lighting, a sage green colour scheme, leather button-back banquette seating, dark wood tables and traditional heavy cutlery and span of glassware. The service is formal and a clutch of managers continually prowl the large room to keep staff on their toes.

There are daily specials and a trolley (of venison on a winter visit) to supplement the short menu which ranges from classic game dishes (roast duck, pheasant etc in season) to rich and complicated creations. From the more ambitious dishes crab Andalouse is a delicious tower of roughly chopped and very fresh crab meat decorated with lobster claws and set in a pale green, cream of watercress sauce. Also recommended are the three pâtés – veal with truffle centre, chicken liver, and quail – beautifully presented on a glaze decorated with a rose-sculptured tomato and lambs lettuce leaves. Aylesbury duck is a popular choice here but their excellent steak – three fillets medicis is a speciality – and rich stuffed chicken breast also has devoted fans. Vegetables get French treatment and are crisp but the cheeseboard is strictly English apart from one goat cheese in olive oil. Rich and filling desserts such as 'proper' apple pie and vanilla ice cream and marron charlotte follow. The Bell is the sort of place to get dressed up for (the dining room is very warm so sleeveless dresses are OK). You can even make a night of it (21 rooms upstairs cost from £46 for two).

From £25 a head including one bottle of wine under £10.

# Boulogne

Boulogne makes for the shortest route from London to Paris and the South of France, which in turn makes Boulogne the most popular channel port. Boulogne is also the favourite port for bons viveurs; Maître Fromager Philippe Oliver has his superb cheese shop there, the market is excellent (Wednesday and Saturday morning in Place Dalton) and there are many very good restaurants. The best include **La Charlotte**, 11 rue du Doyen (tel 21 32 41 24) Vista. Open noon to 2.30pm and 7 to 9.30pm Tuesday to Saturday and **Le Matelot**, 80 Blvd Sainte Beuve (tel 21 30 17 97) Euro. Open noon–2pm and 7.30–9.30pm. Both should be booked and cost from £15 a head.

Outstanding shops include **La Fromagerie de Philippe Olivier**, 43 rue Theirs. Open 9.30am–12.30pm and 2.30–7.30pm, closed Sunday and Monday. English money accepted. It is *the* most outstanding cheese shop where you'll find all the regional favourites and perfect Camembert, and they will pack for the journey at no extra charge. Fab chocolate (Meilleur Ouvrier de France) and pâtisserie (there are tea rooms) can be found at **Lugand**, 9 rue Grande (tel 21 31 56 22) and for charcuterie par excellence **Derrien** (1 Grande Rue). Wine bargains; **Les Vins de France**, 13 rue Nationale; 4 rue de Lille and 34 rue de Brequerecque. All open 9am to noon; 2.30–7pm Tuesday to Saturday; 9.30am–12.30pm Sunday.

Less than an hour's drive inland from Boulogne is the picturesque thirteenth-century walled city of Montreuil and its chateau serves brilliant food. **Château de Montreuil**, 4 Chaussée des Capucins (81 53 04) Amex, Diners, Access and Visa. Open noon–2pm and 7–9.30pm. The Château is run by Christian Germain (ex head chef of the Roux brothers' Waterside Inn) and his charming English wife Lindsay (no relation). The food bears all the hallmarks of Roux food and, if you discount the journey, is far cheaper than eating (and drinking) at either Le Gavroche or Waterside. At lunch they serve a set meal which includes wine and service at 130F and in the evening a four course dinner at 150F. Fear not if your French is sub O level – everyone speaks English perfectly. If you decide to stay the night (rooms from 250F including breakfast) you will find that the rooms are more like suites and overlook the walled garden and or the small pool. Breakfast is as excellent as lunch or dinner and will include freshly-baked croissant, warm cinnamon bread, home-made jams and a selection of seasonal fruit.

# Calais

Now that the channel ports are so accessible and so cheap to visit (Townsend Thoresen do a Pop-Over ticket for £7.50), a meal out of town can be turned into a day in France, and with a little organisation gives time for a meal *and* a chance to stock up the cellar and larder.

Calais is our closest French channel port (only 20 miles and 90 minutes away) but it is saved from gross touristification because most tourists pass straight through en route for elsewhere.

Once off the boat it takes ten minutes to walk to Rue Royal, the beginning of the centre of Calais and probably stocking everything you could want to buy. Walk a little further for the best market (off Blvd Lafayette in a cobbled square) which happens on Thursday and Saturday; brilliant for local cheeses (hard, bright orange Gouda-type mimolette; strong washed maroilles, vieux gris and boulette d'Avesnes); fresh local herbs; duck and other game; fowl and duck eggs; dairy produce; old and new clothes and plants. Shellfish par excellence can be found at **Huitière Calaisienne** (12 Blvd Lafayette); good pâtisserie **Au Croissant d'Or** (48 Rue Royale); goose specialities and sumptuous foody gifts, **Germaine Casteran** (111 Blvd Lafayette) and kitchen equipment, **Cupillard** (51 Blvd Lafayette). Most shops are closed on Sunday and Monday, close between noon and 3pm and stay open til 7/8pm. There is plenty of restaurant choice to suit all moods and pockets. We'd recommend one that caters well for all comers; **Le Touquet**, 57 Rue Royale, Calais (21 34 64 18) open noon till 11.30pm Tuesday to Sunday.

A huge tank full of crab and lobster in the window leaves no doubt that Le Touquet specializes in shell fish. In fact this modest and unpretentious restaurant is one of the best shellfish places in Calais where the locals sit in the window section eating their way through plate after plate of oysters (Fines Claires and Belons), crab, mussels et al. At the other extreme there's a tourist menu which features vegetable soup, roast chicken or steak and frites followed by cheese or ice cream with a quarter bottle of wine for under £4. Numerous other set meals vary in price and sophistication – fish soup with rouille, croûtons and grated cheese followed by chicory rolled in ham in a cheese sauce then rabbit in a mustard and cream sauce *and* cheese is typical for 65F. Their Brouilly is particularly good at 48F.

Le Touquet can seat 200 (there's a funny little casino at the back) is functionally decorated with a tiled floor, ladderback chairs, has slight Tyrolean overtones and, most curious of all, the proprietor is a Donald Pleasance look-alike.

## Chez Max

85 Maple Road, Surbiton, Surrey (399 2365)
Open: 12.30–2pm and 7.30–10.30pm Monday–Friday, 7.30–10.30pm Saturday.

After eight years as head chef at Prue Leith's restaurant in Notting Hill, Armenian-born Max Markarian has flown the roost (so has Leith's entry in the Good Food Guide) and opened his own small restaurant in a suburban high street. Discreet from the outside ('restaurant francais' is the only hint that the place is a restaurant at all), inside is discreet too. Palest eau de nil walls, a weird selection of Eastern abstract art, a tasteless net curtain and a pine dresser do little to comfort diners. However the food more than compensates for the austere setting. The menu shows M. Markarian's love of fish and unlike so many pukka restaurants, he takes the bother (and time) out of ordering by translating each dish thoroughly.

Sweetbreads wrapped in spinach with a chicken and cream sauce were a work of art, and smoked haddock cooked in shallots, white wine, garlic and cream an unusual but successful combination. The pièce de résistance is the half duck cooked in honey and port served with a small fruit salad. The pink breast in its rich sauce is perfectly 'cut' by the fruit and half way through munching the crispy skinned (Chinese-style) leg arrives. The equally excellent small (sic) fillet steak with a wild mushroom sauce paled just for a moment against the splendour of the duck. There is a choice of Brie or Stilton but M. Markarian excells at desserts. Hazelnut meringue with strawberries tastes as monumental as it looks – a tall confection held together with cream – but the light pear mousse served with half a poached pear is a perfect end to a meal and isn't so hard on the cholesterol level. A nice touch is a choice of teas; coffee is served in a cafetiere. There is a decent house Sauvignon at £6.50 otherwise most wines are in the £10 plus range.

About £25 a head.

## The Feathers Hotel

Woodstock, Oxfordshire (0993 812291)
A34 out of Oxford
Open: 12.30–2.15pm and 7.30–9.45pm daily.

It takes 40–60 minutes to get to the pretty and historic village of Woodstock, just 10 miles outside Oxford. The seventeenth-century hotel complete with flagstone floors, open fires, low ceilings and antique furniture throughout is just 100 yards from the gates of Blenheim Palace. The hotel has a bar where visitors can eat in a relaxed setting, a landscaped garden for summer dining or for more formal occasions the attractive pale blue and white dining-room is a very pleasant, homely (in a country house sort of way) restaurant with a couple of window seats. At lunch they serve an outstanding value daily-changing three course set meal at £7.50 (includes service) for which you'd pay double without blanching in London. In the evening an expanded version of the lunch menu costs £10.50 and both are an augmented rotation from the carte.

The extremely able chef specializes in English food with French overtones and includes some innovative as well as some excellent plain dishes on the menu. His fine chicken liver is smooth and delicious and there is always a good country-style soup (such as cream of pea and pear with nutmeg croûtons or mushroom and chive); noisette of lamb with fresh basil and tomato sauce and breaded breast of chicken (that actually tastes of chicken) and pink trout in a sorrel sauce are typical mains. All main dishes are served with several vegetables – almond covered balls of mashed potato, new potatoes, red cabbage and a purée of root vegetables on our last visit – and everything comes in very generous portions.

Dessert choices (savouries are extra at £2.50) range from home-made fruit pies with home-made ice-cream, to sorbets, rich chocolate cake and strawberry omelette but the most popular is the very pretty balls of raw apple on a bed of mint ice-cream and cream inside a tuile and doused in Calvados. The wine list is wide ranging with house wine at £5 but the Maçon at £6.50 is very good value.

Set lunch £7.50, dinner £10.50, alc £15–£20. Double rooms from £32.

## Ho Ho

20 High Road, South Woodford, E18 (989 8021)
South Woodford tube
Open: noon–3pm and 6–11.30pm Tuesday–Sunday.

It takes just under 30 minutes by car to reach South Woodford from Central London, and though South Woodford itself has no particular attractions, we think the Ho Ho is sufficiently outstanding to make the journey (perhaps en route for elsewhere?) worthwhile. The premises used to be an Italian trattoria and the tiled floor, whitewashed walls and archways still suggest a tratt despite the stylish redesign which incorporates the clever use of mirrors, Chinese carvings and photos of latterday China.

The menu is similar to that of its relative of the same name in Maddox Street – inter-regional with a predominance of Peking and Szechuan dishes, as well as spicy Malaysian/Singaporean food known as Nonya. The carte is explicit and helpful to those not particularly knowledgeable about this tasty fare and features several leave-it-to-us-feasts including one devoted to lobster. Favourites such as crispy duck with pancakes, filling and cheap noodle dishes and dumplings rub shoulders with a variety of tempting and not so familiar dishes, and these are the ones that make the journey worth it. Fresh steamed scallops, which arrive still fixed to the shell, swim in a tasty sauce and are topped with chopped black bean and garlic (4 for £4.50). The Imperial mixed hors d'oeuvre (from £4.50 for two) includes tasty smoked fish, broiled prawns, sauced winter mushrooms, barbecued pork, white cooked chicken and hot sweet cabbage and will leave just enough room for the delicious red cooked duck in a rich tangy sauce and a mound of sliced vegetables, served with perfectly contrasting sweet steamed rolls (from £4.50, ¼ duck). Excellent and light weight is chicken soong, a finely-chopped pile of meat and vegetables which are rolled in curls of iceburg lettuce (£3.50). Finish with toffee apples or bananas. The wine list is as varied as the menu and includes Château Bonnet 79 (red and white) which is a snip at £7 a bottle.

From £8 a head for food.

## The House on the Bridge

Eton–Windsor Bridge, 71a High Street, Eton, Berkshire (07535 60914)
Windsor BR–Paddington (via Slough)
Open: noon–2.30pm daily; 6–11pm Monday–Saturday; 6–10.30pm Sunday.

There can't be many more (public) pleasant ways of spending a summer day than dining on the banks of the Thames. The well-appointed House on the Bridge (the one linking Windsor and Eton) is slap on the side of the Thames in the centre of this historic town. The three-storey premises enjoy splendid views of the river and across to Windsor Castle itself. Al fresco freaks can bask on the sun-trap terrace, while interior diners will enjoy the 'sea-breezes' admitted by the restaurant's ever-open windows. A good-proportion of the House's custom comes, of course, from tourists taking in the castle, so the menu is predictably international in flavour – frogs' legs and lasagne are in among the starters, while main courses embrace such indestructible classics as grilled lemon sole and coq au vin, as well as the more up-market Russian Sevruga caviar or lobster. A short range of dishes for two might offer good value – Châteaubriand or veal aurora (strips of veal with a colourful onion, tomato, cream and mushroom sauce). Sunday lunches deal patriotically in roast beef or fresh salmon. There is a cosmopolitan wine list which includes the lively English bottle Wootton Seyval – the perfect fruity gargle for a summer thirst.

About £35 for two.

## Leeds Castle

Leeds, near Maidstone, Kent (0622 65400)
On B2163, just off Junction 8 of M20
Open: 7pm–1am Saturdays; 12.30–3pm Sundays (1 November–31 March only).

The first point to stress is that you don't actually get to eat in the castle itself – it's much too historic and genuinely beautiful to have oiks spilling gravy down the battlements. Instead, the catering takes place inside the nearby Fairfax Hall, a former Jacobean tithe barn restored and converted to accommodate 200 diners in as much comfort as a wooden-beamed hall with mainly communal tables can muster. The high-beamed roof and minstrel's gallery at one end give the impression of eating in an upturned Elizabethan flagship. The hall offers two main deals – a six course 'Kentish Evening Dinner' with music, held every Saturday throughout the year. This includes a tour of the castle, but we'd guess that you'd probably best appreciate the splendid architecture after the winter-only Sunday lunch. £9.50 for four courses with sherry and wine (£6.50 kids, under-5s free), and also including £2.50 admission fee to the castle. Choices on the lunch include first courses of melon, pâté and seafood vol-au-vents, followed by a soup and a selection of hearty English favourites. Of these, the simpler roast rib of beef is likely to be more successful than either the muscular pheasant casserole or wild duck with black cherry sauce. There's also trout with almonds or a vegetarian pie for non-carnivores. Trolley-loads of creamy stodge, coffee and a limited amount of wine (one glass per person) complete the deal. You certainly wouldn't drive the 40 miles to Leeds just for the food, but in combination with the spectacular, moat-surrounded castle, its aviary and wooded grounds (doubling in parts as a golf-course) it's well worth a day out. Please note that advance booking is essential.

Sunday lunch £9.50 a head; Saturday dinner £17.

## The Marquee

1 Bircherley Green, Hertford, Herts (0992 58999)
Hertford BR–Moorgate
Open: noon–2.15pm and 7.30–10.30pm daily.

Camped in an unusual spot – partly in Hertford's modern shopping precinct, partly overlooking the picturesque River Lea – The Marquee cushions its customers from either reality in a cocoon of fabric. The ground floor dining room has thick layers of pink cloth as wall-covering, while the upper floor glows with orange material, flowing tent-like up the walls and into the centre of the room. All of this, plus the gilded mirrors, floral displays and ruffed curtains, suggests that you may have mistakenly wandered into Barbara Cartland's boudoir. Nevertheless, despite its riotous décor and urban setting, The Marquee is still worth a visit for the imaginative English and international menu created by cookery writer Michael Smith (also responsible for The English House).

Many of the dishes are as provocative in taste and colour as the décor – roast Norfolk duckling with green fig sauce, smoked salmon mousse with sour cream dressing, tenderloin of pork stuffed with pickled walnuts and celery. More conservative tastes are catered for by the likes of smoked salmon, beef Wellington, honey-roasted rack of lamb or grilled sirloin steak. Winning starters have included the rough Somerset herb terrine (with chicken liver, ham and ox tongue) or the house speciality, soup Antiboise – fish soup flavoured with Pernod. Puddings extend the flamboyant mood with the traditional English dessert burnt creams with fresh raspberries, home-made pistachio ice-cream or chilled pears with a hot ginger sauce. A lunchtime visit, when there's a prix fixe meal, might give you a better chance to get the measure of the menu and the fabrics.

Set lunch £6.25 (excl wine); alc about £40 for two.

---

## Newington Manor

Callaway's Lane, Newington, near Sittingbourne, Kent (0795 842053)
Off A2, Chatham–Sittingbourne road
Open: noon–2pm and 7–10pm daily.

A sharp right turn off the old A2 Dover Road just three miles outside Sittingbourne will lead you to the charming Newington Manor, a carefully maintained, small 14th-century hall, now operating as a country house hotel and restaurant. It stands in its own verdant grounds, just far enough back from a clutch of drab village houses to sustain the rural illusion. Black and white timbers, oak beams, panelling, brick floors and even a lurking suit of armour greet you on the way to the bar. As befits the surroundings, the restaurant's menu is defiantly English. Changing regularly, it will nevertheless always offer the likes of smoked salmon (baked in a wholemeal pancake), sirloin steak (grilled, finished with a shallot, green peppercorn and red wine sauce), roast guinea-fowl or leg of pork casseroled in red wine with vegetables. Starters might include home-made game pâté, baked fennel in a tomato, wine and garlic sauce, seafood salad (oysters, calamari, prawns in piquant mayonnaise) or an avocado salad, with apple, cheese and onions. The richness of the flavours and sauces might prompt recourse to the proffered sorbets or even to the chef's offer of plain cooked dishes instead. As this is a family-run enterprise, service is pleasantly informal and unstuffy. The small but well-furnished dining-room (high-backed chairs, huge fire-place) has a beautiful aspect onto peaceful lawns and gardens, ideal for a summer evening in the country.

About £32 for two.

## Old Drapery Stores Restaurant

Middle Wallop, near Stockbridge, Hampshire (0264 781301)
On B83084, off A343 Andover–Salisbury road
Open: noon–2pm Monday–Friday and 6.30–11pm Monday–Saturday.

As you might guess from the name this is a converted shop, albeit an old one, which still retains the wooden counter with its brass measuring rod and a rare display of 30s and 40s millinery. There's a comfortable lounge for pre-meal drinks, and a pretty cottage-style dining-room with a garden patio for fine weather. The menu changes seasonally and offers an inventive range of continental dishes, though often with traditional English ingredients – so you might find pigeon breast in pastry with a watercress sauce, rolled breast of veal stuffed with thyme and orange, roast duck with peaches and ginger sauce, or the delicious gooseberry and elder-flower meringue. The menu is structured as a prix fixe for two courses, but with irresistible puddings like blackberry and almond tartlet; and with the good wine list, the bill quickly climbs to familiar London levels. The country idyll is occasionally shattered by the sudden appearance of hedge-hopping planes from the nearby aerodrome.

Set meal £7.50 per person; alc about £30 for two.

## The Old Lodge

High Street, Limpsfield, Surrey (08833 2996)
Off A25 between Oxted and Westerham
Open: 12.30–2pm Tuesday–Friday and Sunday; 7.30–9pm Tuesday–Saturday.

Being awarded a Michelin star after just two years gives some idea of the progress made by the Old Lodge's young team since they took over premises once owned by footballer Steve Kember. The Lodge, in the pretty village of Limpsfield, is an ideal venue for winter dinners – comfortable, warm, beamed lounge, leading into log-fired, oak-panelled dining-room with high, whitewashed barrel ceilings. Their dinner menus are sensible prix fixe affairs ranging from the cheapest three-courser at £12.50, via the more expensive £16.25 to the 'menu exceptionnel' at £18.50 which features chef John Mann's more exotic creations.

The £12.50 meal might offer pot de canard au Calvados or melon with Parma ham as starters, followed by loin of pork with marsala, strips of beef in Madagascar (green peppercorn) sauce or goujonettes de lotte Bretonne (monkfish in butter with artichokes). For the extra £2.75, the move to the £16.25 level offers much more exciting choices – a tender sweetbread salad with walnuts, a delicious hot chicken mousse stuffed with torta cheese or a delicate rosette of smoked salmon with creamed smoked trout appearing among the first courses. Thereafter, the precisely-cooked slices of duck breast in peach brandy sauce, the carré d'agneau au sage, the ragoût de pêcheur amoreux (fish stew with Pernod and cream) and the salmon fillet with grapes and tomato have all scored well. Puddings are also up to one-star standard with crème brûlée, iced raspberry soufflé and Albert's French lemon tart being the pick of the bunch on our visit. The modish presentation of the food doesn't hinder the portions but the atmosphere – a curious combination of formal stiffness and schoolboyish self-satisfaction (witness their incredibly precious 'newsletter') – might grate a little. Well worth the trip however, perhaps for one of their regular 'special evenings' (French provincial, medieval banquet, black tie dinner and dance), and, er, take the Range Rover . . .

Set meals £12.50, £16.25 and £18.50 a head (excl wine).

---

## Paris House

---

Woburn Park, Woburn (052 525692)
M1, turn off at exit 13, left past garage, left again and signs to Woburn. Continue out of Woburn (B528).
Open: 12.30–2.30pm and 7–10pm Tuesday–Sunday.

Access to the Paris House is via the stunning London entrance to Woburn Park. If you are dining rather than lunching, the spectacle of the floodlit, elaborately timbered 'chateau' set in sweeping lawns appears like a mirage. Once inside diners have the choice of pre-meal drinks in a small and rather starchy reception room, or going straight to the table.

A small upstairs room is available for private parties but apart from that very little of the Paris House is actually used for the restaurant. The dining room is stylishly but rather chillingly decorated with a powerful ivy leaf wallpaper, dark green curtains, mount-free antlers and prim tartan upholstered chairs.

The chef de cuisine is Peter Chandler, the first English chef to 'graduate' from a Roux (Le Gavroche and Waterside Inn) training to his own restaurant, which gets Roux support. The menu is short, most dishes are rich and portions are hearty. Cornet of smoked salmon filled with a mousseline of smoked salmon with tomatoes is light though very rich, while the galantine of turkey with an artichoke salad suffered from being served too chilled. The menu offers a fish course (fillet of brill in champagne sauce or monkfish cooked à la bourgignonne) and a choice of five meat dishes. Veal liver with orange is an unusual and successful combination while the boned poussin with a sherry stuffing (which proved to be a bland curd) is a subtle dish spoilt by being served with strongly-flavoured root vegetables. The cheeseboard is an apology from maestro Olivier but *the* pudding is the cold orange and raspberry soufflé. Coffee is served with petits fours of strawberries dipped in chocolate, tuiles and almond biscuits.

With the exception of occasional regional cooking evenings when the meal costs £15 and includes half a bottle of wine, there are no set meals at the Paris House. VAT is not included in the prices and together with the extras (coffee £1.75, cover £1) this is a hands-in-both-pockets sort of place. While food will average £25 a head there is some solace in the house wine; a very good £4.30's worth.

## Partners 23

23 Stonecot Hill, Sutton, Surrey (644 7743)
On A24, Sutton to Epsom
Open: 12.30–2pm Tuesday–Friday; 7.30–9.30pm Tuesday–Saturday.

On the fringes of suburban London, and set in a rather drab shopping parade by the large Woodstock pub, Partners 23 is not exactly the prime spot for a country idyll. Nevertheless, an evening there is likely to be as memorable as any in your average country house hotel, from the point of view of food, if not of décor. The tiny, 30-seater premises were once a transport café, but now with the help of colourful cane screens, some judicious pine-panelling, warm-coloured table-linen, fresh orchids and an imaginative English chef, the Yorkie Bars have been left far behind. Tim McEntire offers smashing four course dinners for £11.50, including coffee and home-made petits fours. Four or five excellent choices are offered at each stage of the meal, and if it sounds like an assault course, be assured that the precision of the cooking and portions allow the food to be fully appreciated. The menu changes regularly, but first courses might include tiny onion and chive tartlets with cucumber and cream sauce or a cottage cheese and spinach terrine wrapped in smoked bacon with tomato sauce. Second courses might offer a refreshing mango sorbet and a beautifully-presented paupiette of sole filled with crab mousse, served in a wine sauce with white grapes. Main dishes cover the spectrum, from salmon trout in dry vermouth, through maize-fed chicken in Hollandaise or pan-fried veal-steak with pink grapefruit and fresh rosemary, to medallions of beef with green and pink peppercorns. All dishes are served with perfect vegetables – baby turnips in cheese sauce, purée of carrots, cucumber with almonds. Desserts are just as colourful – chocolate sponge and orange cream terrine, home-made nougat ice-cream on a fresh strawberry purée or fresh fruits with a fresh fruit sorbet. The 'front of house' operation run by Andrew Thomason is friendly, discreet and immaculate. Lunches are three course affairs, and they occasionally have 'theme' dinners to mark particular events – Election Night for example.

Set dinner £11.50 (excl wine); set lunch £7.50 (excl wine).

## La Petite Auberge

The White Horse, Hascombe, Surrey (Hascombe 258)
On B2130 from Godalming to Cranleigh
Open: noon–2pm and 7–10pm Monday–Saturday.

Familiar images of Surrey as boring commuter-belt country do less than justice to some of its beautiful landscape just an hour's drive from central London. In a particularly attractive wooded stretch just south of Godalming is the White Horse pub which, appreciating the surrounding scenery, has called its restaurant an 'auberge'. Set on a quiet corner with views across open land, the White Horse is an atmospheric, log-fired, oak-beamed, pine-boothed hostelry with more style than the 'stallions' and 'fillies' toilet signs suggest. Bespoke bar snacks offered include moules marinières, deep-fried squid in batter, fish pie and côte de porc, all a cut above the usual ploughman's lunch or hot pies. Furthermore, the small, horse-brasses and skillets restaurant at the rear boasts an extensive menu, of which the table d'hôte selection at £8.25 for three courses can be good value. Home-made watercress soup or a refreshing orange and cucumber vinaigrette might be among the starters along with the more conventional duck pâté. The main courses can find ambition overreaching the kitchen's ability – messy cheese and onion sauce swamping lamb soubise, over-sweet chicken orientale (with bananas, saffron rice and prawns) – so it's probably better to stick to the simpler calves' liver with sage and onion, grilled swordfish steak with lime sauce or even entrecôte au poivre. Home made fruit tarts and gateaux or chocolate ice-cream make up the puds. There's a reasonable wine list and Burton and Friary Meux beers. Walk it all off afterwards in the lovely Winkworth Arboretum nearby.

About £25 for two (restaurant); £8 for two (bar).

# The Pier

The Quay, Harwich, Essex (02555 3363)
Harwich Town BR–Liverpool Street
Open: noon–2.30pm and 6.30–9.30pm daily.

If you fancy a few sea-breezes to blow away the city's cobwebs, The Pier at Harwich couldn't be better placed – it's right on the old quayside overlooking the busy Stour estuary. The container terminal is just around the corner so expect rumbling juggernauts to flash past the window. Otherwise, enjoy the sea view, the riotous décor in the cocktail bar (mermaid murals, waitress in sailor suit, green padded benches) and the splendid array of sea-food in the two brightly-coloured restaurants. With the Essex oyster-beds just an estuary or two away and regular supplies from local fishing boats, you shouldn't be spoiled for either choice or freshness.

Dishes downstairs are restricted to the likes of simple fried plaice and chips (huge piece of tender fish, great chips) while upstairs it's trout in pastry, delicious billy-bye soup (mussels flavoured with saffron, white wine and shredded vegetables), clam chowder, sea-food terrine (turbot, Dover sole, scampi), gargantuan chef's fish pie and halibut casserole. The set lunch might offer a soup and a mussel stew, though even here, the size of the portions should preclude puddings (largely stodge anyway). Walk it off afterwards round the narrow, rambling streets of this historic naval town.

Set lunch £5.75 (excl wine); alc about £11 a head (upstairs), £6 a head (downstairs).

# Simmons

68 The Mint, Rye, East Sussex (0797 222026)
Rye BR–Charing Cross
Open: 7.30–10pm Tuesday–Saturday; noon–2pm Sunday.

For an exciting and interesting day out, a trip to Rye is really worthwhile. The town is steeped in history – as a walled fort in medieval times it was a frequent target for French raiders – and though only part of the old city wall and the Ypres tower remain, you can still get a shiver as you gaze out over the marshes. The architecture of other centuries is also preserved in some of the tiny cobbled streets and a visit to beautiful Mermaid Street and the rambling old inn of the same name is essential. With bookshops, churches and antique markets to browse around, there's enough to keep you occupied for a full day. To complete the trip, enjoy a meal at Simmons, a beautifully appointed little restaurant with oak beams and timbered walls, but comfortably furnished in the modern idiom.

They offer a distinctive English-flavoured menu with touches of Gallic flair and invention. An excellent value prix fixe dinner might offer rich game soup, crudités and a choice of baby chicken cooked with lemon and herbs or blanquette de veau. The à la carte selection could include delicious grilled scallops with herb stuffing or ballotine of duck with lamb sauce as starters. Main courses include simple classics such as beef Stroganoff and entrecôte in red wine and shallots and unusual recipes such as fingers of turbot with almonds or the bizarre venison royal, with white wine, pine nuts and chocolate. Finish with home-made petits fours. Sunday lunches revolve around roast beef and steak and kidney pie, and they'll open for lunch between Tuesday and Saturday if you let them know you're coming.

Set dinner £8.50 a head (excl wine); alc about £15 a head.

---

## The Starr Inn

---

Market Place, Great Dunmow, Essex (0371 4321)
On A120 Bishops Stortford–Braintree road
Open: 7.15–9.45pm Tuesday–Saturday; 12.15–1.45pm Sunday.

A quick thrash up the M11 to Junction 8 and east on the A120 will bring you to the old market town of Great Dunmow, which is so quiet it's even eerily deserted at 5.45pm on a Friday night. The line of cars that later slope down Market Place to the Starr Inn however, give some idea of the exciting activity behind the former coaching house's 18th-century façade. Once inside, there's a warm, cosily-furnished reception room with a huge log fire to banish any 'Midwich Cuckoos' chills. Large blackboards will be brandished at you offering the evening's menu, which is conditioned by the day's market purchases – hence also the display basket of vegetables bagged that morning at Spitalfields or from local farmers.

Each dish is graphically explained with cheerful, fair-ground barker relish and pride – 'We're going to take some Dutch calves' kidneys, slice them thinly across, wrap them in bacon, grill them and serve them with a light mustard sauce'. Six or seven varied first courses are offered (available in combination to make up a full meal), with three fish and six meat or game dishes as main courses. The style of cooking is generally English countryside happily-married to modern French flair. Thus a delicious, garlicky rough veal terrine, studded with pistachio nuts, arrives prettily posed in a light avocado sauce – a combination which nevertheless 'works'; avocado is baked with crabmeat, fresh scallops are steamed while lobster bisque, sautéed herring roes or spinach pancakes might also appear among the starters. After a refreshing sorbet, the fish courses might offer poached brill with salmon mousse, pan-fried Dover sole or escalope of salmon. Among the meat courses, tender slices of Aylesbury duck arrive with rather too much hot cranberry sauce, but rack of lamb is roasted exactly to order, with or without herbs or garlic, and calves' liver with bacon is perfect. Accompanying vegetables are imaginative and excellent (braised red cabbage, Kenyan beans) and puddings include home-made sorbets with fruit and ice-creams, as well as terrific Bakewell tart. The low-beamed, candlelit dining room, decked in pale green napery, is both spacious and intimate. The quality of the cooking just about justifies the London-level prices, and the overpoweringly willing service (it makes Uriah Heep look like Basil Fawlty) will certainly make you feel special.

About £23 a head.

## Tickell Arms

Village Green, North Road, Whittlesford, Cambridgeshire (0223 833128)
Off A10 Royston–Cambridge
Open: 10.30am–2.30pm and 7–11pm Monday–Friday; 10.30am–2.30pm and 6.15–11pm Saturday; noon–2pm and 7–10.30pm Sunday.

With the M11 in operation and most of the A1 expanded to three lanes, it's possible to get up to Cambridge in about 1¼ hours, and a slight detour to the Tickell Arms is an ideal prelude to exploring the ancient university town. Although nominally a pub, the Tickell Arms is much more of a rambling country manor in style. There are no pub signs to identify it – just look for the white fence and the gravel car-park in front of the imposing stone balustrade – and the proprietor Mr Tickell has more than a touch of the country squire about him, booming voice included. His individuality shows itself in a gloomy but atmospheric interior – all dark colours, antique furniture and candelabra – with loud opera or classical music blasting from the stereo. A note on the door declares his prejudices against 'long-haired lefties', 'tee shirts' and 'CND badges', so be warned.

If you pass sartorial and political muster however, you can enjoy some splendidly prepared food, ordered, then collected on a tray, from an efficient counter and tannoy service. Starters could include snails, mushrooms in cream and garlic sauce, smoked salmon, smoked fish pâté, the unusual pastrami and the unappealing conger eel soup. Solid main courses have a touch of style about them too – dressed Cromer crab with sauce béarnaise, excellent quail en cocotte in a white grape sauce, lasagne bolognaise, smoked duck or a vegetable quiche. Delicious puddings include crême brûlée, honey and rhubarb crumble, meringues and a wide range of ice-creams. Drink good, reasonably-priced wines or strong, local Abbott ale. There is a large, airy conservatory at the side of the main house for summer eating. Beware of whopping 33% service charges imposed on orders after certain 'late' times (1.30pm and 10.15pm). Eccentric, individual but well worth a try.

About £10 a head.

---

## Waterside Inn

---

Ferry Road, Bray, Berkshire (0628 20691/22941)
M4, exit 8/9 to Maidenhead, then Bray.
35 minutes centre of London; 15 minutes Heathrow and 10 minutes Windsor Castle.
Open: 12.30–2pm and 7.30–10pm Tuesday–Sunday.

Such is the fame of this stunningly-located riverside Inn (previously a pub) that it has its own council road sign. Bray is a picturesque old English village with characteristic black and white cottages and thirteenth-century buildings. The Inn is decorated in fresh, bright shades of green, and keeps a local Constance Spry very busy. The dining room seats 70 and at lunch and during the summer months gives a spectacular view (the entire front section of the restaurant is plate glass from top to toe) of the river, which bobs with ducks and occasionally punts (a mooring is provided for their guests who really do things in style), a sweeping weeping willow and, ironically, a 'To the Channel' sign.

A central table displays some of M. Roux's team's elaborate culinary work and the menu is appropriate to the Inn's membership of Relais et Chateux, three Egon Ronay stars and two from Michelin. This year's Good Food Guide reckons that Michel Roux cooks less often than of yore though we're glad to say that on our last visit we spotted him en route for the kitchen.

Best value is undoubtedly the Menu Gastronomique at £18; a three course meal with coffee and petits fours (cover included) which changes daily and is different, though of the same high standard, as the carte. Now that the Roux empire is very much a business with Michel and Albert's cookbook on sale, the complexity of preparation that goes into their food is plain to all. Oeufs brouillés aux oeufs – ducks', hens' and quails' eggs, poached, scrambled and coddled with cream and caviare and triangular croûtons is an example and is one of their simpler dishes. Less rich though equally painstakingly prepared is gratin of moules and lobster in Roquefort, so too is the panaché of terrines with Cumberland sauce. Whatever the choice here or at any of the Roux restaurants (Le Gavroche, Le Poulbot, Le Gamin and Gavvers; indirectly La Tante Claire and Interlude de Tabaillau) you can expect superb ingredients; the best of what's available from England, France and elsewhere in the world. As Michel Roux is a specialist pâtissier (Meilleur Ouvrier de France, Paris 1976) don't miss the opportunity to try one of his creations such as feuilleté of pears; panaché de torte citron et délice cassis or the divinely light tierce de sorbets prettily arranged on a bed of feuille de meringue. Coffee is served with petits fours. The wine list has virtually nothing under £10 though there are some half bottles. This is not a place for the faint-hearted or for occasions when the pocket is lightly lined; we think lunchtime is far nicer and would recommend asking for a window seat.

From £30 a head for food.

*Also Good When You Want to Get Out of London:*
New Anarkali Tandoori
Olde Hatchet, The

# Areas

# Index of Cuisines

300

# Set Meals

## Vegetarian (and where vegetarians are well catered for)

## Unlicensed

## Open on Sunday

S Molton
Crepene
Wirdno's Bagel dead – p162